Was
George
Washington
Really
the Father
of Our
Country?

Other books by Robert Marion, M.D.

Learning to Play God: The Coming of Age of a
Young Doctor

The Boy Who Felt No Pain

The Intern Blues: The Private Ordeals of
Three Young Doctors

Born Too Soon (a novel)

Was George Washington *Really* the Father of Our Country?

A Clinical Geneticist
Looks at World History

Robert Marion, M.D.

Addison-Wesley Publishing Company
Reading, Massachusetts
Menlo Park, California   New York
Don Mills, Ontario   Wokingham, England
Amsterdam   Bonn   Sydney   Singapore
Tokyo   Madrid   San Juan   Paris   Seoul
Milan   Mexico City   Taipei

Many of the designations used by manufacturers and sellers to distinguish their products are claimed as trademarks. Where those designations appear in this book and Addison-Wesley was aware of a trademark claim, the designations have been printed in initial capital letters (e.g., Band-Aid).

Library of Congress Cataloging-in-Publication Data

Marion, Robert.
    Was George Washington really the father of our country? : a clinical geneticist looks at world history / Robert Marion.
        p.   cm.
        ISBN 0-201-62255-6
        1. Heads of state—Health and hygiene.   2. Diseases and history.
    3. Human genetics.   I. Title.
    D226.7.M37   1994
    909.08′092′2—dc20   93-26588
                                                                          CIP

Cover design by Rich DeFeo
Text design by Edith Allard
Set in 11-point Garamond by G & S Typesetters, Austin, Texas

1 2 3 4 5 6 7 8 9-MA-96959493
First printing, December 1993

Dedication:

To Diana Finch, my agent and friend,
who's always been there when I've needed her

and

To Nancy Miller, my editor and *best* friend,
who was polite enough to read the entire
manuscript of *Born Too Soon*

Contents

The world has a legitimate
interest in the ancestry of noted men.
Not that heredity alone accounts for any
man . . . but no man can be fully understood
apart from his inheritance of bodily
and mental traits.

—W. E. Barton, 1929

Introduction

As an academic physician who lectures regularly about medical genetics I've been forced to develop a series of talks that both get the essential points across and offer some relief and entertainment to the occasionally hostile crowd of interns and residents. Now this is not as easy as it may sound. After all, any way you dress it up, a lecture on such medically intriguing topics as "The Chromosomal Basis of Inheritance," "Autosomal Dominantly Inherited Conditions," or "Inborn Errors of Carbohydrate Metabolism" still boils down to projecting a large number of blurry slides showing such things as forty-six (give or take a few) vitally important objects that look an awful lot like stretched-out woolly caterpillars, chemical reactions and three-dimensional models of DNA so complicated that, early in their careers, physicians have learned how to fall immediately to sleep as soon as they appear before them. But, fortunately, during the course of my life in academic medicine, I've managed to develop a few talks that have successfully held the house officers' interest.

The first such talk was called "Shopping Mall Genetics." To prepare this lecture, I took a camera to the spectacular Galleria Mall in White Plains, New York and, using a telephoto lens, photographed actual shoppers who I believed were affected with easily identifiable genetic disorders. Using the shoppers' photographs, I constructed a lecture that painstakingly addressed the clinical, pathophysiological, and genetic aspects of the various conditions present in these randomly selected shoppers. While presenting "Shopping Mall Genetics" during Pediatric Grand Rounds, I was pleasantly surprised by the audience's reaction: at the end of the hour, not only was nearly everyone still conscious, but someone even asked a question during the question-and-answer period. Granted, the question concerned the rumor that the mall's J.C. Penney store was scheduled to close, but hey, at least the questioner appeared to be awake.

Trying to capitalize on such unprecedented success, I next moved on to the glamorous world of tabloid journalism. You'd be surprised how many actual genetic disorders are pictured every week within the pages of such widely read publications as the *Star*, the *Globe*, the *National Enquirer*, and my favorite, *Weekly World News*. The talk that grew out of a month of gathering material from these and other tabloids, "Twenty-Two-Pound Baby with Tattoo of Elvis on His Back Born in Pittsburgh!" proved to be another major success. In fact, the only down side of the experience was my incredible, recurring embarrassment at standing in the checkout line, surrounded by friends and neighbors, with all those magazines in hand.

My lecture entitled "Celebrity Dysmorphology: Clinical Genetics of the Rich and Famous" seemed to follow naturally from "Twenty-Two-Pound Baby with Tattoo of Elvis on His Back Born in Pittsburgh!" Since the day I met Ms. Kreuger, whose story appears in the first chapter, in the emergency room at Jonas Bronck Hospital, I've been interested in the disorders that affected famous individuals and how, in turn, these famous individuals reacted and were changed by their diseases. In 1988 I assembled the information I'd collected over the years into a lecture; in 1992 I began to reconstruct that talk into a book. *Was George Washington* Really *the Father of Our Country?* is basically the Classic Comics edition of that lecture.

Ever since the day that, through some spontaneous change in the genetic material, a couple of extra centimeters of gray matter got slapped onto the cerebral cortex of a giant ape, an event that undoubtedly has

significantly changed the course of world history (not necessarily for
the better), members of our species have been fascinated by the presence of individuals who look or act different from the rest. The prehis-
toric record is filled with examples of rock and cave drawings and wood
and stone sculptures of two-headed humans (an obvious attempt to
represent conjoined, or Siamese, twins), dwarfs, and other figures
whose appearance set them apart from the crowd. Since those ancient
days, people with genetic diseases have been idolized, vilified, wor-
shiped, burned at the stake, transformed into court jesters, abandoned
to die on mountaintops, relegated to circuses and sideshows, and even,
on rare occasions, accepted by the mainstream of society. That people
with such disorders have sometimes become leaders of society, respected artists, and stars of the stage and screen is not entirely coincidental or unexpected: to survive in a hostile environment, these
individuals were forced to develop some special strength to overcome
the adversity that nature placed in their path. The stories that follow are
about that special, indefinable strength.

Now I'll be the first to admit that I'm no historian; few new schol-
arly facts are forthcoming in this book. Rather, what follows represents
an interpretation of well-documented historical events through the eyes
of a physician; a clinical geneticist who has treated patients suffering
from such conditions; a doctor who has counseled and observed families, seen what effects, over a lifetime, such diseases have had on patients' minds and bodies. The glue that cements this book into a whole
is that, at the center, each story depicts an individual struggling with
the effects of a genetic disease. As such, rather than biography, this
book more closely resembles a textbook of human genetics, but one
that may shed some unique light on historical events.

The chapters that follow are sprinkled with episodes from my
training and my clinical practice. Although each story is true, all patients' names have been changed; further, some of the details, such as
the names of the hospitals, have been altered to assure anonymity.

This book was written with the help of a lot of people. I'd like to
thank first my teachers, who shaped me into an academic pediatrician

and a practicing clinical geneticist. Specifically, I'd like to thank Drs. Murray Feingold and Lewis Bartoshesky, who took me under their wings during my internship at the New England Medical Center in Boston and introduced me to the field of dysmorphology; and Drs. Steven P. Shelov, Michael I. Cohen, Andy P. Mezey, and the late Lewis J. Fraad, collectively my academic fathers, who nurtured me during my training and provided a protected environment at the Albert Einstein College of Medicine in the Bronx, New York, in which I could continue to grow and learn. Finally, I'd like to thank my pal, Dr. Lewis Singer, director of the Pediatric Critical Care Unit at Montefiore Medical Center, who's kept me laughing during some extremely tough times in the past few years.

Next, this book would certainly have never appeared in print had it not been for the hard work and devotion of my literary agent, Diana Finch, and my editor and close friend, Nancy Miller. It is to Diana and Nancy that this book is dedicated.

Finally, once again, I'd have never gotten to this paragraph had it not been for the help of my parents, Ann and Sam Marion, and the patience and understanding of my kids, Isadora (age twelve), Davida (now nine), and Jonah (coming up on five), who have sacrificed a lot of trips to Sportime USA and Rye Playland so that Dad could sit in front of his keyboard. And of course, thanks to Beth, for her love, understanding, and for putting up with it all.

George III's Urine and the American Revolution

Although some of the details have become a little sketchy in the fifteen years since that day, I would have to say now that it was Ms. Kreuger who, by inadvertently introducing me to the story of King George III, indirectly led me to write this book. I first encountered Ms. Kreuger, then forty-two years old, in the emergency room at Jonas Bronck Medical Center, a large municipal hospital serving the people of the Bronx, New York. It was late January 1979 and I was a pretty hopeless fourth-year medical student mercifully nearing the end of a two-month stint in ambulatory (or outpatient) medicine, a rotation required for graduation from medical school. Ms. Kreuger, who had been rushed to the hospital by a pair of paramedics because of intense abdominal pain, had the misfortune of being my patient.

Immediately before meeting Ms. Kreuger for the first time, I'd had a talk with those paramedics. I was hoping they could tell me exactly what was wrong with the woman and, more important, precisely how to make her better. Unfortunately, they were unable to provide the answers I needed. According to the history they'd received at Ms. Kreuger's house, the woman had been in her usual state of health until about two hours before their arrival, when she'd suddenly been seized by repeated spasms of crampy pain in her belly. Over the next hour, the

1

pains had grown more intense, the spasms coming more frequently until, apparently, the woman had "blacked out," lapsing into what was described by one of the paramedics as a catatonic state that resembled a coma. "It was weird," that paramedic concluded. "It was like she was in so much pain that she'd just lost touch with reality."

"The other thing that was weird," the second paramedic chimed in, "was that nobody in the house seemed all that upset by any of this. All I know is, if that had been my mother or my aunt, I would have been half-crazy about what was happening. But nobody seemed to think very much of it. They said something about this kind of thing happening to her in the past, and that the woman had spent a lot of time in the hospital, but nobody knew for sure exactly what was wrong with her. None of them even asked to come with us in the wagon when we brought her in."

Reluctantly, after I'd realized that I'd struck out with the paramedics, I decided it was time to try to get a history of the present illness from the woman herself. Upon entering the examining booth, I found the patient, who was still fully clothed, her trunk partially covered by a thin white sheet, lying motionless on a stretcher. Plump and with a heavily lined face that made her look at least ten years older than the age listed on her ER sheet, the woman was silent and seemed to be sleeping. Apparently, she wasn't asleep though, as I discovered when I tentatively began to introduce myself. "Ms. Kreuger," I said slowly and as distinctly as possible, "I'm Bob Marion. I'm a senior doctor-in-training, a medical student who will be a real doctor in a few months." (During that year, I always found it difficult to explain to patients exactly what I was and why I was standing at their bedside, bothering them.) "Can you tell me what seems to be the trouble?"

My question was initially met with silence, but then, suddenly, a low-pitched, guttural noise—a sound, I realized, that was not significantly different from the one produced by Lurch, the butler in the old Addams Family television series—began to fill the examining booth. The sound scared me half to death; at first, I couldn't locate exactly where it was coming from, but as it continued, I realized the noise was emanating from the region of Ms. Kreuger's mouth. It seemed as if she was actually attempting to answer my question.

Encouraged by her apparent effort to respond, I decided to press on: "It seems as if you're in a lot of pain," I continued. "Can you point to where it hurts?"

The patient remained motionless, moving not a finger; the guttural monotone started up again.

"The paramedics who brought you in told me the problem was in your abdomen," I pressed on. "Is that right?"

Again, Ms. Kreuger moaned.

"Well, maybe we'll just move on to the exam," I said, more to myself than to the patient, as I realized that my initial response to Ms. Kreuger's disembodied Lurch noise might have been a bit overly optimistic. I peeled back the white sheet, lifted the woman's sweater, and lowered her skirt, revealing a six-inch bulge of pale abdominal skin. Her distended belly was swollen and tense. Placing my stethoscope onto the naked skin, I tried to listen in on any conversation that might be occurring in the abdomen; but rather than hearing the normal bell-like tinkling sounds that the bowel makes when it's healthy and happy, I heard absolutely nothing. The abdomen was distressingly silent, a sign of potentially serious intra-abdominal disease.

After listening for more than a minute and finally convincing myself that the abdomen was truly bereft of bowel sounds, I began to gently palpate Ms. Kreuger's belly. At first, everything was fine; but when I pressed hard against the abdominal wall in the periumbilical region (the area surrounding the belly button), the woman's guttural monotone suddenly became more intense and high-pitched. The noise ultimately crescendoed into something like the tone used during tests of the Emergency Broadcast System.

But ignoring the audio portion of the examination, I concentrated on the physical features and found something even more troubling than the total lack of bowel sounds: the woman's belly was as hard as a rock. Even as a seemingly hopeless fourth-year medical student, I knew what this distressing combination of symptoms and signs meant: Ms. Kreuger had what was known around the emergency room as a "hot belly." Officially called an "acute abdomen," this serious, potentially life-threatening condition results from some horrible, intra-abdominal catastrophic event, such as the rupture of the intestine or of

3

some other organ. I also knew that any patient suffering from an acute abdomen required emergency exploratory surgery in order to identify and treat the underlying problem. I wasn't sure exactly what had gone wrong in Ms. Kreuger's belly but I was sure I knew exactly what needed to be done. At least I thought I did.

Excited by the fact that these few, scattered facts had somehow spontaneously connected in my brain, actually enabling me to come up with a diagnosis and a plan of action, I began searching the emergency room for the general surgery chief resident, the person in charge of the surgical service. Finally locating her in one of the other examining booths where she was hard at work suturing a gaping, nasty-looking laceration in the scalp of a large New York City cop, I burst in, obviously interrupting her concentration, and immediately and excitedly began presenting Ms. Kreuger's case to her; I made sure to point out the urgency of the situation. Impressed by my story, the resident excused herself from the cop in midstitch and followed me as I quickly led her into my examination booth. Although I fully expected the chief resident to rapidly check Ms. Kreuger's belly, pat me on the head and congratulate me on my amazing clinical acumen, and run off to arrange to take the woman immediately to the operating room, instead the resident took one look at the woman who was once again emitting her familiar Lurch moan and herself uttered a groan. "Hello, Ms. Kreuger," the surgery chief resident said, rolling her eyes a little. "I see you've come to visit us again."

Ms. Kreuger responded by continuing to moan.

The resident repeated my exam, feeling the woman's belly quickly; she then turned and began to walk away, signaling for me to follow her. "That's Ms. Kreuger," she explained when we'd reached the hallway. "She's an old friend of ours. She comes in like this every couple of months or so. I know it looks like she's got a hot belly, but there's really nothing wrong with her; nothing we can do anything about, anyway. She's got this rare metabolic disease that, for some reason, causes her to get like this a couple times a year. Believe me, the last thing Ms. Kreuger needs right now is an operation. What she *does* need is a nice warm bed on the medicine service and a few bags full of normal saline with lots of glucose in it pumped into her veins. You'd better call the medicine guys." And with that, the surgery resident turned and went back to her patient.

Confused by the surgery chief resident's reaction, and a little upset that, even though I'd been positive I was right, it apparently had turned out once again that my clinical judgment had proved absolutely wrong, I went to find the senior internal medicine resident who was in charge of the emergency room that day. Like the surgery chief who'd preceded him to the bedside, the medical resident also apparently recognized Ms. Kreuger on sight. But unlike the surgery chief, this resident said nothing; he simply sighed, shook his head slowly from side to side, and then, picking up the nearest telephone, began making arrangements to have the woman admitted to one of the hospital's internal medicine wards.

I was still confused by all this, but then, after a while, Ms. Kreuger's old hospital chart finally arrived from the hospital's record room and the situation began to become clearer. The woman's chart was immense: arranged in three volumes, each consisting of at least five hundred pages, it was filled with the records of more than two dozen hospitalizations, all for virtually the same symptomatology. Starting at the age of twenty-six, apparently the time when she and her family first moved to the Bronx, Ms. Kreuger had been admitted to Jonas Bronck Medical Center every six to twelve months with the sudden, unexpected onset of intense, disabling abdominal pain. Many of these episodes were accompanied by what appeared to be a catatonic state, with the woman completely losing touch with reality, unable to respond to simple questions or commands, to talk, to move her hands and her feet, or even to smile or frown, for days or even weeks at a time. In addition, each attack was accompanied by other unusual symptoms and signs, such as intense joint and back pain, palsies involving the nerves that control the muscles of the face, and insomnia. During the first three admissions, concerns that the woman was suffering from an acute abdomen led the surgical staff to perform emergency exploratory operations. To the apparent surprise and shock of the staff, no trace of intra-abdominal pathology was ever found. So finally, in frustration, during Ms. Kreuger's fourth admission to Jonas Bronck, the surgeons, realizing that they were stumped, called for an internal-medicine consultation. One of our medical school's legendary clinical professors of medicine came to see the woman. A gray-haired senior faculty member who'd worked at the school since its founding, this distinguished physician had devoted his entire professional career to teaching students, interns, and residents about the obscure conditions, often referred to as "zebras," that populate the field of medicine. That legendary clinical professor of medicine had first suggested that perhaps Ms. Kreuger was suffering from acute intermittent porphyria.

Yeah, right! Even I, a sadly incompetent fourth-year medical student, knew that acute intermittent porphyria, or AIP, was a zebra among zebras, a disease that was little more than the answer to an obscure medical trivia question about what disorder causes the urine to turn burgundy red. Acute intermittent porphyria was one of those diseases that legendary clinical professors of medicine everywhere loved to teach medical students about, reciting facts and figures about pathology and physiology until they became nearly orgasmic. But AIP was also a disorder that, at least in our part of the world, affected virtually no one. So, when I read the note written by the legendary clinical professor of medicine that appeared in Ms. Kreuger's chart, I snickered to myself at the predictability of the suggestion. Porphyria! Of course! What else could it be?

My snickering ceased, however, when I turned the page and read the chart's next note. At the request of the legendary clinical professor of medicine, the surgery staff had obtained a sample of fresh urine from Ms. Kreuger. Amazingly, upon standing in room air for less than ten minutes, that urine turned from clear yellow to a deep burgundy red. Chemical analysis of the urine showed a marked excess in the level of two chemicals, porphobilinogen and amino levulinic acid. So, against all odds, Ms. Kreuger actually did have AIP! The shock of this discovery undoubtedly had a profound effect on the legendary clinical professor of medicine; it must have brought tears of joy to his eyes. After all those years, after suggesting the diagnosis dozens, perhaps even hundreds of times, the man had finally managed to get it right!

The knowledge that Ms. Kreuger had AIP also had something of a profound effect on me. From the beginning of medical school, for reasons that still aren't exactly clear to me, I'd developed what would have

to be considered an unhealthy interest in the group of disorders known
as inborn errors of metabolism, rare inherited diseases such as AIP that
cause disturbances in the way the cells of the body break down and dis-
pose of the naturally occurring compounds necessary for the body's
proper physiologic functioning. So that very afternoon, after Ms.
Kreuger had been shipped off to one of the internal medicine wards
and I'd finished my shift in the ER, I got myself over to the medical
school's library, found a book on the group of disorders known as the
porphyrias, and began to read. In that book I first picked up the trail of
George III and his lifelong struggle with the disorder that's come to be
known as "the Royal Malady."

In early June 1788, George III, the ruler of the British Empire
(figure 1), was stricken with a mysterious illness, a disorder that, according to Isaac Ray, a nineteenth-century expert in "insanity," has become the most important single disease process in the history of the
British Empire, an entity that "settled for ever a vital principle in the
British constitution."[1] Beginning with severe, colicky abdominal pain
that, like the pain experienced by Ms. Kreuger, arrived in separate
spasms, the symptoms waxed and waned over the course of the next few
weeks, becoming better one day, only to worsen the next. By September, however, the king, who at fifty years of age was then in the twenty-
eighth year of his reign, seemed much improved, and appeared able to
return to his normal duties. In the days following his apparent recovery,
not much thought was given to the cause of the king's illness. Although
its etiology remained a mystery, the fact that it appeared to be self-
limited seemed to make the issue one of only academic interest.

But unfortunately, the king's improvement was only short-lived.
According to Stanley Ayling, a twentieth-century biographer of George
III, on October 17, 1788, the king suffered what was described as "another 'spasmodic byleous attack,'" an episode accompanied by severe,
intractable abdominal pain and respiratory difficulty.[2] In the days following this second onslaught of the mysterious illness, George's condition seemed to slide steadily downhill: "rheumatick" pains developed in
all his limbs, accompanied by nocturnal cramps and a "skin affection."

Figure 1. Portrait of George III, by Thomas Gainsborough.
From Royal Collection Enterprises, London.

And on October 18, just one day after the renewed onset of abdominal discomfort had begun, Sir George Baker, the king's personal physician, noted for the first time in the daily medical bulletin what would ultimately become an important clue in identifying the underlying cause of George's illness: the king's urine had become "discolored."[2]

Over the next few weeks, George's condition continued to deteriorate steadily. Novel and often baffling symptoms and signs began to appear almost daily. The king developed "lameness" in his legs, which caused him to require a walking stick to get around. He became agitated, his speech seeming forced, his words, which seemed to explode from his mouth much too rapidly, coming randomly and almost incomprehensibly. He began having more and more difficulty falling asleep each night. And there were neurologic symptoms as well: his vision became blurred, his head throbbed, he had swings in his mood from unexplained giddiness to deep depression. And perhaps most distressing of all, he began to suffer from delusions and hallucinations: he imagined that his advisors were plotting against him; he "saw" objects that simply were not there. Dr. Baker and the physicians he called in to provide emergency consultations and advice were at a complete loss to explain the cause of the king's symptomatology. But regardless of their inability to confirm a diagnosis, the physicians did what they could, treating George as they would anyone who presented with these or for that matter any other symptoms. The king was subjected to "the usual bleedings, cuppings and purgings."[3]

But in spite of all the medical attention and treatments, George's condition steadily grew worse. By November, the king's sensorium had become so profoundly deranged that a diagnosis of insanity was considered. During this period, George was observed to carry on conversations with men long dead and with creatures who'd never existed. He had vivid and frightening hallucinations, graphically describing horrible scenes and events that none of the people around him ever witnessed. His agitation became more extreme: unable to sit still for any length of time, the king would race around the palace, sometimes completely naked, at all hours of the day and night. He slept virtually not at all, his insomnia becoming more severe, and he spent hours and hours speaking utter nonsense "with scarce any intermission." More physicians were called in to offer their opinion, including, near the end of December, a Dr. Francis Willis, the noted keeper of a local madhouse, who treated the king with, among other devices, a straitjacket. Over the next few weeks, according to his biographer Stanley Ayling, the king would be physically forced into the straitjacket whenever he became "disobedient or turbulent."[3]

Needless to say, George's illness presented a major crisis to the British government. Because it rendered the monarch completely disabled, incapable of conducting any of his duties, the mysterious disease sent both the royal family and the government into an unprecedented state of disarray and struggle for power that has come to be known as the Regency Crisis. A critical event in British history, the Regency Crisis of 1788 pitted mother against son, government minister against government minister, and ultimately caused passage of the Regency Act, which proved to be groundbreaking legislation. But although, as Isaac Ray has claimed, this episode of the Royal Malady might have been the most important single illness in the history of the British Empire, the episode ended just as suddenly as it had begun: in February 1789, seventeen weeks after he'd complained of abdominal pains for the first time, George unexpectedly began to rally. Miraculously, within days, the king was back to his old self, once again capable of executing his official duties and conducting his business with a clear head and an apparently healthy body.[3]

But George's sudden and unexpected recovery in early 1789 did not represent the end of the mysterious Royal Malady. Two additional episodes of the illness, each characterized by similar symptomatology, would occur during the remaining years of the king's long reign: the first occurred in February and March of 1801, when George III was sixty-two years of age; and the final attack of the Royal Malady, which began in October 1810, was the worst, a protracted episode that spanned the final ten years of the king's life, ending mercifully with his death on January 29, 1820. During this final episode of the illness the Regency laws of 1788 were put into use for the first time: the king's apparent insanity led to the naming of the Prince of Wales as Regent, serving in place of his permanently disabled father.[4] He officially became George IV at the time of his father's death.

And a review of the king's life reveals that these three episodes of the Royal Malady were not the only ones. A fourth major disabling attack occurred in the first half of 1765, five years after he had assumed the crown following the death of his grandfather, George II. Further, the king's life was punctuated by numerous minor attacks, the first occurring as early as 1762. Although each episode was characterized by markedly similar complaints, in no case did any of the attending physicians have any idea what the actual underlying problem was. No one made a definitive diagnosis or instituted a reasonable plan of management, other than the usual "bleedings, cuppings and purgings."

In fact, it wasn't until 1966 that the mystery of the Royal Malady seemed finally to be solved. In that year Drs. Ida Macalpine and Richard Hunter, two British psychiatrists, assembled the pieces of the puzzle that had been spread out nearly two hundred years before and proposed a logical etiology that explained George III's illness. After poring over the daily medical bulletins issued by Dr. Baker and the other physicians who'd cared for the king, these researchers concluded that the seemingly discordant features of the Royal Malady, including the recurrent, spasmodic abdominal pain, the neurologic and psychiatric symptoms and signs, and the presence of sensitive and easily blistered skin and discolored urine, could all be explained by a diagnosis of some form of porphyria. Although their article announcing these findings appeared in the prestigious *British Medical Journal* in January 1966, their observations have not become widely known to the lay reader. Like my patient, Ms. Kreuger, it appeared to Drs. Macalpine and Hunter that George III must have suffered from an inherited form of this class of inborn error of metabolism,[4] a biochemical defect that really begins with the human body's attempt to produce an essential chemical compound known as heme.

We probably know more about hemoglobin than about any of the other naturally occurring proteins and compounds that compose the human body. We know an extraordinary amount about this substance that, because of its role as the transporter of oxygen from the lungs to the deep tissues of the body, is absolutely essential for life. In a way, the structure of hemoglobin can be compared to that of a diamond ring: the diamond portion consists of three molecules of heme, a compound that contains iron and actually serves as the site to which oxygen is bound; the ring portion is made up of four separate but interwoven chains of a protein called globin, whose main function is to hold the heme molecules in their proper position. Two of the four globin chains are called alpha globin; the other two are known as beta globin.[5]

But our knowledge of hemoglobin doesn't end with an understanding of its structure. We know a lot more, including the complicated biochemical pathway that leads to the formation of heme, the chromosomal location of the genes that give the instructions for the formation of the alpha globin chains (coded for by a pair of genes on the seventeenth chromosome) and the beta globin chains (coded for by a single gene on the short arm of chromosome eleven), and the actual sequences of DNA that compose these genes. We even understand the evolution of these protein components, what they looked like in our primitive ancestors, because those compounds are now represented in the form of substances known as embryonic and fetal hemoglobin. We understand the process by which oxygen is trapped and bound to the molecule in the tiny capillaries of the alveoli, the air sacs that compose the lungs, and how that oxygen becomes unbound from the hemoglobin in the capillaries of the body's deep tissue. And unfortunately, we understand all too well the consequences of mistakes, or mutations, that can occur in globin genes, errors that lead to malformed or decreased amounts of either alpha or beta globin chains, defects that cause a wide variety of serious symptoms and complications. Errors in the globin chains lead to such life-threatening but unfortunately common diseases as sickle-cell anemia (caused by a single mistake in one of the thousands of bases that form the beta globin gene) and thalassemia (also known as Mediterranean anemia).[6]

But it's the defects in the production of the heme component of the hemoglobin molecule that cause the disorders known as the porphyrias. The heme biosynthetic pathway is shown in figure 2. (Those readers who are biochemicophobic [that is, possess an unexplained fear of biochemistry], can safely ignore figure 2 without any significant loss of comprehension.) Eight separate and complex enzymatic steps must occur before a mature heme molecule is finally produced.

Since Murphy's Law is a dominant force in all of nature, genetic errors leading to deficiencies of the enzymes at each of these eight steps have been discovered and shown to cause distinct and separate diseases in humans. All of these diseases share two features in common: first, since it's impossible to reach the end of the pathway if one of the intermediate steps is missing, all forms of porphyria result in a deficiency of heme, and therefore in anemia; second, because of the blockage that occurs in the pathway, each of the enzyme defects leads to an accumulation of one or more abnormal substances in the bloodstream, a buildup of the compounds that precede the enzyme block, substances that, in many cases, prove toxic to the skin, the central nervous system, and the liver. Strangely enough, a defect along this heme biosynthetic pathway not only had an effect on English history, but also, according to a theory proposed by some medical historians, quite possibly played a major role in the development of a well-known and apparently ubiquitous ancient legend: the legend of the vampire.

Although nobody's really sure when or where the legend of the vampire actually originated, stories of "the undead" rising from their graves after nightfall to seek nourishment from the living have existed throughout history, appearing as folk tales in such diverse countries as China, Indonesia, the Philippines, and throughout eastern and western Europe.[7] However, although such stories have existed since ancient times, interest in stories about vampirism increased dramatically following the publication of Bram Stoker's classic novel, *Dracula,* in 1897. Today, the heartland of vampirism is indisputably Transylvania, a rural, mountainous province in central Romania, which was the ancestral home of the legendary bad guy, Vlad Tepes (literally, Vlad the Impaler), who was the model for Stoker's character.

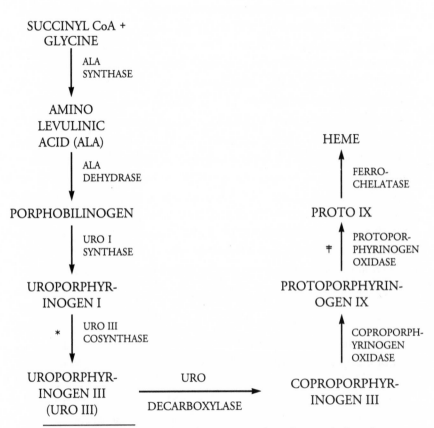

SUCCINYL CoA +
GLYCINE

ALA
SYNTHASE

AMINO
LEVULINIC
ACID (ALA)

ALA
DEHYDRASE

PORPHOBILINOGEN

URO I
SYNTHASE

UROPORPHYR-
INOGEN I

*   URO III
COSYNTHASE

UROPORPHYR-
INOGEN III
(URO III)

URO
DECARBOXYLASE

HEME

FERRO-
CHELATASE

PROTO IX

⸸   PROTOPOR-
PHYRINOGEN
OXIDASE

PROTOPORPHYRIN-
OGEN IX

COPROPORPH-
YRINOGEN
OXIDASE

COPROPORPHYR-
INOGEN III

* Enzyme block in congenital erythropoetic porphyria (Vampire's disease)
⸸ Enzyme block in "The Royal Malady"

Figure 2. The heme biosynthetic pathway.

According to the legend, vampires are formerly living individuals who, either because they have been cursed or excommunicated from the Church, find themselves rejected by the hallowed earth of cemeteries. Unable to achieve a state of peace in their own graves, these cursed individuals are metamorphosed into the undead, finding themselves trapped between the world of the living and the valley of the dead. Unable to transcend their mundane, earthly existence, the souls of vampires are incapable of escaping to heaven; refusing to decay, their bodies require daily nourishment. Because of this perpetual need for sustenance, vampires, who spend the daytime hiding in their graves, must venture out at night to scour the countryside in search of the blood of the living, the only food their bodies can metabolize. When they finally encounter an innocent human, vampires attach their fangs (really just enlarged canine teeth) to the victim's external jugular vein and slowly suck the nourishing blood, eventually satisfying their craving.

Unfortunately, even after this feeding frenzy has ended, the vampire's victims are not able to simply pick up and return to their normal lives. Two bits of bad news soon come to occupy the complete attention of these involuntary blood donors. First, they die: rendered severely anemic by the loss of tremendous quantities of blood, and contaminated as a result of their simply having come into contact with a vampire, the victims become weaker and weaker until death finally occurs. But dying isn't even the worst problem: after they die, these walking blood banks find that they, too, have been transformed into vampires, ultimately coming to compete with the original vampire and his other victims for nourishment. As a result, the existence of a single vampire within a small community will ultimately lead to something of an epidemic of vampirism, as more and more victims rise from their graves, wandering through the countryside after nightfall, searching for more and more blood.[7] Such epidemics will certainly lower morale, not to mention property values.

Throughout the twentieth century, our conception of vampires' appearance has largely been colored by their portrayal in movies, particularly those that have depicted Bram Stoker's creation. Although in

15

recent years Dracula has been transformed into something of a handsome, desirable hunk, a bloodsucking stud whose victims have often been equally desirable women, the original vision of the vampire was very different: "a hideously ugly creature that happens to bear a human form."[8] According to Manuela Dunn Mascetti, author of the book *Vampires: The Complete Guide to the World of the Undead:*

> The vampire's form . . . is available in a grotesquely distorted version, giving us the true horror of the contrast between soft human flesh and rotting death. The physical features are repulsive. . . . The vampire is also psychologically repulsive: he is evil, devoid of any moral code. . . . he drinks blood; he kills without mercy.

Not a very pretty picture.

Now it may seem odd that a brief history of vampirism has appeared smack in the middle of an exploration of King George III and the Royal Malady. Strangely enough, the legend of the vampire may have originated with the birth of one or more infants affected with a form of porphyria.

Congenital erythropoetic porphyria or, as it's more commonly called, Gunther's disease, is a rare but very damaging form of porphyria that results from a nearly complete absence of the enzyme uroporphyrinogen III cosynthase, the fourth step in the journey to mature heme molecules (see figure 2).[9] Because they lack this enzyme, unfortunate individuals affected with Gunther's disease can produce little heme. Due to the metabolic defect, the blood of these people contains excessive quantities of uroporphyrinogen I and coproporphyrinogen I, abnormal metabolites that are fluorescent red and are deposited in the connective tissue and the skin, where, when they come into contact with sunlight, prove to be severely toxic. Gunther's disease is inherited in an autosomal recessive pattern, meaning that parents of affected individuals are carriers of the abnormal gene and that children of carrier parents have a one-in-four chance of obtaining two copies of the normal gene, a one-in-two chance of inheriting one of their parents'

16

abnormal genes and one normal gene, and a one-in-four chance of getting both copies of the abnormal gene. Only in the last case will the child be affected with the disease.

The features of Gunther's disease are usually first seen in early infancy. Often, the first sign that a newborn is affected with the disorder is a bright pink stain in the child's diaper, resulting from the excretion of the toxic metabolites in the urine. The skin manifestations usually appear next: when the child's skin comes in contact with light of any type or intensity, a raised, weltlike rash develops; these welts, technically called "bulli," heal by crusting over, and eventually form large, unsightly scars that gradually become darker or lighter than the surrounding skin. Eventually, hair begins to appear over the face, while on the scalp, the scarring leads to patches of alopecia (loss of hair). As time passes, the skin manifestations lead to hideous facial disfigurement, as well as grotesque distortion of the exposed skin of the neck, arms, and hands. Ultimately, deposition of enormous amounts of uroporphyrinogen I and coproporphyrinogen I in the teeth causes erythrodontia (fluorescent red staining of the teeth), a condition that is pathognomonic for congenital erythropoetic porphyria (that is, it occurs in no other disorder).[9]

Because they usually possess normal intelligence, individuals with Gunther's disease learn early in life what they can and can't do. They quickly figure out, for instance, not to venture out from the safety of their darkened rooms during the day. This avoidance of sunlight serves two important purposes: first, it prevents the worsening of the skin manifestations, which, after all, result directly from exposure to the light; and second, remaining in seclusion during daylight protects such people from the stares, screams of fright, and embarrassing comments that would undoubtedly be directed toward them. The person affected with Gunther's disease usually learns very early in life that it's much better to be lonely in his or her room than it is to be made to feel like a sideshow freak.

To summarize, individuals affected with congenital erythropoetic porphyria are often grotesquely ugly, covered with hair, and scarred beyond recognition. Their outward appearance seems to correspond closely to the description of a vampire quoted above. Because of their photosensitivity, coupled with their psychological sensitivity, people with Gunther's disease learn to go out only at night, much the way vampires emerge from their graves to search for nourishment after the sun has set. And because of the deposition of abnormal metabolites in the structure of their teeth, patients develop erythrodontia, giving the uninformed the unmistakable impression that they have recently been drinking blood. It's not difficult to understand how, in an age when superstition and ignorance ruled the world, the birth of an infant with Gunther's disease could well have led to the beginning of a tale of the undead that ultimately grew into today's legend.

While congenital erythropoetic porphyria is extremely rare—fewer than two hundred cases have ever been reported—porphyria variegata, the disorder that Drs. Macalpine and Hunter believe affected George III, is more common. Occurring in one in a thousand individuals in the British Isles, the gene that causes porphyria variegata reaches its highest frequency in South Africa, where one in every three hundred white citizens is affected. In South Africa, every affected individual is apparently related to a pair of early settlers who emigrated from the Netherlands and married at the Cape of Good Hope in 1688.[9]

The disorder is inherited as an autosomal dominant trait: the presence of a single dose of an abnormal gene, which is passed along from affected parent to affected child, is enough to cause the disorder. People who bear the gene that's responsible for this entity produce only about 50 percent of protoporphyrinogen oxidase, the enzyme that drives the penultimate step in the heme biosynthetic pathway (see figure 2).

Now, under normal circumstances, possessing 50 percent of protoporphyrinogen oxidase is more than enough to assure that normal production of heme will occur; in fact, nearly 90 percent of all people who carry the abnormal gene that causes porphyria variegata are in excellent health throughout their entire lives. But for reasons that are not completely clear, during times of great physical or psychological stress or in cases of anemia, illness, or exposure to certain environmental agents or medications—such as alcohol, phenobarbitol, or sulfa drugs—this amount of the protoporphyrinogen oxidase is simply not enough to get the job done. At such times, the heme biosynthetic pathway becomes blocked off: the affected individual is no longer capable of producing adequate quantities of heme, resulting in a buildup of a group of metabolites, including one called protoporphyrinogen IX.[9]

In high concentrations, protoporphyrinogen IX and these other metabolites are toxic to both the skin and, more important, the central nervous system. When stress occurs, the person affected with porphyria variegata may develop one or more of a whole host of seemingly unconnected, difficult-to-explain medical problems, symptoms and signs that, physiologically, directly relate to the toxic effects of protoporphyrinogen IX. Patients might complain of severe, crampy abdominal pain, often accompanied by vomiting, constipation, or diarrhea. They develop lightning-quick, intense pains in their limbs, head, neck, or chest, pains unassociated with any traumatic injury. Affected individuals have unexplained neurologic symptoms, such as muscle weakness, loss of sensation, seizures, strokes, and coma, the latter few of which can lead to premature death. And they develop a whole host of psychiatric disturbances, including anxiety, restlessness, insomnia, hallucinations, paranoia, and depression.

The clinical features that occur in porphyria variegata are identical to those that occurred at one time or another in my patient, Ms. Kreuger. However, as I've already mentioned, Ms. Kreuger did not have porphyria variegata; she suffered from a related entity known as acute intermittent porphyria, a disorder that's caused by the deficiency of uro I synthase, the enzyme that catalyzes the third step in the heme biosynthetic pathway (see figure 2). These two disorders share nearly all of their clinical features in common; the only feature that distinguishes them at the clinical level is that porphyria variegata is also associated with skin lesions. Because protoporphyrinogen IX is toxic to the skin as well as to the central nervous system, individuals affected with porphyria variegata often develop rashes, similar to, but far less severe than, those seen in patients affected with congenital erythropoetic porphyria. But skin manifestations never occur in acute intermittent porphyria; although quite toxic to the central nervous system, excessive amounts of porphobilinogen and amino levulinic acid (the metabolites that build up as a result of the failure of uro I synthase to do its job) have no effect on the skin.[9]

The clinical symptoms and signs that occurred during the episodes of the Royal Malady clearly match those seen in cases of symptomatic porphyria variegata. As Drs. Macalpine and Hunter report in their 1966 article:[4]

> Reviewed in this light, the symptomatology and course of the royal malady reads like a text book case: colic and constipation; painful paresis of the arm and legs; vocal paresis, visual disturbance and other signs of bulbar involvement; radicular pain; autonomic disturbances with marked tachycardia and sweating attacks; and encephalopathy ranging from insomnia to excitement, raging delirium, stupor and fits. The only feature not recorded is hypertension, because blood pressure was not measured.

One may conclude that George III suffered from one of the forms of porphyria. Because of the presence of skin manifestations, the type was most likely porphyria variegata. Although his four major and numerous minor episodes of the disease began apparently without any warning, the episodes were undoubtedly prolonged and the symptoms made more severe as a result of the king's medical treatment. All those "bleedings, cuppings and purgings" unquestionably worsened the king's anemia. Since anemia is a known trigger of both acute intermittent porphyria and porphyria variegata, the medical care King George received apparently worsened the crises that were caused by his disorder.

This conclusion, that the Royal Malady represented a well-known and not-all-that-uncommon form of porphyria, raises at least two intriguing questions. Was George III's illness an isolated example of this disorder or was the disease present in any of the king's royal ancestors? And what effect did porphyria have on George's life, on his long reign, and on the running of the government during the years 1760 to 1820?

First, as already stated, both porphyria variegata and acute intermittent porphyria are typically passed on from affected parent to affected child. Although the abnormality in the gene might have originated as a random change that occurred in the genetic material at or before the time of George's conception, a change that is known as a spontaneous mutation, it is in fact more likely that the gene was passed on to him by one of his parents. Through careful analysis of George III's forebears, other affected relatives might be identified.

This optimism must be tempered by the fact that, as already discussed, unlike many other autosomal dominantly inherited disorders, the vast majority of individuals who carry the gene responsible for both types of porphyria never know that there's anything different about them. As such, in analyzing the pedigree, we'd expect to find, at best, spotty representation of the disease in other members of the royal family, with evidence of the disease skipping generations and of affected individuals suffering from markedly variable expression of the gene. With this in mind, are there in fact other members of the family of George III who appear to have been affected with porphyria?

The answer to the first question is a resounding yes. In 1967 Drs. Macalpine and Hunter, the undisputed heroes of this story, joined this time by a third colleague, Dr. C. Rimington, followed up their original article on the Royal Malady by performing an exhaustive review of the medical histories of the individuals who form the various branches of George III's family tree.[10] The annotated pedigree they painstakingly documented, reproduced here in figure 3, appears to blossom with other instances of individuals affected with a disorder whose features overlap significantly with those suffered by George III during his episodes of the Royal Malady.

Amazingly, although the lack of complete records makes it impossible to say for sure, Drs. Macalpine, Hunter, and Rimington have proposed that the gene responsible for the Royal Malady may have been introduced into the royal family of Great Britain as early as 1542, nearly two hundred years before the birth of the infant who would become George III. It was in that year that Mary, Queen of Scots, was conceived. From the time of her adolescence, Mary, described by Drs. Macalpine, Hunter, and Rimington as "one of the great invalids of history,"[10] suffered from repeated episodes of severe, colicky abdominal pain, attacks that, like those that would afflict her descendant, George III, two centuries later, were frequently accompanied by vomiting, joint pains, and psychiatric disturbances. Perhaps the worst and most characteristic episode of her illness occurred in 1566, when, suddenly and without any warning, Mary, who was then twenty-four, developed severe nausea accompanied by insomnia. Within hours, the symptoms that at first resembled little more than a mild case of viral gastroenteritis rapidly grew more severe and worrisome.

On the second day of Mary's illness, the queen developed severe pain in her back and side, intense discomfort exacerbated and made intolerable by virtually every slight movement, even inhaling and exhaling. Next, Mary's nausea worsened, and she began to vomit. Over the next two days she retched incessantly, more than sixty times, until bright red blood began to stain the vomitus.

But although these symptoms must have been very disturbing to both her and her family, the pain and vomiting weren't the worst problems produced by the disorder. Once, mercifully, the vomiting ended, Mary became delirious, losing her ability to both speak and see. Next, she developed convulsions, and following one seizure, the queen lapsed into a coma. Her situation seemed dire; although no explanation could be offered for the illness and no treatment given to improve her condition, the young woman was sinking rapidly, moving inexorably, it seemed, toward death. But, amazingly, only ten days after the episode had begun, Mary's illness spontaneously resolved. Miraculously, she returned, relatively unscathed, to her premorbid state.

Similar episodes recurred throughout Mary's short and sad life, which ended in 1587, not because of any complications directly relating to her unusual illnesses, but rather because she was beheaded for plotting to overthrow her cousin, Queen Elizabeth I. (It is certainly possible that the neuropsychological effects of Mary's illness caused her intransigence and illogic, factors that led her to attempt, against all odds and sound advice, to overthrow her cousin's government and seize power; indirectly, Mary's illness may have played a role in her death.) But in 1566, after she'd married Henry Stuart (a cousin also known as Lord Darnley), Mary gave birth to a son who, upon the death of the childless Elizabeth I in 1603, ascended to the throne as James I, thus becoming the first member of the Stuart dynasty to become king of

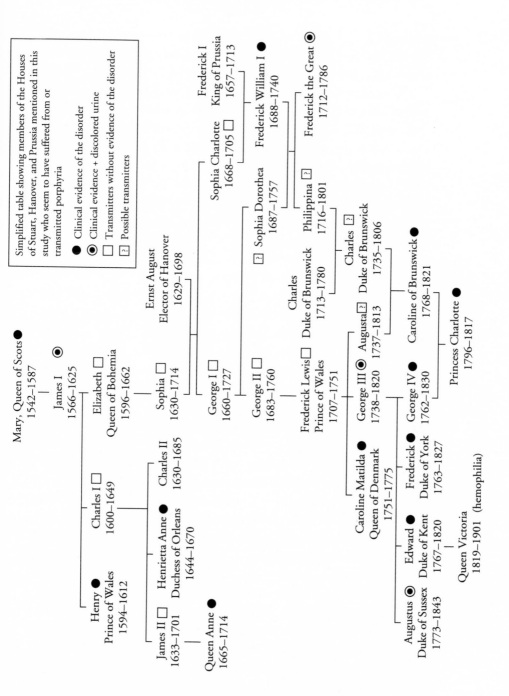

Figure 3. An annotated pedigree of George III (modified from reference 11).

England. Like his mother and his great-great-great-great-grandson, George III, King James I suffered from a peculiar recurrent illness that remained undiagnosed during his lifetime.

According to Drs. Macalpine, Hunter, and Rimington, throughout his adult life, King James I was repeatedly affected with attacks of abdominal colic, often accompanied by nausea, vomiting, and diarrhea. During these attacks, he was found to occasionally have a rapid and at times irregular pulse, as well as pains in his limbs and trunk, which were described in detailed medical reports by his physician, Sir Theodore Turquet de Mayerne, as arthritis and often accompanied by weakness. During these episodes the king was noted to suffer from behavioral instability characterized by alternating states of sadness, uncontrolled weeping, irritability, and euphoria, as well as insomnia, and fits of unconsciousness. Often, the episodes of illness would be accompanied by the passage of dark, "bloody" urine that, according to the king himself, resembled port wine.[10] Although these episodes appear nearly clinically identical to the ones suffered by his mother, one detail of James's illness is different, one essential clinical feature, documented by the royal physician, that in itself nearly confirms the diagnosis of porphyria variegata.

In the summer of 1611, during what would turn out to be one of the king's milder episodes of illness, Mayerne noted that after exposing himself to the "blazing sun" for a prolonged period, James's face, especially his forehead, broke out in a rash of blisters. Although the other symptoms, which included headache, vomiting, and arthritic limb pain, were relatively short-lived, the vesicular rash remained, resistant to treatment with ointments and salves, throughout the summer, finally resolving in late September, "when the sun was less violent."[10] This description is inconsistent with anything other than the photosensitivity seen in the various types of porphyria. Based on the description of these illnesses, King James I suffered from porphyria variegata.

James I fathered three children: his eldest, Henry, Prince of Wales, born in 1594, predeceased his father by thirteen years; Elizabeth, born in 1596, became Queen of Bohemia and was the direct ancestor of the Hanoverian dynasty, the branch of the family to which George III belonged; and Charles, born in 1600, upon the death of his father went on to become King Charles I. Although their positions in the pedigree indicate that all three of James's children inherited the gene responsible for porphyria variegata from their father, neither Elizabeth nor Charles exhibited any symptoms of what would later come to be known as the Royal Malady. Only Prince Henry manifested any symptoms of the family's disease.[10]

In fact, some of the more severe neurologically induced complications from an episode of the Royal Malady probably led to the premature and unexpected death of the then eighteen-year-old Prince of Wales on November 6, 1612, an event that thrust his younger brother, Charles, into the role of heir-apparent. Beginning on October 10 of that year, Henry developed an illness that nearly paralleled the episodes suffered by his father and grandmother. Initially characterized by high fever, abdominal pain, diarrhea, restlessness, and insomnia, the symptoms waxed and waned throughout the remainder of October, finally crescendoing in early November, at which time the prince became affected with a whole host of new and unexplainable symptoms and signs: his pulse raced, he had trouble breathing, his muscles became weak and twitched uncontrollably; he suffered from headaches, tinnitus (ringing in his ears), photophobia (sensitivity to light), delirium, and seizures. Finally, on November 5, the prince slipped into a deep coma, possibly the consequence of a stroke, from which he would never awaken. Knowing what we now do about the remainder of the prince's family history, it would be hard to believe that this illness represented anything other than a severe episode of porphyria variegata.

Neither King Charles I, who ascended to the throne upon the death of his father in 1625 and ruled England until 1649, when he was beheaded for treason, nor either of his two sons, Charles II, who became king when the monarchy was reestablished in 1660 and ruled until his death in 1685, *and* James II, whose reign lasted from 1685 to 1688, appeared to show any symptoms or signs of porphyria. But analysis of the family tree strongly suggests that the gene was present in at least two of them. Both Charles I and James II had children who showed evidence of the familial disease.

One of those offspring who clearly was affected with the Royal Malady was Queen Anne, the only child of James II, who proved to be

the last member of the Stuart dynasty. All through her life, Anne was afflicted with an illness that was described by her physicians as "the flying
gout," a disorder manifested by, among other features, intense pains in
the limbs and abdomen and "hysterical affectations."[10] When Anne,
who was childless, died suddenly in 1714 at the age of forty-nine, after
having fallen mysteriously into a coma that followed a period of "stupe-
faction, broken by occasional fits of delirium,"[10] the gene for the disorder in this branch of the family tree died with her. But the gene for
porphyria variegata lived on in other branches of the British royal family, transmitted through yet another descendant of Mary, Queen of
Scots. Analysis of the pedigree shows that, although she herself was unaffected, Elizabeth, Queen of Bohemia, daughter of King James I, sister
of Henry, Prince of Wales, and Charles I, and great-great-great-grand-
mother of George III, carried the gene for porphyria variegata into the
Hanoverian dynasty.

After searching through the historical records, Drs. Macalpine,
Hunter, and Rimington conclude that although none of the individuals
were affected by the disease, the gene for the Royal Malady had to be
present in the next four generations of British monarchs. The life histories of Elizabeth's daughter Sophia, her grandson George I, her great-
grandson George II, and her great-great-grandson Frederick Louis,
Prince of Wales, fail to reveal a single example of a manifestation of porphyria. It was only in the case of Frederick Louis's son, George, the man
who would ultimately become George III, that the gene next caused
significant symptoms and signs of disease.

Two pieces of evidence support the conclusion that this asymptomatic transmission of the gene actually occurred. First, as has been
discussed above, the majority of individuals who carry the gene for porphyria variegata are asymptomatic. The second piece of evidence is far
more convincing: not one but two members of this line fathered children who appeared to be affected. Elizabeth's grandson, George I, had
a son, Frederick Wilhelm I, and a grandson, Frederick II (known to
history as "Frederick the Great"), both of whom were kings of
Prussia, who appeared to be affected with the Royal Malady. History
has seen fit to consider the recurrent episodes of limb and abdominal

pain suffered by both of these men as cases of severe, recurrent gout; however, the symptoms from which they suffered closely paralleled George III's. And Elizabeth's great-great-grandson, Frederick Louis, Prince of Wales, had at least two children who were affected: George III and his younger sister, Caroline Matilda, Queen of Denmark. Thus there is evidence that, prior to the birth of George III in 1738, England had experienced nearly two hundred years of the effects of the Royal Malady on the ruling family.

In fact, all the evidence, every symptom and sign that composed the Royal Malady, as well as the extensive review of the medical history of all the members of his family tree performed by Drs. Macalpine, Hunter, and Rimington, seems to point incontrovertibly to the fact that George III suffered from porphyria variegata. And yet there's a crucial piece of hard evidence missing: confirming the diagnosis of this, or of any other form of porphyria, depends on the discovery of a "smoking gun," on the demonstration of the deficiency of the specific enzyme and the buildup of the abnormal metabolites in the blood and urine of the affected individual. Since circumstances (namely, the fact that he died more than 170 years ago) render it impossible to perform a complete chemical analysis of George III's blood and urine, it appears, unfortunately, as if we're stuck, unable to know for certain whether George III actually suffered from a form of porphyria.

Or are we?

There are a lot of bad things about genetic diseases. They tend to be chronic illnesses that cause years of disability and suffering. They often lead to premature death. And because they tend to be transmitted from parent to child, they nearly always cause feelings of profound guilt on the part of the parents, who blame themselves for passing along the abnormal gene. But this very transmission from parent to child may, in the case of George III, actually provide the "smoking gun" that would confirm the diagnosis. Although King George III has been dead for more than 170 years, and his grandfather, King George II, died nearly 235 years ago, their genetic material lives on

27

today, transmitted through the centuries in the sperm and eggs of their direct descendants. Because of this extraordinary property of DNA, it might be possible to identify living relatives of George III who carry the abnormal gene, people who, through their linkage to the Stuart and Hanoverian dynasties, might be able to provide us with proof beyond a shadow of a doubt that the Royal Malady did in fact represent a distinct case of porphyria.

Apparently understanding this concept, George III did his best to assure that twentieth-century geneticists would be provided with a surplus of blood and urine samples. Following his marriage to Charlotte Sophia of Mecklenburg-Strelitz in September 1761, he set about fathering children at a breakneck pace. The couple produced fifteen offspring, including six girls and nine boys. But unfortunately, circumstances beyond the king's control worked against us: none of the six daughters, who included Princesses Charlotte, Augusta, Elizabeth, Sophia, Amelia, and Mary, bore any children. And of his nine sons, two, Prince Octavius and Prince Alfred, died in infancy. Two others, Prince Frederick, Duke of York, and Prince Augustus, Duke of Sussex, remained childless. And three had children who themselves produced no offspring[11]: George, Prince of Wales, who ruled England as George IV from the time of his father's death in 1820 until his own death in 1830; Prince William, Duke of Clarence, who, as William IV, succeeded his brother, George, ruling until his own death in 1837; and Prince Ernest, Duke of Cumberland, who, according to the biographer Stanley Ayling,[11] grew up to be "the most unpopular man in England," ultimately becoming King of Hanover.

Therefore, only two of the children fathered by George III established ongoing lines: Prince Edward, Duke of Kent, whose only child, Victoria, ruled as Queen of England from 1837, when her uncle, William IV, died, until her own death at the age of eighty-two in 1901; and Prince Adolphus, Duke of Cambridge, whose daughter, Mary, produced live-born children. Review of the records reveals that neither the Duke of Cambridge nor his daughter Mary showed any symptoms or signs of porphyria; and, although Edward, the Duke of Kent, like his father, suffered from "frequent bilious attacks" accompanied by pain and weakness of the limbs and skin rashes,[10] neither his daughter, Queen Victoria, nor any of her offspring seemed to demonstrate a single feature of the Royal Malady. Since, in autosomal dominantly inherited entities, each offspring of an affected parent has a one-in-two chance of inheriting the abnormal gene and an equal chance of getting the normal gene, and since parents who inherit this so-called "normal" gene cannot themselves have children who are affected, these observations are certainly not inconsistent with a diagnosis of porphyria variegata. They do, unfortunately, make it a bit more difficult to come up with that all-important "smoking gun."

But the gene for porphyria variegata clearly did not originate with George III; it was passed along to him through generations of English monarchs, individuals who had other children who, although they did not themselves become kings or queens, just the same had the identical chance of passing the gene for the Royal Malady along to their offspring. Perhaps one of these other descendants of the Hanoverian dynasty could be found to be living today and suffering from the features of porphyria variegata.

Once again, it was Drs. Macalpine, Hunter, and Rimington who investigated this possibility.[10] They discovered two contemporary women who, through their relationship to members of George III's family, qualified for examination. The first of these subjects, referred to by the authors as Patient A, was the great-great-great-granddaughter of George II's youngest child (George III's aunt), Princess Louisa. According to their article, during her sixth decade of life, Patient A developed a case of pneumonia and came under the care of a "distinguished physician who is a recognized authority on porphyria."[10] After having observed numerous episodes during which the woman's urine became bright red, the physician suspected a diagnosis of porphyria. For this physician, the diagnosis was confirmed by the finding of large amounts of the abnormal metabolites coproporphyrin, uroporphyrin, and porphobilinogen in the woman's urine.

The woman described by Drs. Macalpine, Hunter, and Rimington as Patient B was also a descendant of George II, related in a more complicated way than Patient A; the product of a mating between descendants of both of George's daughters, she was the great-great-great-granddaughter of both Princesses Mary and Louisa. Then in her seventh decade of life, Patient B had a history reaching back to adolescence of recurrent episodes of a condition whose components correspond remarkably to those that made up the Royal Malady. Characterized by severe abdominal pain, much "worse than labour pains," and constipation, the episodes were exacerbated by the administration of certain medications, including barbiturates and sulfa drugs, and included arthritic-like limb pains, sun sensitivity with easy blistering of the hands and feet, and the passage of dark, red urine. Although laboratory analysis of Patient B's stool and urine was performed at a time when no acute exacerbation of the illness was occurring, the results revealed elevated levels of coproporphyrin, protoporphyrin and protoporphyrinogen IX.[10] This analysis proves incontrovertibly that the woman suffered from porphyria variegata and offers conclusive evidence that the Royal Malady of George III actually did represent the manifestations of porphyria variegata.

Compared with some of George III's episodes, it didn't take Ms. Kreuger all that long to recover from the coma-like stupor into which she'd slipped a few hours before appearing in the emergency room that afternoon fifteen years ago. During that ambulatory-care rotation I did as a fourth-year medical student, we were encouraged to "make rounds" on the patients who, after we'd had a hand in managing them in the outpatient department, had been admitted to the hospital. Trying my compulsive best to get a grade of honors in the rotation, every day after completing my shift in the emergency room I dutifully went up to the ward to visit the woman. For the first few days, Ms. Kreuger remained pretty much unchanged, lying in her bed, producing no sound other than that Lurch-like moaning noise that had so endeared her to me in the first place. But then, one afternoon less than a week after she'd been admitted to the hospital, I entered the four-bed room on the internal medicine ward and found her sitting up in bed, reading a copy of *Newsweek*. After once again fumbling over an introduction and trying to explain who I was and what I was doing there, I asked how she was feeling. "Better," she replied in a normal but weary-sounding voice. Although she seemed to be tired and in more than a little pain, she appeared to be happy to have some company, even though that company was a lowly fourth-year medical student.

"I understand from reading your chart that you get attacks like this every few months," I said. "Do you ever know in advance when they're going to start?"

"No, not really," she replied. "Usually what happens is, out of the clear blue, my stomach starts to hurt. That's usually the first sign I have that it's starting up. The pain gets worse and worse and the next thing I know, I'm waking up in a hospital bed with a headache and all sorts of other problems. This time, it looks like the nerve that controls the left side of my face doesn't seem to be working. Did you notice that?"

When she'd started talking, I had noticed that the muscles on the left side of her face seemed to be paralyzed. I nodded my head.

"This problem has happened to me before," she continued. "Judging from past experience, the paralysis should last about a month or so. Then, for some reason no one can explain, the nerve just starts to work again."

"It must be terrible," I said.

"No, it's not so bad," she answered. "At least, it hasn't been that bad since the doctors finally figured out what was wrong with me. Even though I understand that it's a serious disease, and that there's a possibility that I might die during one of these attacks, you'd be amazed at how much easier it is to take once you know what's wrong and that, at least most of the time, the symptoms aren't going to last forever. But before they knew I had porphyria, things *were* pretty terrible. For years, nobody had any idea why I was getting so sick so often."

"I guess no one else in your family is affected," I said.

"Actually, I don't really know that for sure. I've been told that the form of porphyria I have runs in families, but I was adopted when I was less than a year old. I've never been able to find out anything about my birth parents, so I don't know if either of them had the disease."

"Do you remember when you had your first attack?" I asked.

"When I was fifteen," Ms. Kreuger replied. "I remember it as if it were yesterday: I was in so much pain that I thought my belly was going to explode. My parents rushed me to the local hospital in Pittsburgh, which is where I grew up. The doctors diagnosed acute appendicitis and they opened me up. Of course, they didn't find anything wrong. Then, about a year and a half later, I had my second attack. They decided to operate on me again, and, of course, they still couldn't find anything wrong. But that time, right after the surgery, I became unconscious. I was out for nearly a month; even though nobody knew what was wrong with me, the doctors all thought I was going to die. Then, one morning, I just woke up and felt fine. My nurse told my parents it was a miracle.

"Over the next few years, I kept getting the attacks every few months. Each time, my parents would take me to one hospital or another, and each time, the doctors would want to do exploratory surgery. After they'd cut me open three or four times and hadn't found anything wrong, they finally decided I was faking the whole thing just to get attention. They decided I was having all these attacks because . . . well, because I was just completely loony."

"I've read that happens a lot with people with porphyria," I interrupted. "It's not unusual for doctors, at one time or another, to diagnose them as having a psychiatric disorder."

"Well, that's certainly what happened to me," Ms. Kreuger continued. "I got sent to see a psychiatrist, who asked me a lot of questions about my parents and my background, trying to figure out exactly what it was that had finally pushed me over the edge. The psychiatrist finally decided that my attacks were somehow caused by the fact that I'd been adopted, and he recommended that I immediately get started on a course of intensive psychotherapy."

"That must have been very helpful," I said.

"I must admit, it really did change my life," she replied. "Unfortunately, it didn't exactly change it for the better. I started going to see the psychiatrist two and three times a week. I was a senior in high school then, and I was spending so much time in the shrink's office that I had to drop out of all my extracurricular activities at school.

I lost just about all my friends, who figured that I must have really been deranged. It caused all sorts of problems in my family. My parents started fighting a lot: my father blamed my mother because it was her idea to adopt me; my mother blamed my father for treating me like a guest in our house, rather than like a real member of the family. They fought about what to do with me, whether to put me away in an institution or keep me at home. And, of course, nobody paid any attention to anything I said; since the doctors had decided I was crazy, everybody figured that any idea I came up with, or any suggestion or decision I made, was just the rantings and ravings of a crazy person. And to make matters worse, while I was in the midst of this intensive psychotherapy, my attacks started to get worse. The psychiatrist figured it was because we were finally starting to make some progress in dealing with the issues that were actually bothering me, and so he suggested that we increase the number of sessions. Of course, the worsening of the attacks had nothing to do with my therapy; my attacks were getting worse because the porphyria was getting worse."

"How did you finally escape from the psychiatrist?" I asked.

"Simple. I decided to move away from my family. When I was twenty-six, I moved in with my mother's sister and her family here in the Bronx. Since I felt that the visits to the shrink weren't doing me the least bit of good, I decided not to look for a new therapist once I got settled in New York. But two weeks after I got here, I had another attack."

"That's when you came here for the first time?" I asked.

"That's right," she replied. "They did more surgery on me, and guess what they found."

"Nothing was wrong," I answered.

"That's correct. I'll tell you, I've had so much abdominal surgery, I finally suggested to them at one point that, rather than stitching me up next time, they just install a zipper. But then, finally, after all those years, one of the doctors here figured out that I had porphyria. Now everything's fine."

"Everything except that you wind up getting admitted to the hospital every six months," I said.

"Like I said, even that's not so bad. Just knowing that I'm not crazy, and that I'm eventually going to get better is what's important. And my aunt and her family are pretty good about it, too."

Our talk was obviously wearing on Ms. Kreuger, and so I decided to depart. Although she was much improved, she remained in the hospital, steadily regaining her strength, for another few days. Then, over the next weekend, she was discharged to home. Since her discharge, I've never had the opportunity to see her again.

But now, thinking about the effects that porphyria must have had on George III's life and on the running of the British government during the years 1760 to 1820, I'm struck by a great many of the details that Ms. Kreuger described to me during those days of her hospitalization. Although, not surprisingly, there are a number of parallels between the lives of these two individuals whose situations were so different and who lived so many years apart, there are also, undeniably, differences. Matters were much more complicated for the King of England: rather than having only a smattering of family and friends concerned about his well-being, as had Ms. Kreuger, George III was a central figure in society and in history. The king was surrounded by a large, ambitious family, many of whom would do virtually anything to gain control of the government. He had powerful friends and ministers, who, during the times of crisis that punctuated his life, were forced to choose sides. He had millions of subjects in England as well as in the British colonies flung throughout the world, people over whom he reigned and who depended on him and his decisions. Just imagine what life must have been like in the British Empire when this very important man was suddenly and repeatedly struck down and incapacitated by mysterious episodes of what appeared to be acute insanity. The mystery of the Royal Malady undoubtedly had significant effects on the course of the history of England.

But, these major differences aside, George III and Ms. Kreuger do share a lot in common. For instance, like the damaging effect Ms. Kreuger's illness had on her relationship with her adoptive parents, the Royal Malady served to tear apart George III's family. The attack that began in June 1788, described in detail above, led directly to the so-called Regency Crisis, a political free-for-all in which members of the British royal family, including the king's eldest son, the Prince of Wales, and the king's most trusted cabinet ministers struggled to gain the upper hand. The free-for-all led to vehement infighting among members of the king's immediate family. In November 1788, after seeking the opinion of his own private physician, the Prince of Wales, hoping to gain control of the government, declared his father "a complete lunatick," claiming that the king was permanently insane.[12] Although the prince was joined by his brother, William, in this conclusion, their mother, the queen, who hoped and prayed for her husband's rapid and complete recovery from the curse that had come to plague him, deeply resented her sons' attitudes, as well as the manner by which the prince had seized control of the king's duties "as though he were already dead or judged incurable."[12] Not surprisingly, this episode created a serious and long-standing rift between Queen Charlotte Sophia and her eldest sons, who, at the height of their hostility, accused their mother of being "as much deranged as the King."[12]

Although the Regency Crisis ended with George III's nearly miraculous recovery in February 1789, this episode of the Royal Malady had two major effects: first, it allowed Parliament to settle on a workable plan to be instituted upon the incapacitation of this and future monarchs; and second, as was the case in Ms. Kreuger's family, it led to a serious schism within the king's family that would not and could not be fully mended.

The parallels between Ms. Kreuger's illness and the Royal Malady don't end with the effects their disorder had on their families. Early in the course of her disease, after repeated exploratory laparotomies had failed to uncover any pathology, Ms. Kreuger was judged to have a serious psychiatric disturbance. A search of the events of her early life was then undertaken to identify any possible triggers for her abnormal behavior, a search that ended with the conclusion that her symptoms were in some way caused by her adoption at a very early age. A similar search has been carried out in the life of George III: from the time that the diagnosis of insanity was made by his physicians in 1788 until the time that his condition was definitively diagnosed as porphyria

variegata by Drs. Macalpine and Hunter in 1966, repeated attempts
were made to identify the problems in the king's past that contributed
to his becoming deranged. In the case of Ms. Kreuger, the examination
was carried out by her psychiatrist; in the case of George III, however,
the search was conducted by many historians.

Those historians have advanced numerous theories in attempting
to explain the king's insanity. According to the noted British scholar
John Brooke, one group of twentieth-century authors have tended to
see the king not as psychotic, but rather as an ineffectual man who,
keenly aware of his own lack of ability to serve as monarch of so vast
and powerful a country, and unwilling to admit openly to those fail-
ings, faked the episodes of insanity in order to escape his responsibilities.[13] A second group concluded that it was the shock and shame of
the loss of the American colonies following the undignified defeat of
the supreme British forces at the hands of the ragtag Continental
Army that led to the king's slow spiral toward madness. Yet another
theory held that it was simple sexual frustration that caused the king to
lose his mind, frustration brought about by the combined effects of his
strict personal moral code that prevented him from taking a mistress
and the fact that Queen Charlotte Sophia was considered by some to
be something of a "shrew," a difficult and calculating woman who,
through providing or withholding sexual favors, essentially ran the
king's life.[13]

Of course, although all of this speculating provided generations
of British historians with a good, steady income, the realization that
George's symptoms sprang not from idiopathic insanity, but rather
from a form of porphyria proved all of these theories nothing more
than fantasies. As was the case when the legendary clinical professor of
medicine made the spectacular diagnosis of acute intermittent porphyria in Ms. Kreuger, the brilliant and undoubtedly correct conclusion reached by Drs. Macalpine and Hunter freed George III for all
time from the "stigma" of insanity. But it was not only the reputation of
George III that benefited from this retrospective diagnosis: Queen
Charlotte also benefited greatly. Now, rather than being portrayed
throughout history as an insensitive shrew who drove her husband

insane, her husband's diagnosis has allowed her to be remembered as a caring woman who loved her chronically ill husband, defended him against attack from all quarters, and, sexual politics aside, provided him with fifteen children.[13]

Ms. Kreuger told me that before her diagnosis of porphyria had been made, everyone around her, including her family, friends, and acquaintances, dismissed her thoughts and ideas as nothing more than the rantings and ravings of a crazy person. Is this another parallel between her life and the life of George III? Were the words and decisions of the man who was King of England during one of the most turbulent eras in its history dismissed by those around him? And, more important, was the course of world history altered by the fact that a man with porphyria variegata was ruler of probably the most powerful empire then in existence?

By all accounts, George III was an unduly stubborn, rigid man who, once he'd made a decision, stuck by it against all advice, no matter how sound. When time proved that his decision had been unwise, George learned to live with the consequences. According to the historian John Brooke, during the American Revolutionary War, George III firmly adhered to a policy toward the American colonies that was unwise and ultimately proved disastrous.[13] For example, his politically unsound, seemingly illogical decision to support the Tea Act of May 1773, which directly benefited the privately owned East India Company while further burdening the disenfranchised and already-angry colonists, directly led to the Boston Tea Party, an event that placed on simmer the pot that ultimately would boil over into the Revolutionary War.[14]

It is possible that these historically important, politically unsound decisions were directly related to the king's underlying disease. George III, facing battles both at home and abroad, was undoubtedly under a great deal of personal stress during the days that led up to the start of the American Revolution. As already mentioned, stress, whether physically derived in the form of an infectious disease or psychologically induced, can, in individuals who carry the gene that causes porphyria variegata, trigger a buildup of the metabolite protoporphyrinogen IX, leading to symptoms of the disease. Conceivably, the psychological stress George experienced during those weeks might have led to a minor episode of the Royal Malady, one which caused no abdominal pain, skin manifestations, or discoloration of urine, but featured an impairment in the king's ability to reason.

But even if the king wasn't functioning under the influence of a minor attack of the Royal Malady during the days that led up to the American Revolution, it's still possible that the effects of George's inherited disease played a role in his decision-making process. It must be remembered that between attacks of his illness, the king's sensorium was perfectly lucid; when free of the Royal Malady, he had insight into what his condition could do to him. And like Ms. Kreuger during the years before her diagnosis was made, George III probably lived in constant fear of his disease.

Think of what the king's life must have been like. He clearly understood that he was affected with a disorder that, during acute exacerbations, caused him nearly unbearable pain and, even worse, episodes of insanity. He also knew that these periods of illness occurred unpredictably, without even a moment's warning. George probably understood that any decisions he made during the periods he was under the influence of his disease were likely to be illogical and potentially hazardous; but as king, and as the grandson of a king, he also understood that, in order to be an effective monarch, he had to exude confidence, to show those around him that he believed in his abilities as a leader. It is perhaps for this reason that he seemed so stubborn and rigid: in adhering to decisions, even those that seemed unwise, he was simply doing his best to convince his subjects that despite the Royal Malady he could still be an effective ruler.

But reading anything more into the effect of George's porphyria on the American Revolution would be naïve. The late eighteenth century was a time of great turmoil, not only in England and its colonies, but in the rest of the developed world as well. Europe was being swept by the Industrial Revolution, an event that transformed the workplace and altered forever the economy and, with it, the international balance of power. Ideas were changing throughout the world; revolutionary concepts were being introduced in the American colonies, in France, and in other countries.

Undoubtedly, the American Revolution would have been fought whether or not George III had become King of England following the death of his grandfather. But in trying to understand the origins of that war, the state of the king's health should not be ignored: George III probably had porphyria variegata; his reign was clearly interrupted by multiple episodes of the Royal Malady; and because of his understanding of the effect of the disease on his life, his style of running the government—from the way he made decisions to the way he remained inflexible when those decisions blew up in his face—was undoubtedly influenced by both his fear of the disease and of being judged an incompetent ruler. As such, George III's disease surely affected the timing of the American Revolutionary War, how it was fought, and, ultimately, how it ended.

References

1. Isaac Ray, Insanity of King George III, *American Journal of Insanity* 12 (1855): 1.
2. Stanley Ayling, *George the Third* (New York: Alfred A. Knopf, 1972), 330.
3. Ibid., 331–45.
4. Ida Macalpine and Richard Hunter, The insanity of King George III: A classic case of porphyria, *British Medical Journal* 1 (1966): 65–71.
5. Lubert Stryer, *Biochemistry* (San Francisco: W. H. Freeman and Co., 1975), 62–112.
6. J. S. Thompson and M. W. Thompson, *Genetics in Medicine,* 4th ed. (Philadelphia: W. B. Saunders Co., 1986), 79–92.
7. Paul Barber, The Real Vampire: Forensic Pathology and the Lore of the Undead, *Natural History,* October 1990, 74–382.
8. Manuela D. Mascetti, *Vampires: The Complete Guide to the World of the Undead* (New York: Viking Studio Books, 1992), 9.
9. Urs A. Meyer and Rudi Schmid, The porphyrias, in John B. Stanbury, James B. Wyngaarden, and Donald S. Fredrichson, eds., *The Metabolic Basis of Inherited Disease,* 4th ed. (New York: McGraw-Hill Book Co., 1978), 1166–220.

10. Ida Macalpine, Richard Hunter, and C. Rimington, Porphyria in the royal houses of Stuart, Hanover, and Prussia: A follow-up study of George III's illness, *British Medical Journal* 1 (1968): 7–18 .

11. Ayling, *George the Third,* 179.

12. Ibid., 333–39.

13. John Brooke, Historical Implications of Porphyria, *British Medical Journal* 1 (1968): 109–11.

14. Ayling, *George the Third,* 246.

Was George Washington *Really* the Father of Our Country?

It's July 9, 1799. In England, King George III is enjoying a period of good health between attacks of the Royal Malady; in northern Virginia, George Washington, the leader of the opposition forces during the American War of Independence, and therefore George III's foe, is sitting at a desk in his study on the first floor of his home, Mount Vernon. No longer young nor powerful at sixty-seven years of age, the ex-president is hard at work on a document that's stretching on and on, covering page after page of the special paper ordered for just this occasion. Periodically, Washington, pausing from his work, stares out the windows of the home in which he's lived since childhood and sadly breathes an audible sigh. Then, his reverie finally broken, the old man returns to his work with renewed conviction.

On that day, as he worked on the document that would become his official Last Will and Testament,[1] George Washington, the most famous man in the then-short history of the United States, was forced to take a long, hard look back at his life. Without question, as he set down on paper what he wanted done with all the possessions he'd amassed during his lifetime, the old man realized how much he'd managed to accomplish during the relatively few years he'd spent on Earth. In that document, twenty-nine pages long, Washington listed all of his

41

possessions, laboriously spelling out the names of each of his 317 slaves (Washington believed that his slaves were nothing more than possessions), mentioning where each lived, what job each held, and to whom each was married, so that, upon the death of the master, each could be granted his or her freedom. He listed the vast number of parcels of land he'd accumulated over the years, tracts spread throughout Virginia, along the Ohio and Great Kanawha rivers, even reaching into such relatively distant regions as the Northwest Territory, Maryland, Kentucky, Pennsylvania, and New York. For each tract of land, after describing how it was acquired and some facts about its distinctive physical features, Washington estimated its value. And finally, he listed all his other assets, the farming equipment he'd imported from England, his personal possessions, his cash on hand.

And as he sat at that desk on that morning, reliving in his mind the various periods of his life, in addition to feeling proud at having accumulated all those possessions, George Washington must also have realized how extraordinary his life had been. By almost any standard, the ex-president was a true Renaissance man, successful in virtually every endeavor, reaching and exceeding nearly every goal he'd ever set for himself. Amazingly, he'd proven successful in four separate and distinct careers. First, from a childhood characterized by what today would be considered only middle-class comfort, Washington had transformed himself into a wealthy farmer and landowner. Second, although historians would never conclude that he'd been an out-and-out military genius, he had, during his long and distinguished military career, become the most famous man in colonial America. Having first forced himself to the public's attention at the tender age of twenty-two as a result of his heroism while serving as a colonel in the Virginia regiment during some of the darkest days of the French and Indian War,[2] Washington had become a household name after his appointment as commander-in-chief of the Continental Army, the body of armed resistance that wore down the better-trained and more luxuriously equipped British troops commanded by King George III, thus earning the independence of the American colonies from England.[3] Third, almost by necessity, he'd next become a respected statesman, a "founding father" of the newly independent nation, participating as a delegate from Virginia in both the First and Second Continental Congresses, playing a major role in the drafting of the new nation's Constitution, and ultimately, by unanimous choice of the Electoral College, becoming its first president, defining and shaping, through his pioneering spirit and his sense of leadership, the job for all chief executives who followed him. And finally, although firm evidence is scarce, he'd worked to establish what was apparently a successful marriage, through good times and bad, with Martha Dandridge Custis from the time of their wedding on January 6, 1759, until the day of his death more than forty years later.[4]

But despite all his success, it's possible that George Washington didn't spend a great deal of time in his study that day savoring his stellar, superhuman accomplishments. Rather, those moments of meditation may have been spent dwelling on his one immense failure. For there was one goal that Washington had never been able to accomplish, one shortcoming that, quite possibly, not only ruined Washington's reverie during the last days of his life but also had a major effect on the type of government established at the very birth of the United States. Throughout those forty years of marriage to Martha Dandridge Custis, the couple remained childless; Martha Washington neither bore a child nor even conceived a single pregnancy.[5] And although rumors about Washington having sired children with his slaves or with other women have been in circulation since before the first president's death, there is no documentation nor any real evidence to support this claim. In colonial Virginia, a man who died without a son was viewed as an immense failure. So, as he worked at his desk that day, the writing of that Last Will and Testament only pointed out once again that, regardless of everything he'd accomplished, the line ended with George, that there'd be no more Washingtons after him, no sons to carry on the family name and establish a dynasty, no daughters and sons-in-law to take over and continue the work he'd begun at Mount Vernon.

The fact that the Dandridge Custis–Washington union was marred by infertility has, of course, been well known since the eighteenth century. But the reason for that infertility, the cause of George and Martha's inability to reproduce, has never been objectively considered. One important piece of evidence strongly indicates that the

problem did not lie in any gynecological or endocrinological disorder
of Martha's: her marriage to George was not her first. In 1749, at the
age of seventeen, Martha Dandridge married Daniel Custis, a wealthy
landowner from New Kent County, Virginia. Custis, who was twenty
years older than Martha, died suddenly and unexpectedly in 1757 at
the age of forty-five. But in the eight years between their wedding and
Daniel Custis's death, Martha, in fairly rapid succession, had given
birth to four children. Although two of the children died in infancy,
the second pair, Patsy and John Parke (Jacky) Custis survived, spending the latter parts of their childhood and adolescence with their
mother and stepfather, George Washington.[6] The existence of Patsy
and Jacky pretty much verify that the infertility in the Dandridge
Custis–Washington marriage was not due to any problem in Martha;
rather, it had to lie in George.

It shouldn't come as much of a surprise that the marriage of at
least one of the founding fathers of the United States was touched by
infertility. Unfortunately, the problem was then, and still is today, very
common. Technically defined as the failure to establish a pregnancy
after one full year of unprotected intercourse, infertility today affects
about one in seven marriages. And it should also not be surprising that
the cause of the Washingtons' difficulties appears to have resided in
George; when it comes to the causes of infertility, the sexes have long
ago established equality. In about half of the cases in which an etiology
can be identified, the problem lies in the male partner.[7]

An actual cause, however, can be established in only a fraction of
all cases of infertility. In the remainder of couples, no etiology is ever
identified with certainty. It would seem to be even more difficult to determine the underlying cause of George Washington's inability to father
a child since it's been nearly two hundred years since the man's death. Is
there any way, by reviewing the pieces of evidence scattered during
Washington's life, actually to diagnose a problem?

The task of identifying the cause of George Washington's infertility is made at least a little easier by the fact that the role of the male in
conception and childbearing is limited. For all physiologic intents and

purposes, it is completed once one of the father's sperm cells, after hurtling through the warm, dark recesses of the uterus at breakneck speed (relatively speaking) and slamming head-on into the zona pellucida (the membrane that surrounds the egg), manages to digest its way through the membrane and finally merges its genetic material, carried in a tiny packet called the pronucleus, with the pronucleus of the egg. As described in table 1, the male must fulfill only five requirements in order for this miracle of fertilization to occur.[8]

The first requirement is that the male must be able to manufacture sperm. To do so, three components of male anatomy are necessary. First, the testes, the actual hardware of sperm production, must be present and in good working order. Next, the spermatogonia, the primitive cells that, through their repeated division, actually give rise to the functional sperm, must possess the ability to properly reach maturity. And finally, the pathway the mature spermatozoa take from the safe confines of the testis to the outside world must be present, well formed, patent, and clear of any obstruction. For the first and second components to function, the male endocrine system must be functioning adequately, with appropriate chemical signals being passed back and forth between the hypothalamus (a gland buried deep inside the brain), the pituitary gland (a second gland in the brain), and the testes.

But being able to produce sperm does not guarantee that a man will be fertile. The spermatozoa that are made must also be produced in adequate numbers. Normally, more than two hundred million sperm cells, suspended in about half a teaspoon of semen, are present in a single human ejaculate. While such huge numbers of sperm may be nice to have around, such an immense total is not really all that necessary. In fact, it's believed that in order for conception to take place, a minimum

Table 1.   The Five Requirements of Male Fertility.

1. You must make spermatozoa.
2. The sperm must be manufactured in *huge* quantities.
3. You must be able to ejaculate.
4. The sperm you make must be able to swim like a fish.
5. The sperm must meet an ovum at just the right time.

of only about twenty million spermatozoa is necessary. The production of too few sperm, a condition known as oligospermia and defined as a count of less than this critical value of twenty million sperm in a single ejaculate, will, without the introduction of a method to concentrate the sperm or to pool multiple ejaculates, nearly always result in infertility.

Next, simply producing such huge quantities of sperm cells will also not guarantee success. For fertilization to take place, the spermatozoa, the "footballs" in the game of conception, must be delivered onto the proper "playing field." The sperm must be deposited, through the process of ejaculation, onto the female's cervix or into the back portion of the vagina. For all intents and purposes, ejaculation is under the control of portions of the sympathetic and parasympathetic nervous systems, and thus is governed by nerves originating in the lower portion of the spinal cord.

And, of course, successfully ejaculating adequate numbers of sperm onto the gridiron of conception is still not assurance enough that paydirt will be hit. Once those sperm cells have reached the correct position, they must still be fit enough to swim downfield toward the egg, make their way through the zona pellucida, and fuse their pronucleus with the pronucleus of the egg. If the sperm cells are injured or paralyzed, if they're malformed or poorly made, they may prove to be immotile and therefore never have a chance of reaching the goal line.

Finally, all of these criteria must be fulfilled at just the right moment: when the egg is ready to be fertilized. If the timing is off, even by a few hours in some cases, nothing much will happen. So, infertility may result from inadequate understanding of the timing of ovulation, which always occurs two weeks before the woman's next menstrual cycle begins, from the sperm being deposited in the wrong place, or from having intercourse too infrequently.

As listed in table 2, the causes of male infertility include a wide variety of disorders. Azoospermia, the complete absence of sperm cells in the ejaculate, may result from an arrest in the maturation of the sexual machinery, a problem that itself may be due to disturbances within the endocrine system, such as absence or deterioration of the pituitary gland. Azoospermia may occur due to an abnormality in the composition of the sex chromosomes, as is the case in a disorder called

Klinefelter syndrome, in which an extra X chromosome is present in every cell of the body (a chromosome complement of 47,XXY instead of the normal 46,XY), or in the XYY syndrome, in which an extra Y chromosome is mixed in. Azoospermia can arise from serious damage to the testes caused by exposure to certain drugs, from infections, such as mumps, or from exposure to high doses of radiation, which might itself result from the administration of radiation therapy for certain types of cancer. Finally, apparent absence of sperm cells in the ejaculate can be a consequence of the failure to form or remain patent of the seminiferous tubules and duct system, the pathway the spermatozoa must take to get from the testis to the outside world. Such a problem can result from certain chronic diseases, such as cystic fibrosis.

Oligospermia, the presence of too few sperm cells in the ejaculate, can also result from many different causes. In cryptorchidism, a condition in which the testes fail to descend from their site of embryonic origin in the abdominal cavity to their normal adult position within the scrotum, some sperm will be produced, but because of the increased temperature of the abdominal cavity, many fewer than normal will be

Table 2.   Causes of Male Infertility.

1. Absence of Spermatozoa (Azoospermia)
   Due to absence of testes (caused by a chromosomal abnormality
   [Klinefelter or XYY syndrome], exposure to toxic drugs, infections
   [mumps], or unknown), arrest of maturation of spermatogonia
   (caused by XYY syndrome or a varicocele), or obstruction of the
   duct system (due to cystic fibrosis or Klinefelter syndrome)
2. Insufficient number of Spermatozoa (Oligospermia)
   Caused by cryptorchidism, a varicocele, exposure to drugs or infections, or due to unknown causes
3. Inability to ejaculate
   Caused by spinal injury, surgery, vascular disease, exposure to toxic
   drugs, diabetes mellitus, or due to psychological disturbances.
4. Nonmotile sperm
   Due to Kartagener syndrome, prolonged abstinence, unknown
   causes
5. Normal physiology, but infertile
   Due to abnormal coital habits, infection, or immunologic causes

manufactured. The production of too few sperm because of elevated temperature of the testis can also result because of a varicocele, an abnormal tangle of blood vessels within the scrotum that's described as looking like a "bag of worms"; in a varicocele, an excessive amount of blood flowing through the abnormal vessels causes a slight increase in the temperature inside the scrotum, a change that damages the testes, rendering them unable to produce adequate numbers of sperm. Finally, as in azoospermia, oligospermia may result from the effect of certain drugs, infections, and certain other "spermatotoxic" agents present in the environment.

Paralyzed, or nonmotile, sperm often result from a genetic disorder known as Kartagener syndrome, in which the sperm cells themselves are abnormally made. Men with this disorder usually suffer from a series of related medical problems, including recurrent infections of the sinuses and lungs. Also, their hearts are reversed, located in the right side of the chest instead of the left, a condition known as dextrocardia. And as in the other categories, immotile sperm may also result from exposure to certain drugs, infections, and environmental agents that can impair the sperm cell's ability to swim.

Finally, inability to ejaculate may result from the effect of certain drugs, from surgery or injury to the spine or the penis, or from chronic medical conditions such as diabetes mellitus. And failure to get the sperm to the egg on time can result from abnormal or unusual coital habits, from a failure to understand the timing of ovulation, or from psychological problems.

Considering that the male's role in reproduction is terminated at the time of conception, this is still a fairly long list of problems. Having reviewed all such causes of male infertility, is there evidence that George Washington suffered from any of them? Unfortunately, the passage of time, coupled with the fact that the life of the real George Washington lies buried beneath layer upon layer of myth and legend, makes it difficult to be certain about almost anything that occurred during his life. But there are a few incontrovertible facts about Washington, pieces of evidence that actually do allow us to rule out immediately a fair number of these conditions.

For instance, throughout most of his lifetime, George Washington enjoyed excellent health. It's inconceivable that he might have been affected by any serious or chronically debilitating medical condition, such as cystic fibrosis, diabetes mellitus, or Kartagener syndrome. Outside of numerous episodes of bloodletting, the last of which probably accounted for his premature death,[9] Washington never underwent any real surgical procedures, and certainly no operations were performed on him that might have resulted in damage to either his testes or his central nervous system. Similarly, there's no evidence to support the contention that he took any medications, nor that he was exposed to any environmental agents that might have proven toxic to this section of his anatomy. He had his fair share of infections: the dread "ague and fever" (possibly malaria), which first struck when George was sixteen and made return visits through the rest of his life;[10] intestinal dysentery, which resulted in major difficulties for Colonel Washington during the French and Indian War;[11] and a mild case of smallpox that struck when he was about eighteen. Yet there's no record of Washington having suffered from mumps after puberty, or from any other gonadotoxic infection.

Finally, as to the question of abnormal coital habits and misinformation about how conception occurs, there is at least circumstantial evidence that Washington had an excellent understanding of the process of fertilization. As a farmer, the future first president became something of an expert in the field of animal husbandry. According to his biographer, James Thomas Flexner, Washington was "much concerned with breeding horses and hounds."[12] After his "retirement" from public life that followed his exploits in the Revolutionary War, George became fixated on the idea of establishing a line of "supermules," superior, but of course sterile (as all mules are) offspring of matings between the best of his Virginia-reared mares and a prized jackass that had been a gift from the King of Spain.[13] George's ultimate success, after what amounted to more than a few failures in trying to get the jackass interested in his mares, not only served, by establishing a breeding stock, to underpin the entire race of mules prevalent to this day in the southern section of the United States, but also sheds a great deal of light on what the first president of the United States understood about the birds and the bees. From this evidence, it appears certain that his inability to father a child did not result from George Washington's failing to understand the mechanics of fertilization.

But although these few conditions can be dismissed without much difficulty, elimination of the other causes of male infertility cannot be so easily accomplished. The fact is, we'll never really know for sure whether George Washington had undescended testes (cryptorchidism) or a varicocele, whether he suffered from some hypothalamic or pituitary disturbance that impaired his testicular development, or if he was affected with a chromosomal abnormality such as Klinefelter syndrome or 47,XYY syndrome. Although there's no evidence that allows us to dismiss any of these conditions out of hand, there's also no "smoking gun," no facts providing irrefutable proof that Washington suffered from one of these problems.

Or is there?

From the perspective of the 1990s, when human genetics is undergoing an astonishing revolution, when major breakthroughs in the localization of the genes responsible for common diseases are reported virtually every week in *The New York Times,* when the human genome is being biopsied and dissected as part of a federally funded program, the Human Genome Project, it's hard to believe that, as recently as 1956, we didn't even know for sure the exact number of chromosomes present in normal human cells.[14] In that year two cytogeneticists, H. J. Tjio and A. Levan, using techniques that had only recently been developed, were able to demonstrate with certainty for the first time that the correct number of chromosomes in the nuclei of human cells was forty-six, not forty-eight as had previously been believed. Arranged in pairs, with one copy of each pair contributed by the mother and the other copy coming from the father, forty-four of these chromosomes are referred to as the autosomes, while the remaining pair consists of the sex chromosomes. Normal females have two X chromosomes; normal males have one X and one Y. Obviously, in the fewer than forty years that have passed since Tjio and Levan's discovery, we've come an awfully long way in our understanding of the functioning of these microscopic "lollipops" of DNA, structures that, through their presence in every cell in the body (except red blood cells), carry the genes that are suspended on them like beads on a string from parent to child.

Tjio and Levan's discovery led to a revolution in genetics that was in some ways just as spectacular as the revolution we're experiencing today. Within five years of the appearance of their findings, dozens of articles appeared in the medical literature reporting the chromosomal basis of disorders such as Down's syndrome (caused by an extra, or third, copy of the twenty-first chromosome), Patau and Edwards syndromes (disorders associated with serious birth defects and early death, caused, respectively, by an extra copy of chromosomes thirteen and eighteen), and a whole host of other conditions whose etiologies had previously been a mystery.

One of the articles that followed Tjio and Levan's paper was written by A. A. Sandberg and his colleagues and published in the prestigious British medical journal *Lancet* in 1961. In this report, the authors described a man of normal intelligence and appearance who had fathered a large number of children, a few of whom had been born with significant medical disorders.[15] The man's case was noteworthy, Sandberg and his colleagues believed, because studies performed on his skin cells had revealed that instead of the normal forty-six-chromosome complement they'd expected to find, the man had forty-seven, the extra one being a second copy of the Y. Thus, the man had a chromosome complement, or karyotype, of 47,XYY.

In the years following the Sandberg article, many other men with the 47,XYY karyotype were identified. It turns out that this disorder is relatively common, occurring in about one in every thousand liveborn males. Although most men with the so-called XYY syndrome are normal in nearly every way—many are not even aware that they possess an abnormal chromosome complement—a pattern of subtle clinical findings that occurs with increased frequency in these individuals has been identified. Affected men tend to be tall, with an average adult height in excess of six feet; their shoulders are narrow, and their hands and feet are larger than expected. The facial appearance of these men is not strikingly different from that of their siblings, but in general they tend to have a prominent glabellar region (the portion of the forehead that meets the bridge of the nose), some degree of facial asymmetry, and long, well-formed ears. The teeth have been shown to be larger than normal and, in addition, tend to have minor defects in their structure: for example, the lateral incisors are shovel-shaped and show deeper lingual fossae (the area of connection between the tooth and the gum) than in men with normal chromosome complements.[16]

In addition to these morphological features, there are also some medical differences between men with the XYY syndrome and men with normal karyotypes. For instance, it has been reported that during adolescence affected males tend to develop severe acne on their face, neck, and back.[17] Although the acne usually improves with age and ultimately disappears as the affected individual passes into adulthood, a pockmarked complexion may remain throughout the man's life.

Although most men with the syndrome are capable of producing normal amounts of viable sperm, and therefore have little or no trouble fathering offspring, various abnormalities of the genitalia have been reported. These abnormalities include cryptorchidism (failure of the testes to descend during fetal life from the abdomen into the scrotum), hypospadias (a defect in the formation of the penis in which the external urethral meatus, the opening through which urine passes to the outside world, is located not at its normal position at the very tip of the penis but at some other point, such as on the underside of the penis, at the junction between the penis and the scrotum, or somewhere farther down on the scrotal sac), and smaller-than-normal testes. Also, the testes may be abnormally formed, leading to decreased spermatogenesis, which results in oligospermia or even azoospermia.[17] As a result, as already suggested, there is believed to be a somewhat higher incidence of infertility in men found to possess a 47,XYY chromosome complement than in the general population.[8]

In addition to these morphological, medical, and reproductive differences, a host of neurodevelopmental alterations occur more commonly in individuals with a 47,XYY karyotype than in the general population. Although the intelligence of most men with the syndrome is normal, at least one in three affected individuals has some specific developmental disability. In early life, such disabilities may manifest themselves as delayed acquisition of speech or as poor language development, and problems with fine motor coordination may also occur. During the school years, an increased frequency of educational disturbances, such as learning disability and dyslexia, may be seen.[16] One consequence of these developmental and educational difficulties is that men with XYY syndrome may wind up with low self-esteem, which by itself may lead to behavioral disturbances.

To summarize, most men affected with the XYY syndrome are, at least to the untrained eye, normal in virtually every way: in their appearance, their behavior, and their fertility. In fact, if it weren't for one particular observation, one peculiar and still openly disputed feature of this entity that has, through the years, led to a continuing avalanche of controversy, the XYY syndrome would have amounted to little more than a brief and boring footnote in medical genetics textbooks. But that one observation, made by Dr. Patricia Jacobs, a British cytogeneticist, and her colleagues in 1965, has caused this disorder to take on an identity different from any other congenital syndrome, to become well known not only to medical geneticists, but to psychiatrists, criminal lawyers, and to the lay public as well.[18] The information reported by Dr. Jacobs and her colleagues is startling, and I can verify that, at least in my experience, it seems to be true.

Near the end of my fourth year of medical school, having already pretty much decided on what I wanted to do with the rest of my professional life, I did a one-month elective rotation in clinical genetics. One afternoon in the middle of that month, I was assigned the task of examining a patient named Edgar Morales. Edgar, who was then eight years old, had been referred for a genetic evaluation by the psychologist at his elementary school because, in the words on his referral form, he had demonstrated "an unusual facial appearance, mild cognitive developmental delay, and aggressive and violent behavior that occasionally poses a danger to him and those around him."

I have to admit that after reading that referral form, I wasn't exactly jumping with joy at the prospect of seeing this child. The school psychologist's description made me expect the kid to be a genuine monster, an angry and dangerous little animal, and I wasn't thrilled about having to close myself off in an examining room alone with him. But once I gathered up my courage and went to look for the kid and his mother in the genetics clinic's waiting area, I found myself pleasantly surprised and somewhat confused: the boy, sitting calmly on one of the waiting area's chairs reading a Superman comic book, looked to be the antithesis of aggressiveness and violence.

After introducing myself, I invited Edgar and his mother into the office. His mother, understanding that I was going to start off the session by taking the boy's history, asked if it would be all right if Eddie stayed out in the waiting room until he was needed. I told her that would be fine with me.

In contrast to her son, Mrs. Morales that day seemed edgy and tense. After we'd entered the office and taken seats, she began to tell me an amazing story. According to his mother, Edgar, the youngest of three children, born when his mother was thirty-three and his father thirty-four, was from the beginning of his life different in subtle ways from his two older brothers. "He did everything he was supposed to do at the same time his brothers did it," the woman explained carefully. "You know, he sat up at the right time, he walked at the right time, we didn't have any problems toilet-training him. All those things were fine."

"Well, then how was he different?" I asked.

"He always seemed to be . . . I don't know exactly how to put this . . . angry," she replied. "I don't like to use the word 'angry,' though, because what was happening with him wasn't exactly anger. And really, there never has been anything for Eddie to be angry about. We always gave him whatever he wanted, but nothing we did ever seemed to satisfy him."

"Can you give me an example of what you mean?" I asked, not having a clue as to what the woman was talking about.

She thought for a moment and then responded. "When he was two, he started biting people. I mentioned it to his pediatrician, and he reassured me that it was nothing to worry about. He said it was just a stage Eddie was going through, and it wasn't abnormal or anything. The doctor promised me it would eventually pass. But instead of passing, it's just gotten worse and worse. He bit everybody: me, his brothers, his father, anyone who came in contact with him. I tried everything I could think of to get him to stop: I punished him, I made him stay in his room, I took away treats, but nothing seemed to do any good. After a while, he had bitten so many of the other kids in our neighborhood that none of the other mothers would let their children play with Eddie."

"Has there been anything other than the biting?" I asked.

"Yeah. Lots more. I guess he was about three when he started getting into fights for the first time. These weren't just little arguments or anything, they were real fistfights, with kicking and biting and scratching. And like with the biting, he'd fight with everybody: kids bigger than him, kids his own age, boys, girls, even little babies being wheeled around in carriages. It got so bad that, by the time he was nearly four, I couldn't even take him out to the playground anymore."

"Did you try to get any help for him at that point?" I asked. I have to admit, being only a fourth-year medical student, I was way out of my league when it came to trying to figure out what was going on with this boy.

"I thought about it," she answered. "By that point, our pediatrician was beginning to realize there was something really wrong with my son, and he referred us to a place where Eddie could get a full psychological evaluation. But my husband didn't let me take him; he kept saying there wasn't really anything wrong, that Eddie was just a little wilder than our two other boys had been, that it was just a phase he was going through, and that he would eventually just grow out of it. But after the fires started late last year, even my husband couldn't deny it anymore; he finally admitted that we had to do something. . . ."

"The fires?" I interrupted.

"Yes. Last December, we had two fires in our apartment. The first time, it was a wastepaper basket in the boys' bathroom. I figured one of my oldest son's friends who was at our apartment that day threw a lighted cigarette or a match into it, so I just put it out and had a little talk with them. My son and his friend both swore they didn't have anything to do with it, but there didn't seem to be any other explanation. Then, about a week later, the same thing happened again in the basket in Eddie's bedroom. But this time, Eddie and I were the only ones at home. Since I knew I hadn't had anything to do with that fire, I asked Eddie if he knew how it had started. He didn't say a word. He just kept looking up at me with this goofy expression on his face."

"Have there been any more fires since December?" I asked.

Mrs. Morales rolled her eyes. "Oh yes," she responded, "at least half a dozen. So far, they've all been small and easy to put out. Each time, Eddie has been somewhere close by. He's never talked about it, so I don't know exactly why he does it. I'm not sure, but I think it must be that he likes watching the flames."

"It must be pretty scary," I said. I'd never heard anything like this story. According to his mother's description, Eddie Morales appeared to be an eight-year-old pyromaniac.

"It's really terrifying," Mrs. Morales said in response to my comment. "We all understand that we can never leave him alone in the apartment, not even for a minute. One of us has to stay with him at all times, just in case something should happen. And every time I hear a fire siren or see a fire truck in our neighborhood, I always feel this tightening in my stomach: I'm sure it's going to turn out to be one of Eddie's fires."

We spoke for a while longer, and then, after I'd finished taking the history, I went out into the waiting room and fetched Edgar. The time I spent examining the boy verified the initial impression I'd had of him: the kid seemed absolutely fine. During the examination, he proved to be alert, friendly, and extremely cooperative for a child of eight; not once did he try to bite me, or punch me, or in any way express aggressive tendencies. Sure, he was tall for his age, and he didn't look all that much like his mother, but these things seemed minor. My overall impression was that Edgar was completely normal, but that his mother and possibly the school psychologist needed professional help. I was convinced that the problem in this family lay in the mother, who was having hallucinations about her son's behavior, and not in Edgar.

Since I was an inexperienced medical student, it was required that I review my findings with an attending physician before sending any

patient home. In the case of Edgar Morales, that turned out to be quite
a fortunate rule because, as I unraveled the boy's story to Dr. Lillienfeld,
one of the attending physicians in the genetics clinic, a look of wonder
illuminated her face, an expression that probably represented the external reflection of a lightbulb switching on in her brain. When I finally
got to the part about Mrs. Morales worrying every time she heard a fire
siren, Dr. Lillienfeld yelled, "Stop right there. Has anyone done chromosome studies on this kid yet?"

"No," I replied. "This is the first time he's been referred to a
geneticist."

"Well, get back in there and get a sample of his blood right now!
This kid's got XYY syndrome!"

Dr. Lillienfeld was so convinced of Edgar's diagnosis, which
was ultimately confirmed when the boy's chromosomal analysis was
completed, because of the body of evidence that by that time had
accumulated indicating that men with a 47,XYY chromosome constitution exhibited "dangerous, violent, or criminal propensities."[18] As already mentioned, this observation was initially suggested by Dr. Patricia
Jacobs and her colleagues, who while performing routine chromosome
studies on blood samples taken from 197 mentally subnormal men in-
carcerated because of their aggressive and antisocial behavior, discovered that eight of the men, or nearly 4 percent of the total, had a
47,XYY or 48,XXYY (a variant of XYY syndrome) chromosome complement. This was an extraordinary finding: considering that the frequency of the 47,XYY karyotype in the general population is, as
mentioned above, about one in every thousand males, this number was
something like forty times that which would be expected by chance.

The observations of Dr. Jacobs and her colleagues were quickly
confirmed by other cytogeneticists working with similarly institutionalized populations. Although the overall frequency of an XYY chromosome complement in the men studied was actually somewhat lower
than Dr. Jacobs's original figure, coming out to approximately 2 percent, the association was found to be even more striking when the
study group was restricted to institutionalized men of tall stature.

When only men of six feet in height or greater were included in the evaluation, the frequency of the 47,XYY karyotype in the population reached a nearly astounding 20 percent.[19]

As might be expected, these reports in the scientific literature didn't exactly go unnoticed outside the medical community. Two major groups grabbed onto the newly published information and simply wouldn't let go. The print and broadcast media created a genuine sensation. It was discovered, perhaps not surprisingly, that stories centering on a genetic factor that caused men to commit violent crimes both sold papers and raised ratings. Through the efforts of journalists, the Y chromosome quickly became known to the general public as "the chromosome of crime," and "the murder chromosome." Men with an extra Y chromosome were incorrectly referred to as "supermen," individuals who, as a consequence of their extra dose of some vague and indistinct "maleness factor," were supposed to be twice as aggressive as normal males. This extra dose of aggressiveness, it was argued in the media accounts, caused their "macho" behavior to fall outside what was considered the "socially acceptable" range.

The second group who found a novel use for this new scientific information was the legal community. Suddenly, a new defense strategy had been handed to attorneys defending men accused of committing violent crime. Why not argue that these men had XYY syndrome, and that their antisocial behavior was inherent and biological, transmitted through an error in their genetic composition, and therefore completely outside of their control? Such a defense strategy was, in fact, used in the widely publicized trial of Richard Speck, an unemployed seaman and laborer charged with murdering eight nurses in an apartment in Chicago during the night and early morning of July 13 and 14, 1967. After all, his lawyers argued during the trial, which took place in the spring of 1968 in Peoria, Illinois, Speck had some of the characteristic features that had already been recognized as components of the XYY syndrome: he was tall, he'd had bad acne as an adolescent, and he was diagnosed as having mild mental retardation. If he'd been born with this chromosomal abnormality, his attorneys continued, then he should not be held accountable for the murders.

It was a terrific argument, and the team of attorneys who defended Speck did a great job of selling it to the jury, but there was one significant problem that the lawyers simply could not overcome. When the nuclei of his white blood cells were examined under a microscope, it was discovered that Richard Speck had a normal 46,XY chromosome complement. Although, on April 15, 1968, the jury convicted Speck of the murders and he was sentenced to die in the electric chair (a sentence that, upon the banning of the death penalty in Illinois, was ultimately commuted to eight consecutive terms of fifty to one hundred years in prison, then the longest prison sentence in American history), the trial opened the door to other uses of the "killer-chromosome" defense in criminal trials. And in fact, this strategy was used, and apparently worked well, in the case of Daniel Hugon, a French citizen with an XYY karyotype who, after being convicted of murdering an elderly prostitute in Paris, was given a less severe sentence than might have been expected, presumably because of his chromosomal anomaly.[20]

But in addition to providing an opportunity to sell newspapers and a novel approach to defending criminals, the association of the 47,XYY karyotype with violence raised an important ethical and civil rights issue. Since this disorder was felt to be commonly associated with violence, did society have the right, or perhaps even the duty, to restrict the freedom of an individual with a 47,XYY chromosome complement before he's had the opportunity to break the law? Faced with this question, it was essential that information regarding the extent of the problem be obtained. Specifically, it needed to be ascertained whether all men with XYY syndrome are at risk to commit such antisocial behavior, a conclusion that would arguably lend support to a move to restrict the freedom of affected men, or if this behavior might be limited to some smaller segment of the entire XYY population, a finding that would argue against such civil rights restrictions. These questions could only be answered through a carefully performed prospective study, a project in which all the XYY males within a sizable population are identified and evaluated.

Such a study was actually performed in Denmark in the 1970s.[21] The researchers identified and contacted all men greater than six feet in

height who were born in that country between January 1, 1944, and
December 31, 1947. The men who were willing to cooperate with the
study, representing 90 percent of all of the men who had been initially
contacted, were examined, were given a battery of tests, and had blood
taken for chromosome analysis. Of the 4,139 men examined, twelve
with a 47,XYY chromosome complement were identified, giving an
overall frequency of nearly three per thousand (remember, this is a
sample limited to men over six feet in height; the incidence is therefore
higher than would be expected in the general population). Review of
records revealed that five of these twelve men, nearly half of the group,
had, during the course of their lives, been convicted of one or more
criminal offenses, a difference that was statistically significant when
compared with the group of men of comparable height who'd been
found to have a normal chromosome complement. Only one of the
crimes committed by the XYY men was considered to be an act of aggression against another person. The others were described as typical
crimes, those, like theft, arson, and burglary, that didn't fit the profile of
a "macho" crime, and that, actually, were indistinguishable from offenses committed by individuals who had normal karyotypes. At the
end of their study, the researchers reached the following conclusion:

> There can be little doubt that men with the chromosome
> constitution 47,XYY run a higher relative risk than normal
> XY men to show antisocial behavior and to get into con-
> flict with the law.[20]

Higher risk, yes, but not so high, it must be argued, that their freedom should be restricted. The results of the Danish study confirmed
that men with XYY, although more likely to break the law, were neither
a danger to themselves nor to the rest of society. As such, no efforts
have ever been made to register men with XYY syndrome, to track their
activities, or to restrict their civil rights.

More recently, some studies that found fault with the work that
had been previously performed have failed to show any relationship between criminality and the XYY karyotype. However, the Danish study
is still pretty convincing; I believe its conclusions cannot be ignored.

The reason that men with this chromosomal abnormality manifest these particular behavioral disturbances remains a mystery. As the years have passed, however, it has become more and more clear that many men with a 47,XYY chromosome complement seem to be afflicted with a specific personality disturbance that may have something to do with this excess incidence of criminal behavior. Men with the XYY syndrome often exhibit traits such as infantilism, lack of emotional control, increased impulsiveness after emotional stimulation, excessive numbers of temper tantrums, aggression against authority figures, and a poor sense of self, personality disturbances that certainly could lead to persistent difficulties in adjusting to the social environment. But why the presence of an extra copy of the Y chromosome should cause such disturbances is still unknown.

But what does the XYY syndrome have to do with George Washington? Am I really trying to propose that the much beloved first president of the United States, perhaps the single most important man in the history of America, was afflicted with a chromosome abnormality documented to cause personality disturbances and associated with deviant, even criminal behavior? The answer to the latter question is a resounding maybe.

I have to admit that, as I thought about the possible causes of George Washington's infertility, two strong images kept running through my mind, frozen pictures from stories that nearly every American schoolchild knows. Even though only one of the stories is actually based on fact, both have become important threads in the fabric of myths and legends that now surrounds and guards the true story of the life of the first president. In my opinion, both stories, even the one that seems to have arisen in the vivid imagination of an early Washington biographer, provide evidence that George Washington possessed at least some of the features now known to be components of the XYY syndrome.

The true story involves Washington's famous false teeth, a physical feature that has become permanently attached to the legend of the first president largely through the efforts of Gilbert Stuart, the portrait artist who painted the most lasting image, now known as the Athenaeum portrait (figure 1), of the first president. It is well known that all through his life, George Washington suffered greatly from dental disease. At the age of twenty-six, his close friend George Mercer offered this description of Washington's oral cavity: "His mouth is large and generally firmly closed, but which from time to time discloses some defective teeth."[22] In nearly every year of his adult life, George Washington developed "an aching tooth and swelled and inflamed gums." According to Flexner, the future president used all sorts of devices, including "sponge" toothbrushes, tinctures of myrrh, and other dentifrices, in attempts to get some relief from his nagging problem. But in every instance, his efforts failed. Each aching tooth was ultimately extracted until, by 1789, the year in which he assumed the presidency, only one tooth remained in his entire mouth. Soon, even that lone tooth was gone, and Washington spent the final eleven years of his life cursed with having to wear bizarre and disfiguring dentures.

These false teeth were constructed in 1789 by John Greenwood, a New York dentist and apparently, at least if we can believe the descriptions of what he did to George Washington's mouth, a closet sadist. From the very first day they were loaded into the president's mouth, the contraptions, which had been fashioned out of hippopotamus ivory to which spare human teeth had been attached by gold rivets, failed to even come close to fitting properly, projecting outward much too far, and causing Washington's lips to bulge as if swollen. And to add insult to injury, by the time the damned things finally and mercifully collapsed in 1797, the teeth had turned an unsightly black, the result, the dentist concluded, of long-time exposure to such acidic substances as port wine.[23]

So it would be safe to assume that, by September 1795, when Washington posed for Gilbert Stuart for the first time, the dentures were on their last legs. According to reports, the artist and the president did not exactly hit it off. Washington could not have been in a very good frame of mind during those sessions: in addition to the constant discomfort caused by his dentures, the president had never felt comfortable being stared at. Trying to make him more comfortable during one of the early sittings, Stuart said to his subject, "Now sir, you must

Figure 1. The Athenaeum portrait of George Washington, by Gilbert Stuart. From the National Portrait Gallery, Washington, D.C. and the Museum of Fine Arts, Boston.

let me forget that you are General Washington and that I am Stuart the painter." To which Washington replied, "Mr. Stuart need never feel the need of forgetting who he is or who General Washington is."[24]

Stuart painted three portraits of the president. In each case, the artist portrayed exactly what he saw, smoothing out none of the rough features, masking no minor or major physical flaw. In each painting, Washington's lips are portrayed as pulled in an unnaturally tight line, distorting the natural contour of the middle of his face, a consequence, it seems, of the bulging dentures. The lips are pursed, as if the man were getting ready to whistle. These images of Washington's midface have led to the telling and retelling of the story of his poorly fitting false teeth.

So what does this have to do with the XYY syndrome? As already mentioned, men with this disorder often have subtle dental abnormalities. Their teeth, in both the deciduous and permanent dentition, are larger in size than teeth of men with normal chromosome complements. And the teeth themselves can be abnormally formed and positioned: the lateral incisors have been shown to be "shovel-shaped," and there tends to be a deeper lingual fossa than normal, an anomaly that could very well lead to premature decay and ultimately, tooth loss.[16] As such, the story of George Washington's false teeth could be a clue to the cause of his infertility.

The second tale that kept running through my head as I was considering the possible causes of the first president's infertility is the one that has put cherry pie on our plates as the unofficial food of modern Washington's Birthday celebrations (now, of course, known as President's Day). Apparently an invention of Mason Locke Weems, a much vilified early biographer (or "fictionalizer" as the more contemporary biographer, James Thomas Flexner, has referred to him) of Washington's—who, after all, was only trying to spice up the man's history in order to sell a few more books—it is the tale of George Washington's father's cherry tree.[25]

Consider the story. It is early spring in the Virginia of 1738 or 1739, and Augustine Washington, then in his early forties, has set out for a walk on the family's property, a breathtakingly beautiful five-hundred-sixty-acre tract of farmland along the Rappahannock River. Recent business setbacks involving his holdings in an iron mine in the region have deeply disturbed the elder Washington, causing him to have serious concerns about the family's financial future. But as he strolls along, his mundane worries begin to lift as, with joy, he anticipates the sight of his favorite cherry tree, then in full bloom, which stands on a small hill just up ahead. But something's wrong: as he approaches the hill, Augustine, initially shocked at what he sees, quickly becomes indescribably furious.

Augustine Washington's tree has been chopped down. Its trunk has been permanently and irreparably severed from its root system by the repeated, apparently senseless blows of a hatchet. Although the blossoms remain bright pink on the tree's branches, the fallen body of the tree is lying on the ground adjacent to the scarred trunk, the whole thing obviously permanently destroyed.

After stopping for a moment and taking a few deep breaths, an attempt to regain control of his emotions, Augustine Washington finally walks on, trying to somehow understand the senselessness of this wanton act of destruction of such natural beauty. Soon, he comes upon his son George, the eldest child of his second marriage, who at that time is six or seven. Augustine is shocked to find that the boy is brandishing a small hatchet. The father, trying desperately not to prejudge his son, asks little George if he knows the identity of the slayer of the tree. "Yes sir," the child replies without hesitation. "I cannot tell a lie. It was I who chopped down that cherry tree, using my little hatchet."

The father, still upset at the loss of his tree, but all the same overjoyed that his son, in spite of the understood consequences, has decided to tell the truth, immediately forgives the boy. And Augustine and George live happily ever after (or at least until April 12, 1743, when the father suddenly and unexpectedly dies).[26]

Wonderful story. But think about the implications of the tale, which, after all, was supposedly invented by Weems in order to point out the inherent truthfulness of the first president. With absolutely no provocation, for apparently no underlying reason, the young George Washington felt the urge to do harm to a prized possession of his father,

65

and willfully began putting hatchet to trunk. Through his blows against that cherry tree, the mythologic George Washington demonstrated both poor impulse control and aggression against an authority figure, two important traits seen again and again in individuals with a 47,XYY karyotype. In fact, isn't there a similarity between young George Washington's attack on that cherry tree and the actions of my patient, Edgar Morales, who, also demonstrating poor impulse control and a need to lash out against authority, felt a compulsion to set fires in the wastebaskets in his parents' apartment?

But in the Weems tale, George Washington's reaction to being confronted by his father is even more pathologic than that demonstrated by my patient. After all, at least Eddie Morales had sense enough to remain silent when his mother asked if he had anything to do with setting those fires; even he understood the consequences of telling the truth. The mythologic young George Washington didn't even have sense enough to lie, to invent a story for his father, which would have been normal, appropriate behavior for a child of six or seven.

I fully understand that the story of the cherry tree is fictitious, but I think it's relevant for two reasons. First, although invented by Weems, the story most likely arose out of some true episode in George Washington's early life. And second, and perhaps more important, it does prove to be representative of a pattern of behavior seen repeatedly in Washington's later life. As we'll see in a moment, during his career in the military, George Washington again and again showed poor impulse control and a need to lash out against authority; but for now, like the true story of his false teeth, the fictitious image of George Washington with that little hatchet in his hand represents another potential clue to the etiology of the first president's infertility.

Other than these two anecdotes, however, is there any real, solid evidence that George Washington might have had XYY syndrome? Obviously, chromosomal studies of the first president's cells have never been performed, nor, after the nearly two hundred years that have passed since his death, are they likely to be performed in the near future. As such, it's impossible to demonstrate by karyotype analysis that the first president's infertility was caused by this condition. But how about the physical findings and neurodevelopmental features associated with the disorder? Did Washington's body habitus, facial features, and personality traits conform to what we now know to be the features of the XYY syndrome? A full review of the evidence is warranted.

Let's consider the physical features first. As already stated, most men with a 47,XYY karyotype are taller than average, with a mean adult height in excess of six feet, and they tend to have large hands and feet. There is a great deal of evidence to support the fact that George Washington demonstrated these characteristic features. When, in March 1758, the twenty-six-year-old George Washington met his future wife, Martha, for the first time, his friend, George Mercer, described the future president in this way: "Straight as an Indian, measuring six feet two inches in his stockings. . . . His bones and joints are large, as are his hands and feet."[27] In 1795, after Washington had spent all that time posing for Gilbert Stuart, the painter described the president using these words: "His shoulders were high and narrow and his hands and feet remarkably large."[28] Washington's tall stature is even more striking considering the fact that, in the latter half of the eighteenth century, the average height of American males was slightly below five and a half feet tall. It's no wonder that Flexner chose the word "gigantic" to describe the appearance of the first president.[29]

And what of George Washington's facial appearance? As previously mentioned, men with the XYY syndrome tend to have prominent, raised glabellar regions (the portion of the face where the forehead meets the bridge of the nose), some degree of facial asymmetry, and long, well-formed ears. Did Washington exhibit any of these features? Here's how the president's countenance was described by the painter Gilbert Stuart:

> There were features in his face totally different from what I had observed in any other human being. The sockets of the eyes, for instance, were larger than what I ever met with before, and the upper part of the nose broader.[28]

No comment is made by either the artist or any other contemporaries about the president's ear size, probably owing to the fact that Washington wore his chestnut-colored hair long, effectively covering the ears. Similarly, no mention is made of the symmetry of his face. Unfortunately, since all the portraits painted by Gilbert Stuart show the president facing either toward the right or the left, examination of these paintings fails to reveal any helpful information regarding that symmetry.

Also, there is no mention made in any biography of Washington's having had acne during adolescence, another frequent feature of XYY syndrome. However, there is at least some indirect, circumstantial evidence that the president may have borne the consequences of such a problem. Numerous biographers have commented upon the fact that George Washington's face was pockmarked, especially in the malar region (the area surrounding his nose).[30] Although Flexner states that these scars probably were a consequence of the case of smallpox that Washington contracted in December 1751, they could just as easily have represented the vestiges of an early struggle with cystic acne.

Still, at this point my contention that our first president might have had XYY syndrome rests, at best, on very shaky ground. After all, most of the evidence I've just cited is circumstantial. Sure, George Washington was tall, he did have long hands and feet, he had a prominent nasal bridge and bad teeth, and he was infertile, but that's not nearly enough to prove conclusively that the man had a 47,XYY chromosome complement. Without karyotypic confirmation, a lot more evidence—behavioral evidence—is needed. But other than the fictitious story about the cherry tree, is there any evidence that George Washington had behavior problems similar to those seen in individuals with XYY syndrome?

George Washington first rose to the public's attention just prior to the start of the French and Indian War. In 1753, at the tender age of twenty-one, George was selected by Robert Dinwiddie, the lieutenant governor of Virginia, to be the emissary of King George II, grandfather of George III, ruler of Great Britain and, therefore, of the colonies as well. It was young George Washington's task to carry a message from Virginia through the Shenandoah Valley, to Legardeur de St. Pierre, commander of the troops occupying Fort Le Boeuf, a French outpost near Waterford, Pennsylvania. A rumor had circulated that St. Pierre and his men were planning an invasion of the land east and south of their outpost, territory that had previously been claimed by the members of the Ohio Company, an organization owned by a group of wealthy British landowners. Lieutenant Governor Dinwiddie had instructed his emissary to inform the Frenchman to stay where he was, or desperate action might follow.[31]

Now, George Washington had not been selected for this task because he'd proven to be a fearless warrior, or because he'd demonstrated a strong sense of responsibility in the past, or even because he'd been shown to be a great leader of men. In fact, Dinwiddie had chosen him simply because he was one of the only men of "acceptible" social background who had any knowledge of the untamed wilderness that was the Shenandoah Valley. Washington had amassed this knowledge in years past, when he'd worked as a surveyor. George Washington was chosen to carry the message to St. Pierre because he was judged to be the person least likely to get hopelessly lost.

The good news is that he didn't get lost. After a horrendous journey, he and his band of men finally reached Fort Le Boeuf; Washington relayed the king's message to St. Pierre, whose response, loosely translated from the original French, was "Nuts to you!"

At that point, Washington, believing that there was more than a little urgency involved, was set on returning to Virginia as soon as possible, and that's when the bad news portion of the story occurred. Because of delays encountered along the way, the Virginians had reached Fort Le Boeuf in mid-December, and the weather had turned bitter cold. Having originally planned to float home on the river system that connects western Pennsylvania with Virginia, Washington found that this plan was now simply impossible: the rivers had all frozen solid. That's when the future president, in one of the first decisions he'd ever make as a leader of men, opted to take the land route home.

Now there were experienced trappers accompanying Washington on this trip, four backwoodsmen who were acting as guides. Apparently, each one of these experienced campers believed their leader was crazy. They strongly advised Washington to set up camp, settle in, and wait a few weeks until the weather cleared. But George Washington would hear none of it. He told the trappers that it was urgent that he get back, that he had to inform Lieutenant Governor Dinwiddie of the potentially serious threat emanating from the Frenchmen at Fort Le Boeuf. Never mind the fact that those Frenchmen, like Washington and his band, were all prisoners of the extreme winter weather; the man simply decided that it was imperative that the group press on. And so press on they did.

The journey that small band of men took is described by James Thomas Flexner in this way:

> His horses' legs sank deep into snowdrifts and were cut at the ankle by sharp crusts of ice. The horses staggered with hunger because all forage was frozen over. Thirst became a horror for man and beast: all water had turned to ice so cold that, if sucked, it would burn the mouth. In midst of the utter desolation, the cavalcade moved more and more slowly.[32]

Somehow, the group ultimately did manage to make it back to their home base, despite an attack by Native Americans and the effects of frostbite. But the real question is, Was any of this really necessary? Rather than placing the men under his command in such extreme jeopardy, wouldn't it have made a lot more sense if he had simply waited out the weather, taking the advice of the experienced and wiser guides? This story certainly appears to be an example of both poor judgment and poor impulse control.

But after all, this was one small incident. Can't we write off this poorly formulated decision to Washington's immaturity and inexperience? Actually, this sort of thing happened repeatedly during the military career of George Washington. Again and again, he made decisions that weren't well thought out, that required taking often unnecessary chances.

Many times during his career, while caught in the heat of battle, Washington seemed to forget what was happening and act impulsively. During the French and Indian War, he needlessly rode his horse between two firing columns of men; his horse was killed, his own clothes became riddled with bullets, but, amazingly, he remained uninjured.[33] A similar scenario occurred during the Revolutionary War: "In subsequent years," Flexner writes, "during the Revolution, Washington was again and again to take the most foolhardy risks, but the bullets . . . never touched his body."[34]

And not infrequently, his actions and decisions placed the men under his command in great and unnecessary jeopardy. During the Battle of Trenton, for example, fought in 1777 during the Revolutionary War, Washington had his troops attack the British-held city in central New Jersey during a blinding winter storm. Marching nine miles through hail, snow, and sleet, in freezing temperatures, many of the Continental soldiers died of exposure before approaching anywhere near where the battle was to take place. Although his action did catch the British and their Hessian mercenaries offguard and ultimately resulted in victory, the price paid in suffering was great. There's no question that Washington's poor judgment and his impulsiveness, as well as his failure to listen to the advice of those who had more experience than he, cost the lives of many men who would otherwise have survived. But in the end, despite the mistakes he'd made and the lives he'd lost, Washington won the war. And by the time that war had been won, Washington had managed to establish a place for himself in the hearts of his countrymen.

And finally, after all, what it all comes down to is that George Washington became commander-in-chief of the Continental Army and eventually president of the United States because he was a revolutionary. The man achieved his great fame and became a hero because he chose to rebel against George III, King of the British Empire, victim of porphyria variegata, and the most important authority figure at that time. George Washington thus became famous because he rebelled against authority—as my patient had, as many other men with XYY syndrome have. That George wasn't labeled a criminal, wasn't considered a danger to society, was simply the result of circumstances beyond his control. George Washington just happened to be on the side that ultimately won the war. Sure, Washington is considered a hero today. But had the Continental Army lost the war, had America remained a

British colony, is there any doubt that George Washington would today be considered a criminal and a traitor to his country?

———————

I have to confess that, although there does seem to be a strong case that George Washington was affected with XYY syndrome, the evidence is just not conclusive. But despite the difficulty in making this case, there remain some irrefutable facts about the man's life. One important fact is that George Washington had no heirs, no sons to carry on his family's name, and this clearly must have affected him greatly during the course of his life. It also apparently had an effect on the type of government that became established in America.

In May 1782, after the Continental Army had finally defeated the British and the independence of the American colonies had been assured, Lewis Nicola, one of Washington's colonels, sent the commander-in-chief a letter urging him to accept the responsibility of becoming king of the United States.[35] Washington apparently considered the proposal, but ultimately declined, replying to Nicola that "I must view with abhorrence and reprehend with severity" a conception that was "big with the greatest mischief that can befall any country."[35]

But would George Washington have been so quick to decline the proposal to become king had he had a son? Washington clearly understood that the lack of a young male Washington meant that no dynasty could be established. After the demise of George I, first King of America, there would have been no George II to take his place. Had George Washington had a male heir, his decision might well have been different; had Martha been able to bear him a child, the United States might today be existing under the effects of more than two hundred years of uninterrupted rule by members of the House of Washington.

References

1. James Thomas Flexner, *George Washington: Anguish and Farewell (1793–1799)* (Boston: Little Brown and Co., 1972), 453.
2. James Thomas Flexner, *Washington: The Indispensable Man* (Boston: Little Brown and Co., 1974), 36.
3. Ibid., 180.

4. Ibid., 41.

5. Ibid., 42.

6. Elswyth Thane, *Washington's Lady* (New York: Dodd Mead and Co., 1960), 1.

7. L. I. Lipshultz, S. S. Howards, and J. P. Buch, Male infertility, in J. Y. Gillenwater, J. T. Grayhack, S. S. Howards, et al., eds., *Adult and Pediatric Urology* (Chicago: Year Book Publishers, Inc., 1987), 1256.

8. R. J. Sherins and S. S. Howards, Male infertility, in P. C. Walsh, R. F. Gittes, A. D. Perlmutter, et al., eds., *Campbell's Urology* (Philadelphia: W. B. Saunders Co., 1986), 657–65.

9. Flexner, *Washington: Indispensable Man,* 397–402.

10. James Thomas Flexner, *George Washington: The Forge of Experience (1732–1775)* (Boston: Little, Brown and Co., 1965), 41.

11. Ibid., 124–31.

12. Flexner, *Washington: Indispensable Man,* 191–92.

13. Ibid., 191–92.

14. H. J. Tjio and A. Levan, The chromosome numbers in man, *Hereditas* 42 (1956): 1–6.

15. A. A. Sandberg, G. F. Koepf, T. Ishihara, et al., An XYY human male, *Lancet* 2 (1961): 488–89.

16. R. J. Gorlin, M. M. Cohen, Jr., and L. S. Levin: *Syndromes of the Head and Neck,* 3rd ed.; New York: Oxford University Press, 61–62.

17. C. A. Moore and D. O. Weaver, Chromosome XYY, in M. L. Buyse, ed., *Birth Defects Encyclopedia* (Dover, Mass.: Birth Defects Information Services, 1990), 400–401.

18. P. A. Jacobs, M. Brunton, M. M. Melville, et al., Aggressive behaviour, mental subnormalty and the XYY male, *Nature* 208 (1965): 1351–52.

19. J. S. Thompson and M. W. Thompson: *Genetics in Medicine,* 4th ed. (Philadelphia: W. B. Saunders and Co., 1986), 143.

20. F. Vogel and A. G. Motulsky, *Human Genetics: Problems and Approaches,* 2nd ed. (New York: Springer-Verlag, 1986), 579.

21. H. A. Witkins, S. A. Mednick, S. Schulsinger, et al., Criminality in XYY and XXY men, *Science* 193 (1976): 547–55.

22. Flexner, *Washington: Forge of Experience,* 192.

23. Flexner, *Washington: Anguish and Farewell,* 308–309.

24. Ibid., 311.

25. M. L. Weems, *The Life of George Washington with Curious Anecdotes Equally Honorable to Himself and Exemplary to his Young Countrymen,* 5th ed., 1806.

26. Flexner, *Washington: Forge of Experience*, 17.
27. Ibid., 190.
28. Flexner, *Washington: Anguish and Farewell*, 311.
29. Flexner, *Washington: Forge of Experience*, 80.
30. Ibid., 50.
31. Ibid., 54–77.
32. Flexner, *Washington: Indispensable Man*, 14.
33. Flexner, *Washington: Forge of Experience*, 26.
34. Flexner, *Washington: Indispensable Man*, 36.
35. Ibid., 170.

A Not-So-Short
(Actually Average-Sized)
Look at the Life
of Napoleon

*E*verybody knows that Napoleon Bonaparte, the Emperor of France, was a tiny, even minuscule man, a military leader virtually dwarfed by everyone, friend and foe, who surrounded him. Today in the late twentieth century, his diminutive height has been widely accepted to be the driving force behind Napoleon's aggressive personality, the internal cause of his overwhelming need to conquer all of the world. In fact, in both the psychological and lay literature, the terms "Napoleonic complex," and "little Napoleon" have become synonymous with short-statured individuals who, to compensate for their lack of height, feel the need to become both domineering and dominant.

But aside from the question of his short stature, Napoleon Bonaparte had other peculiar physical characteristics. According to Arno Karlen, author of the book *Napoleon's Glands,* between the ages of thirty-six (the year he had himself crowned emperor) and forty, Napoleon Bonaparte's body underwent a dramatic and apparently spontaneous transformation. Rather rapidly during those years, the emperor metamorphosed from a slim, fit, energetic, and mentally focused military leader into something entirely different:

> His face became round, his hands pudgy, his hair sparse and silky; he developed a paunch. . . . Carnot, his minister

of war, wrote during the Russian campaign: "I no longer
know him. He used to be lean, shy and silent. Now he is
fat and garrulous. He is sleepy and his mind wanders."[1]

The emperor himself apparently noticed at least some of the
changes in his body: of the gynecomastia (excessive development of the
male mammary glands) that had rather suddenly developed, he commented to his physician, "Any beauty would be proud of my bosoms."[2]
Most of these striking alterations in body shape that appeared in
midlife were still present when the former emperor died in April 1821.
Dr. Walter Henry, a British physician present at Napoleon's autopsy, an
examination that revealed that the former emperor, like his father, had
apparently died of stomach cancer, noted that the corpse was quite fat,
with pale, delicate skin almost without body hair. He wrote:

> The pubis much resembled the mons veneris in women.
> The muscles of the chest were small, the shoulders narrow,
> and the hips wide. The penis and testicles were very small,
> and the whole genital system seemed to exhibit a physical
> cause for the absence of sexual desire and chastity which
> had been stated to have characterized the deceased.[1]

Since the time that these changes began occurring in Napoleon's
body habitus in 1805, a debate has been raging among Napoleonic
scholars concerning what exactly happened to the emperor that caused
this unusual metamorphosis. Although the verbiage produced by this
debate has managed to fill more than its fair share of books and jour-
nals, no completely satisfactory explanation has thus far appeared.

What exactly are the abnormalities that were apparently present in
Napoleon after he was crowned emperor? Historical accounts reveal
that, although earlier in life he had clearly possessed what would be
considered a masculine body configuration, at around the time he
was crowned emperor he developed gynecomastia, obesity with something of a feminine distribution of fat, and sparsity of body hair. In addition, some historians believe that Napoleon suffered a significant
lessening of his sex drive and question whether his penis and testes

shrank. Assuming that at least some of these features were actually present, is there any way to fit them together into a single, unifying diagnosis?

The best way to attempt a diagnosis is to choose the single feature that is both the most medically significant and the least controversial (that is, a feature generally accepted by all observers) and review all its possible causes. Since it was a feature about which Napoleon himself commented (and therefore, we can assume, actually was present), gynecomastia is probably the best starting place for this diagnostic search.

Although it's not rare during adolescence, the development of significant gynecomastia in middle-aged men is somewhat unusual. In most cases, no etiology can be identified. When the gynecomastia is accompanied by other features, however, it is often possible to come up with a clear-cut diagnosis.

Enlargement and development of the mammary glands results from the effects of estrogen on the tissue that form the breasts. In humans, most of the body's estrogen, which is the major sex steroid in females, is produced by the cells of the ovary. Interestingly, the biosynthetic pathways through which estradiol, the major active form of estrogen, and testosterone are formed are closely linked. Both compounds are created out of a precursor called androstenedione, which itself, after a series of complicated biochemical steps, is somewhat ironically produced from good old cholesterol, the most universally hated component of food among humans. In the testis, a series of enzymes turns the androstenedione into testosterone. In the ovarian cells, testosterone is also produced; however, the vast majority of this ovarian testosterone is further acted upon by a series of additional enzymes that ultimately produce the active estradiol.

During puberty, it is the physiologic interrelationship between the active forms of testosterone and estrogen that determines whether male or female secondary sex characteristics will develop. In the normal male, the presence of high levels of testosterone causes the penis and testes to grow, the voice to deepen, the quantity of facial and body hair to increase, the libido to begin to rule the boy's life, and all the other changes that characterize normal male pubertal development. In the normal female, excessive amounts of estrogen produce the growth of the breasts, redistribution of fat, broadening of the hips, and other changes that characterize the typical female body habitus.

So, in simple terms, gynecomastia, the abnormal growth of breast tissue in the male, occurs when an excess of estrogen appears in a body in which testosterone should be ruling the roost. Logically, there are only two ways something like this could happen: either the male begins somehow to produce estrogen, or a lot of external estrogen is either accidentally or intentionally taken into the body.

Now there are only a few conditions that can cause estrogen excess to occur in the male. The simplest-to-diagnose cause is the intake of drugs that have estrogenic effects. A whole host of medications, including certain antihypertensive and antipsychotic medications, as well as drugs of abuse such as heroin and methadone, have been found to have such effects. We're pretty sure Napoleon didn't take any of these medications.

Certain cancerous tumors are also known to cause gynecomastia. Presumably, the cells of these tumors, which include cancers of the adrenal glands, the testes, and the liver, either produce excessive amounts of estrogen or destroy the ability of the testes to produce normal amounts of testosterone. Although Napoleon did die of cancer, the form of the disease from which he suffered is not known to cause changes that might lead to gynecomastia.

Additional causes of enlargement of the male breasts include familial and idiopathic gynecomastia (in which no obvious pathophysiologic mechanism can be identified) and marked obesity, but the most interesting causes feature an abnormality in the endocrine system's delicate system of checks and balances.

For either estrogen or testosterone to be produced, signals in the form of hormones called gonadotropins must be released from the pituitary gland in the brain. The production of these gonadotropins is controlled by chemicals called gonadotropin-releasing hormones, which are themselves produced by the hypothalamus in the brain. The hypothalamus has the ability to sense the levels of testosterone and estrogen in the blood; it produces its signal in response to what it considers abnormally low levels of these hormones.

Any tiny imbalance in this very complicated system will wind up knocking over the whole delicately constructed house of cards. Such perturbations are well known and must be considered possible causes of the midlife change in Napoleon's body.

In fact, since the time that he developed his symptoms, doctors have theorized about various endocrinologic alterations that might have caused Napoleon's bodily reconfiguration. Theories include one in which the emperor's problem resulted from the burning out of his thyroid gland; another states that his pituitary gland simply ceased to function properly, a condition that ultimately led to abnormalities of growth, sexuality, and emotion; a third points to the possibility that Napoleon suffered from Klinefelter's syndrome (see the previous chapter on George Washington); and still a fourth theory suggests that Napoleon really had no medical problem at all, that in fact the changes that occurred in his body were simply the normal consequences of the aging process in a man who led a largely sedentary life-style.

Unfortunately, there are problems with each of these theories. None fully explains all of the features of Napoleon's metamorphosis. I'd like to offer an alternative suggestion.

Recently, while evaluating a group of young men with supposed idiopathic gynecomastia (that is, no clear etiology for the breast enlargement could be identified), Drs. Mariano Castro-Magana, Moris Angulo, and John Uy of Winthrop University Hospital in New York identified three individuals who, during or after adolescence, manifested a deficiency of an enzyme called 17-ketosteroid reductase.[3] This enzyme, which exists within the testis, catalyzes the final step in the production of testosterone.

If a deficiency of 17-ketosteroid reductase occurs during fetal life in a genetic male (that is, an individual possessing one copy of an X chromosome and one Y), little or no testosterone will be produced, and externally the child will appear to have either relatively normal female genitalia or genitalia that appear ambiguous. But according to the article by Drs. Castro-Magana, Angulo, and Uy, if a deficiency of 17-ketosteroid reductase manifests itself in a male later in life, perhaps during or after puberty, the effect would be that of acquired hypogonadism:

that is, a sudden deficiency of testosterone, an increase in estradiol, and all the consequences that might result from this, including gynecomastia, decrease in body hair and libido, redistribution of fat, wasting of the testes and penis, and an impairment in spermatogenesis that could lead to infertility.

Amazingly, this list of features virtually parallels those that were present in Napoleon after he became emperor, except for two previously unexplored features: the wasting of the testes and penis and the impairment in spermatogenesis. Is there evidence that he had these two abnormalities?

The question of an impairment in spermatogenesis is easiest to address. Such an impairment, accompanied by a loss of libido, would have led, at the very least, to reproductive difficulties. But on the surface, this doesn't seem to have been the case: apparently, Napoleon fathered a number of children. Or did he?

There's a great deal of speculation about this question. It is known that his first marriage, to Josephine de Beauharnais, ended mainly because she failed to provide him with an heir. But after his marriage to Josephine ended, Napoleon is said to have "impregnated two other women, felt reassured, took a second wife, and fathered more with her and with mistresses."[1] So the question of infertility in Napoleon would seem to be easily dismissed.

And yet, numerous authors have argued that the offspring of Napoleon's second marriage, to the Archduchess Marie Louise, were actually not fathered by the emperor himself, but rather by a self-selected stand-in. According to these stories, Napoleon, fearing that his vast empire would be in danger of extinction if an heir was not in place, chose some of the men closest to him to impregnate his second wife.[1] In fact, in his book entitled *Napoleon: Bisexual Emperor,* the Scottish physician Dr. Frank Richardson suggested that the chief stud was none other than one of the emperor's brothers.[1]

Regardless of the true answer to this question, the emperor's real inability to produce an offspring during his first marriage might, in fact, offer enough evidence of the difficulties that would be expected to support a diagnosis of late-onset variant of 17-ketosteroid reductase deficiency. But what about the wasting of the penis? Did Napoleon manifest this feature of the disorder?

Under normal circumstances, there would be no way today, more than 150 years after his death, to definitively answer this question. But, fortunately, we actually have the opportunity to get at least something of an answer. And this, at long last, brings us to the fascinating story of Napoleon Bonaparte's penis.

Early in the course of writing this book, well before I began investigating the question of Napoleon Bonaparte's condition, an article in the book review section of *The New York Times* caught my attention. Entitled "Exhuming a Dirty Joke," the article, written by the novelist John Vernon, discussed at great length the search Mr. Vernon had undertaken to uncover the present location of the emperor's penis.[2] According to legend, Napoleon's penis had been removed from the ex-emperor's body sometime after his death by an overexuberant "relic seeker," who later sold the item to a collector. After some investigation, Mr. Vernon ultimately discovered that the relic in question had, at some time in the past, been purchased at auction by Dr. John K. Lattimer, "a surgeon at the Columbia Presbyterian Medical Center" in New York.

Now although he's mentioned here for the first time, this is certainly not the last we'll hear of Dr. Lattimer. An internationally known urologic surgeon and currently the chairman emeritus of the Department of Urology at Columbia University, Dr. Lattimer has also received acclaim in two other, though somewhat related fields of endeavor. First, he is a well-known collector of medical memorabilia, possessing a burgeoning collection that includes, among many other objects, the spectacles worn by Abraham Lincoln at the time of his assassination, and the shirt collar worn by John F. Kennedy at the time of his assassination. Second, Dr. Lattimer is a biohistorical scholar; he has written extensively on the health of Abraham Lincoln and is the author of a book that compared the similarities between the Kennedy and Lincoln assassinations. And, as related by John Vernon in his article, he is also the man who bought Napoleon Bonaparte's penis at auction.

I'm not exactly sure how this latter situation actually came to be. According to the story I've heard from an acquaintance of Dr. Lattimer's, after the relic had passed out of the possession of the descendants of the Abbe Ange Paul Vignali, the man who was Napoleon's chaplain, it was bought and sold again and again by antique dealers in Europe and the United States. Finally Dr. Lattimer, outraged that it had once again reached the auction block, a situation he found disgraceful and degrading to the memory of Napoleon, bought the relic and, in an attempt to return some dignity to the object and to spare Napoleon's memory from the gawkers of history, donated it to the Squire Urological Collection at Columbia.

Because of my interest in its size, I telephoned Dr. Lattimer and asked if I could see it. Appropriately, he told me that viewing the penis was frowned upon by the members of the Board of Trustees at Columbia, the group that will forever determine its fate. But actually gazing at the object wasn't essential; I realized that having a world-renowned urologist describe it to me would be as good.

Dr. Lattimer explained to me that the penis had never been preserved in formalin, but had been air-dried, a process that essentially left it mummified. When I asked him to describe it, the urologist quickly told me to just look at my little finger. "It's pretty much the same size and shape," he added. Not having any frame of reference with which to compare it, I asked Dr. Lattimer if, in his opinion, the penis was significantly smaller than other specimens that had been prepared in this way. The urologist replied that he'd had some experience examining mummified penises in the past and, to his eye, Napoleon's was not appreciably different in size or shape from the others he'd seen.

Although Dr. Lattimer freely admits he's not certain that the object in his possession actually came from the body of the Emperor Napoleon I, it really doesn't matter all that much. The question of whether or not Napoleon had the later onset form of 17-ketosteroid reductase deficiency or, for that matter, any other disease that accounted for his midlife metamorphosis will probably never be conclusively answered.

82

Until now I've avoided discussing how Napoleon's diminutive
stature may have affected a search for the cause of his midlife changes.
But what about the emperor's lack of height?

When I set out on my investigation of Napoleon's shortness, I felt
confident that it was simply going to be a matter of studying his other
physical attributes, reviewing the list of genetic disorders associated
with diminutive height, coming up with a reasonable match, and making a diagnosis. I figured it should have been a cinch.

The key phrase in the previous paragraph is "should have been."
When I began looking into what has been written about the appear-
ance of the man who during his life had been referred to as "the Little
Corporal," I discovered, much to my surprise, that Napoleon I, the
Emperor of France from 1804 to 1814, was in fact not short at all.
During the autopsy that was performed on his body following his
death on May 5, 1821, on the island of Saint Helena in the Mediterranean Sea, Napoleon was found to be over five feet, six inches tall, at
least equal to the average of adult men in early-nineteenth-century
France.[1] Amazingly, it seems that Napoleon Bonaparte was, in fact, of
normal stature!

How could this have happened? How could such an absolutely
unfounded and incorrect belief have become so deeply imbedded in the
minds of most of us living in the latter portion of the twentieth century? How could an entire theory of behavior based on something that
simply was not true have been propagated and accepted? The problem,
apparently, lies in a simple misunderstanding involving a system of
measurements.

Through recorded history, attempts to develop a method of measuring objects that is both accurate and universally acceptable have
caused serious diplomatic problems. Basically, the whole thing boils
down to an issue of chauvinism: the citizens of one country, having
come to believe that the system of weights and measures adopted by

their ancestors perhaps hundreds of years before is, without question, the easiest to work with and to understand, simply refuse to accept, to use, or to even try to understand the workings of an alternate system that has become the standard in a neighboring country. This problem exists even today, as a struggle to dominate the method of measurement rages in the world of the late twentieth century; in this battle the supporters of the metric system, represented by the peoples of France, Great Britain, China, Egypt, Canada, and most of the rest of the civilized world, are pitted against a minority of holdouts, mostly centered in the United States, who have steadfastly clung to an antimetric approach to measuring things. Year after year, the question arises as to which standards are the most appropriate and most acceptable, those of the metric system or those of the so-called English system. Is the meter a superior and more elegant method of expressing length than the lowly foot? Is the liter a better way to measure volume than the quart? Could the kilogram possibly be a more appropriate method of describing weight than the pound? Throughout this century, plenty of supporters have lined up on either side of these questions.

In medicine in the United States today, we seem to be stuck right in the middle of this debate, attempting simultaneously to use both of these warring systems. This is especially true in the field of pediatrics: at the hospitals in which I work, the weights of newborn babies are nearly always initially recorded in grams. Of course, when we tell a mother that her infant weighs 3,200 grams, she usually has little or no conception of what this means. So, in order for parents to understand how large their baby is, it's necessary for us to "translate," as if into a different language, this gram measurement into what most mothers and fathers like to refer to as "real numbers," (in the example used, this would be 7 pounds, one-half ounce).

This discrepancy between the more scientifically acceptable metric system and the more comfortable English system does not stop at birth. Almost everything that must be calibrated and calculated, from the dose of many medications, to the amount of formula an infant needs to take in per day, to the amount of urine that should be produced during a one-hour period, is done on the basis of the patient's weight in kilograms. Since most parents are able to report, fairly accurately, their child's weight in pounds and ounces, pediatricians are forever having to convert from one system to the other. It's because of this that, to us pediatricians, the pocket calculator has become as indispensable a medical instrument as the stethoscope.

During the life of Napoleon Bonaparte, a similar failure existed on the part of the population of one portion of the civilized world to comprehend the system of measurement utilized in another. At that time, most countries in Europe used the English system, employing the foot as the standard unit of length. Originally based, as is implied by its name, on the length of an average human foot, the English foot eventually became fixed as a unit of measure equivalent to exactly twelve inches or, alternately, to exactly one-third of a yard.

Although the people of prerevolutionary France also used the term "foot" to describe their unit of measure, the French foot was unfortunately not exactly equivalent to the English version. Known as *pied de roi,* the French foot, which was exactly equal to the length of the foot of a former French king, was equal in length to exactly 0.3248 meters, or 12.78 inches.[4] To put it another way, the French foot was just over three-quarters of an inch longer than the English foot. And it was because of this slight variation between the French and English feet that the misunderstanding about Napoleon's height developed.

According to the measurement system then in use in France, Napoleon Bonaparte, during adulthood, stood 5 feet 2 inches tall.[1] Using the conversion factors mentioned in the previous paragraph, the emperor's stature is therefore equivalent to about 1.68 meters, or, in the English system, nearly 5 feet 6½ inches, a height that, as previously mentioned, was about average for a western European male during the late eighteenth and early nineteenth centuries.

However, most people who lived outside of France apparently didn't understand the difference between the French and the then-more-widely-used English systems of measurement. The problem was compounded by the fact that, because he lived during an age when there were no cameras and no television, relatively few people outside of France had actually ever laid eyes on Napoleon Bonaparte. True, there were portraits painted of the man and they were sometimes reproduced, but these paintings usually showed the emperor as a solitary figure, either standing or sitting by himself; only rarely was Napoleon portrayed as part of a tableau, standing amidst a group of other people, individuals who, because they were presumably of normal stature, could be used as a basis of comparison. Because they never had the opportunity to see him in person, people outside his sphere of influence were forced to rely on descriptions of the man that were passed from person to person. Outside of France, the reports that Napoleon was 5 feet 2 inches in height were undoubtedly interpreted to mean that the emperor was a runt, smaller by far than his average countryman.

It was Dr. Alfred Adler, the eminent Austrian psychiatrist and founder of the school known as individual psychology, who first proposed that Napoleon's short stature was the driving force behind Napoleon's bellicose behavior.[1] Dr. Adler believed that the development of one's personality was not a random, haphazard event, but rather depended heavily upon self-determination, and that the individual could either consciously or subconsciously compensate for most of life's difficulties, whether derived from emotional trauma or physical shortcomings, and, eventually, overcome them.[5] An early believer in the importance of the inferiority complex, Alfred Adler argued at around the turn of the present century that Napoleon's tyrannical nature, his need to conquer and to rule everything and everyone, was simply a subconscious effort on his part to overcome his supposed short stature, the physically derived shortcoming (no pun intended) that presented, at least according to Dr. Adler, the most significant difficulty in the emperor's early life.

Now I have to admit, I agree with many of the points Dr. Adler makes in his book. Not only have I repeatedly seen the effects that physical disabilities have on the development of the personalities of my young patients born with congenital malformations, but the personalities of nearly all of the people whose lives are chronicled in this book were affected by one or more physical or emotional abnormalities. And it is true that there were many incidents that Dr. Adler might have used to explain why Napoleon Bonaparte turned out the way he did, many important early life experiences that the psychiatrist could have selected as a cause for an inferiority complex. For example, Dr. Adler might have argued that Napoleon felt inferior because, having been born in

Corsica, an Italian region that had, only a few years before his birth, been annexed by the government of King Louis XV, he was made to feel that he was an outsider, comfortable neither as a Frenchman nor as an Italian. He could have made a case for the fact that, having been sent away to a military boarding school in Champagne, France, before he was ten, a situation that forced him to spend the formative years of his childhood and adolescence alone, without any contact with his parents or siblings, Napoleon naturally developed an inferiority complex.[1] Or the psychiatrist might have claimed that, as a result of Napoleon's alleged small penis, discussed in detail above, he developed a psychiatric condition known as "organ inferiority."[5] But, unfortunately for him, Adler decided to argue that Napoleon's inferiority complex was caused by the one physical feature that Napoleon clearly wasn't affected by.

And so, one thing is clear: the man who was called the Little Corporal was not short. At 5 feet 6 inches, he was of average height.

After learning that George Washington couldn't have been the father of our country and that Napoleon wasn't short, does anyone out there still believe that Abraham Lincoln was tall?

References

1. Arno Karlen, *Napoleon's Glands and Other Ventures in Biohistory* (Boston: Little, Brown and Co., 1984), 20–30.
2. John Vernon, "Exhuming a Dirty Joke," *New York Times Book Review,* July 12, 1992, 1, 34, 35.
3. M. Castro-Magana, M. Angulo, and J. Uy, Male hypogonadism with gynecomastia caused by late-onset deficiency of testicular 17-ketosteroid reductase, *New England Journal of Medicine* 328 (1993): 1297–301.
4. Martine Heitner and Sheldon C. Heitner, personal communication, May 1993.
5. H. and R. Ansbacher (eds.), *Individual Psychology of Alfred Adler; A Systematic Presentation in Selections from his Writing* (New York: Basic Books 1956).

Mr. Lincoln and Dr. Marfan's Syndrome: The Making of the President, 1860

During the height of the presidential campaign of 1860, a campaign that would culminate on Tuesday, November 6, with his election as the sixteenth president of the United States, Abraham Lincoln, the candidate of the Republican Party, received the following letter, dated October 15, 1860, from Grace Bedell, a young admirer from the village of Westfield in Chautauqua County, New York:

> Dear Sir
> My father has just [come] home from the fair and brought home your picture. . . . I am a little girl only eleven years old, but want you should be President of the United States very much so I hope you wont think me very bold to write to such a great man as you are. . . . I have got 4 brother's and part of them will vote for you any way and if you will let your whiskers grow I will try and get the rest of them to vote for you you would look a great deal better for your face is so thin. All the ladies like whiskers and they would tease their husband's to vote for you and then you would be President.[1]

On October 19, despite what must have been a hectic schedule, Mr. Lincoln took time out to reply to Grace: "My dear little Miss . . . As to the whiskers, having never worn any, do you not think people would call it a piece of silly affect[at]ion if I were to begin it now?" However, despite any misgivings he might have had about the impression his action would leave with the general populace of the United States, within three weeks of that response, President-elect Lincoln, for the first time in his life, began to grow a beard.[1]

This apparently innocent exchange of letters, the first written by a preadolescent girl who presumably had no strong political motivation, no hidden agenda, nor anything of substance to gain by the writing of it, and the nearly immediate response from the presidential candidate during what was undoubtedly one of the busier periods of his life, underscores two significant factors about the man who has come to be known as the Great Emancipator. First, Miss Bedell's comments regarding the candidate's facial appearance confirm that to his contemporaries, Abraham Lincoln, to put it as kindly as possible, was an unusual-looking man, an individual who, as his biographer, Stephen B. Oates, has stated, appeared to be composed of body parts that simply did not fit together exactly right.[2] Second, and certainly more important to the course of history, Lincoln's response, both the letter to Grace Bedell and his subsequent action, indicates that the future president was extremely sensitive about the way he looked. He apparently understood all too well that his appearance was unusual and homely; he knew that he "stood out in a crowd," and that this ease of identification was not necessarily due to the brilliance of his mind, nor to the lightning quickness of his wit, nor to the sensitivity and understanding that was his nature, but rather, it resulted from his strange and unattractive appearance. Apparently, Abraham Lincoln was so sensitive and uneasy about the way he looked that he was willing to take the unsolicited advice of a little girl who not only had never met him, but, in fact, had never even seen him in person.

Abraham Lincoln's response to Grace Bedell's letter says a tremendous amount about what the man actually thought of himself. And yet, in all the years that have passed since his death, in all the biographical studies that have been published, this aspect of Abraham Lincoln's existence, the effect that his unusual appearance had on the formation of his character, as well as its effect on the evolution of his political philosophy, has apparently never been formally addressed. But understanding the effect that his disproportionately tall stature and homeliness had on Lincoln is undoubtedly important; without understanding this, it may be impossible to comprehend fully what motivated the man whose mere election to the presidency would literally split the nation in two.

———————

There is little argument about the way Abraham Lincoln appeared to his fellow countrymen: as seen in figure 1, the man literally towered over his contemporaries. At a time when the median height of adult American males was 5 feet, 6 inches,[3] Lincoln, at 6 feet, 4 inches, was nearly a foot taller than the average. And his biographies indicate that it had always been this way for him: he had attained this massive height

Figure 1. The president and his officers: Lincoln is a good head taller than the other men pictured.
From Stefan Lorant's *Lincoln, A Picture Story of His Life* (W. W. Norton).

early in life. Described at age seven by a neighbor as "a tall spider of a boy," Lincoln went through a rapid growth spurt between the ages of eleven and sixteen and, according to Carl Sandburg, had already attained his adult height by the time he was seventeen.[4] And his great size was further accentuated by the leanness of his body: as an adult, Mr. Lincoln's weight varied between only 160 and 185 pounds.

But it wasn't just Lincoln's extraordinary size and narrow build that set him apart from the rest of the populace. As already noted, the man simply didn't seem to fit together properly. It was as if he had been randomly stuck together, created out of a series of disparate spare parts, formed from a collection of accumulated odds and ends that had originally belonged to a great many different individuals, almost as if he were actually a composite sketch. Because of the way his body seemed thrown together, it probably makes sense to explore the man section by section.

It seems logical that a tour of Abraham Lincoln's discordant body segments should begin with the most unusual and outstanding: these would be his extremities, arms and legs that were simply much too long for the man's trunk and head. According to Oates, "when he was sitting, he was no taller than an average man; but when he stood, he kept rising until he towered over his friends."[2] "It was his legs that gave him his height," the biographer added, "so long that he seemed to be standing on stilts."[5] And going along with those stilt-like legs were almost clown-like feet, so large that they required size fourteen shoes, a fact that would assure that, throughout his life, the future president would require that all his footwear be specially made to order.[6]

Lincoln's upper extremities were as disproportionately long as his lower ones. Mr. Lincoln himself recognized this: during the Civil War, while observing a regiment of oversized and burly Maine lumbermen in 1862, the president commented that "I don't believe . . . there is a man in that regiment with longer arms than mine."[7] And in 1907, the sculptor J. H. Bartlett, after studying Leonard Volk's 1860 cast of the president's hands, observed that the upper extremities were large and long, and that "the first phalanx of the middle finger is nearly half an inch longer than that of an ordinary hand."[8]

But in contrast to the striking length of his extremities, Lincoln's head seemed relatively small, and his face, as pointed out by Grace Bedell in her letter, was too long and much too thin. In photographs, such as the one shown in figure 2, Lincoln's eyes appear smaller than they should be, an appearance exaggerated by the fact that his lids droop slightly, a condition known as ptosis. His ears are large and stand

Figure 2. Lincoln's face prior to his beard. Note drooping of lids (ptosis), large lop-ears, long nose, sunken cheeks, and heavily-lined skin.
From Stefan Lorant's *Lincoln; A Picture Story of His Life* (W. W. Norton, 1969).

off from the plane of his face in what could be described as a mild lop ear deformity; the nose is long and straight, the cheeks sunken, and the skin, even at a relatively early age, was heavily wrinkled and leathery in appearance.

In contrast to the small head and long limbs, the length of the president's neck and trunk appear more appropriate for a man living in the mid-nineteenth century. However, there were still some unusual features to be noted among these two body segments: Lincoln's neck was described as "scrawny" and "too thin to fill the collar of his dress shirt, even when it was pulled tight with a black cravat."[9] The shoulders were narrow and sloping, and, according to his law-partner-turned-biographer, William H. Herndon, his chest was so thin that he appeared to possess a "sunken breast."[10] Thus, the overall impression that one takes away from a study of Abraham Lincoln's body morphology confirms, as has already been pointed out, that the various parts of the sixteenth president of the United States simply did not fit together.

Although the unusual nature of Abraham Lincoln's appearance is well accepted among his biographers, the cause of his odd morphology has remained something of a puzzle. In a letter regarding this issue, William Herndon wrote to an acquaintance in the medical profession, "I would consult some of the best . . . physicians on this very question. . . . Please get your most learned men to assist us."[10]

Herndon's plea appears to have been ignored during the remainder of the nineteenth century, but more recently, some attempts have actually been made at making a retrospective diagnosis that would explain Lincoln's appearance. Since 1962 a handful of articles have appeared in the medical literature speculating that Lincoln's unusual body habitus might have actually represented the external manifestation of some underlying, generalized disease process. Most of the speculation has grown out of an article by Dr. A. M. Gordon that appeared in a 1962 issue of the *Journal of the Kentucky Medical Association*. A physician studying an inherited condition known as Marfan syndrome, Dr. Gordon suggested there that Lincoln might have suffered from this very disorder.[11] Dr. Gordon's original article became the first volley in a debate regarding Mr. Lincoln and Dr. Marfan's syndrome that has slowly simmered since the time of its initial publication.

———————

From the beginning, it was the unusual skeletal manifestations that attracted the most attention. In 1896, Dr. Antoine Bernard-Jean Marfan, the first professor of pediatrics to be appointed in the city of Paris, was asked to evaluate a five-and-a-half-year-old girl named Gabrielle. Although the girl was in excellent health and apparently of normal intelligence at the time of her visit with Dr. Marfan, she had, since the time of her birth, been noted to have a very unusual body configuration: tall and thin, with disproportionately long, spider-like extremities; in retrospect, she must have looked quite a bit like Abraham Lincoln. Although Dr. Marfan was one of the founders of pediatrics in France and had therefore had the opportunity to see a great many unusual patients during his career,[12] he had apparently never seen a patient quite like Gabrielle. So unusual were her features, so struck was the professor by the appearance of the young girl's arms and legs, that he reported her case in a French medical journal, naming the condition "dolichostenomelia" (meaning long, thin extremities) and accompanying the description with drawings of her hands and feet (figure 3), the latter of which he described using the term *pattes d'araignee* ("spider legs").[13] Gabrielle, therefore, became the first patient to be reported in the medical literature with a condition that has subsequently come to be known, in honor of the man who first brought it to medical attention, as "the Marfan syndrome."

And since Dr. Marfan's initial description of Gabrielle, it has been the skeletal features that have been the easiest to recognize and to compile. In addition to tall stature with disproportionately long extremities and arachnodactyly (the technical term currently employed to describe the spider-like fingers and toes), common skeletal manifestations seen in individuals affected with the Marfan syndrome include "funnel" or "pigeon" chest deformities (technically, pectus excavatum and pectus carinatum, respectively), curvature of the spine (scoliosis), laxity, or

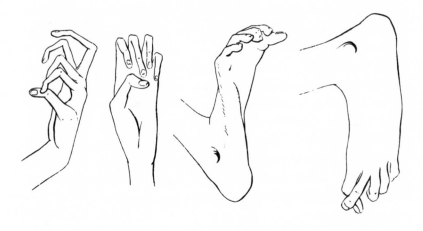

Figure 3. The drawings of Gabrielle's hands and feet that appeared in Dr. A. B.
Marfan's original article.[13]

hyperextensibility of the joints, and pes planus, or, as it's more commonly known, flat feet.[14]

But Marfan syndrome, which occurs in about one in every 10,000 Americans, is far more than just the skeletal abnormalities described above. Because the underlying abnormality involves a defect in the formation of connective tissue, the "glue" that essentially holds most of the human body together, it became clear in the years following Marfan's initial report that major organ systems other than the skeleton are affected in all patients who suffer from the disorder, systems that, because of the anomalies that characteristically occur, usually result in profound disabilities and markedly foreshortened life expectancy.

The first and certainly most serious internal manifestation of the syndrome is the involvement of the heart and aorta, the body's largest artery, the vessel that carries blood away from the heart to the remainder of the body. The fact that the cardiovascular system is affected in Marfan syndrome became apparent sixteen years after Gabrielle's case appeared in the medical literature. In 1912, Viktor Salle, a German pathologist, reported the findings of an autopsy he'd performed on a two-month-old infant with dolichostenomelia who had suddenly and unexpectedly died. On the autopsy table, Dr. Salle discovered that the infant's heart had essentially exploded: the aorta had ruptured, flooding the chest with blood.[15]

It is this explosion of the aorta, unfortunately an almost inevitable consequence of the presence of the gene that causes Marfan syndrome, that is clearly the disorder's most dire and dreaded feature. In affected individuals, the wall of the ascending portion of the aorta (the part that extends from the heart upward, toward the head) is weakened; eventually, as time passes and the toll accumulates from years of pounding blood forced under high pressure out of the pumping chamber of the heart, the wall begins to thin and blow up like a balloon, much the way an old radiator hose might after years of constant service. In the aorta, this weakened, dilated segment forms what is known as an aneurysm; while the aneurysm is slowly developing within his or her chest, the person affected with Marfan syndrome may experience some chest pain, but most of the time, the dilatation of the aorta occurs without any accompanying symptoms. Slowly, the wall continues to thin and dilate, becoming steadily thinner and more balloon-like with each contraction of the heart, ultimately reaching three or even four times its normal diameter. The process continues until, suddenly, usually in dramatic fashion, the aorta bursts, as it apparently did in the infant examined by Dr. Salle, causing immediate, unexpected, and unexplained death.[14]

Such a scenario has unfortunately played itself out over the years in some athletes, especially, as might be expected as a result of the tall stature that occurs in Marfan syndrome, in basketball players. However, perhaps the best-known instance of the rupture of an aorta leading to tragedy occurred not in a basketball player, but rather in Flo Hyman, a star of the 1984 U.S. Olympic women's volleyball team. During the heat of a game in Japan in January 1986, Ms. Hyman, who excelled at her sport principally because of her unusual size and her excessive arm span, and who was apparently totally unaware that she was affected with any medical condition, suddenly collapsed, dropping heavily and dramatically to the floor of the volleyball court. Attempts at resuscitation, both immediately in the gym and later at a nearby hospital to which she was taken, proved to be in vain. An autopsy revealed that she had the characteristic cardiovascular features of Marfan syndrome, and had died as a result of a ruptured aortic aneurysm.[16]

Had she been known to have had the Marfan syndrome, Flo Hyman's death could have been predicted: until recently, early demise from rupture of the aorta was a nearly inevitable consequence of Marfan syndrome. Among seventy-two of his patients who had died, Dr. Victor McKusick, one of the world's earliest and best-known experts in Marfan syndrome, found that the average age at death was only thirty-two years.[17] But a recent breakthrough in the management of patients with Marfan syndrome has happily altered what had become clearly the natural endpoint of the disease. In 1986, the same year in which Flo Hyman tragically died, a novel treatment was reported, a surgical procedure in which the weakened portion of the aorta is electively removed and replaced by a plastic graft before it has a chance to explode.[18] Experience has shown that, following such surgery, which itself introduces only a very low mortality rate, the risk of sudden death resulting from rupture of an aortic aneurysm is reduced nearly to zero. This dramatic breakthrough has given new hope to people with Marfan syndrome; it has nearly assured that with proper care and close follow-up, affected individuals can expect to lead longer, cardiac disease–free lives.

Another major internal manifestation that is nearly a constant feature of Marfan syndrome involves the eyes. Not unlike the skeleton, the eyeball, or globe, tends to be long and thin, leading to extreme nearsightedness, or "high myopia" as the condition is more accurately called. This high myopia usually requires the use of thick eyeglasses; frequently, the severity of the nearsightedness will lead to detachment of the retina, itself often a cause of permanent blindness. Also, as a consequence of the ubiquitous defect in the connective tissue, as many as eight out of ten people who suffer from the disorder develop dislocation of the lens of their eyes, a condition technically known as "ectopia lentis"; such dislocations often lead to the development of cataracts, another common cause of loss of vision.[14] Although not as dramatic and life-threatening as the cardiovascular consequences of the disorder, the visual defects that result from the presence of the abnormal gene can certainly be severe.

To be sure, there are abnormalities that occur in other body systems in individuals affected with Dr. Marfan's disorder: there can be spontaneous collapse of a lung, or "pneumothorax," resulting from the rupture of a "bleb" on the surface of the pleura, the covering of the lung; there have been abnormalities of the nervous system reported, such as "dural ectasias," defects in the covering of the spinal cord. But to the physician, it is the manifestations of the skeletal, cardiovascular, and ophthalmologic systems that really form the hallmarks of the Marfan syndrome.

A final feature that must be mentioned is the familial nature of Marfan syndrome. In 1931, three decades after Marfan's initial report of Gabrielle's unusual features, H. Weve first noted that the syndrome seemed to show a hereditary pattern. Passed along from affected parent to affected child, the disease is now known to be clearly inherited in what is known as an autosomal dominant pattern of inheritance.[19] In 1990 a major breakthrough in the genetic basis of the disorder occurred: by studying families in which many individuals in multiple generations have been affected, a group of Finnish scientists discovered that the defective gene responsible for the Marfan syndrome is found on chromosome 15, one of the twenty-three pairs of chromosomes that make up the human genome.[20] This finding has more recently led to another major breakthrough: using a technique known as "reverse genetics," scientists in different laboratories have identified the substance whose deficiency is actually responsible for the symptoms and signs of the disorder.[21] Known as "fibrillin," this protein, which has been shown to be absent in all patients with Marfan syndrome who have thus far been evaluated, is an essential component of something called "the myofibrillar array," the basic backbone of certain types of connective tissue. These two recent discoveries will, in the very near future, lead the way for an additional breakthrough: namely, they will allow the diagnosis of Marfan syndrome to be made through the use of a simple blood test.

But, alas, such simple tests are currently not available for use in the general population.[21] Until now, to prove the diagnosis of Marfan syndrome, it has been necessary to rely completely on clinical findings.

Ideally, in order for the diagnosis of Marfan syndrome to be confirmed, the patient should be tall, with disproportionately long arms and legs, arachnodactyly, curvature of the spine, funnel or pigeon chest deformity, lax joints, a weakened, dilated aorta, high myopia and dislocated lenses of the eyes, spontaneous pneumothoraces, dural ectasias, and a history of a parent who is or was similarly affected.

But unfortunately, life for us clinical geneticists is not so simple. In the vast majority of people who appear to be affected with Marfan syndrome, one or more of these cardinal features of the disorder are not present. How then can we conclusively determine if an individual is affected with this serious, life-threatening disorder? In 1986, during a meeting held in Berlin, a panel of the world's leading experts in the field of the Marfan syndrome developed an acceptable system for confirming the diagnosis of the disorder, a system that is based on the presence of a certain number of clinical criteria. In simple terms, the diagnosis of Marfan syndrome should only be made in patients in whom at least two of the following four criteria are met:

1. involvement of the skeleton;
2. involvement of the cardiovascular system;
3. involvement of the eyes; and
4. a family history of Marfan syndrome, proven by these criteria.

This criteria system for diagnosis now allows us a way to review the record in order to assess objectively whether Abraham Lincoln did in fact have Marfan syndrome.

Although, as previously mentioned, it was Dr. A. M. Gordon who initially speculated that Lincoln might have been affected with the Marfan syndrome, the staunchest support for this position came later, in 1964, from Dr. Harold Schwartz. In an article entitled "Abraham Lincoln and the Marfan Syndrome" that appeared in the *Journal of the American Medical Association*,[22] Dr. Schwartz, who was then an instructor in internal medicine at the University of Southern California School of Medicine, reported that in 1959, he had made a diagnosis of Marfan syndrome in a seven-year-old boy who was a descendant of Abraham Lincoln's paternal great-great-grandfather, Mordecai Lincoln II. After constructing a complete family history, reproduced in figure 4, and considering the fact that Abraham Lincoln had had what could only be referred to as a "Marfanoid habitus," Dr. Schwartz concluded that the association was not just mere coincidence. Rather, he believed, the evidence pointed to the fact that Lincoln, and in fact all of the eleven relatives who connected him to the seven-year-old patient, whether they suffered from any symptoms or not, had to be carriers of the gene that produced the disorder.

After carefully gathering and analyzing the existing evidence, Dr. Schwartz concluded, as could clearly be deduced from the description presented above, that Lincoln's "unusual morphological organization," as he referred to the president's body habitus, represented the skeletal manifestations of the disorder. But what of the other features? In Dr. Schwartz's opinion, did Abraham Lincoln possess at least one of the other three criteria necessary for confirmation of the diagnosis of Marfan syndrome?

According to his original article, and the one that followed in 1972,[23] Dr. Schwartz concluded that not only did Abraham Lincoln show evidence of one additional criterion, he showed evidence of *all* of them. Dr. Schwartz argued that the presence of Marfan syndrome in his seven-year-old patient, who shared a minuscule fraction (1/4,048) of his genetic material in common with Lincoln, confirmed the presence of the gene for the disorder within the family. The internist further pointed out that Lincoln suffered from eye problems: with evidence of "strabismus" (a squint) and the requirement of glasses for correction of "severe hyperopia" (farsightedness), Dr. Schwartz concluded that the history was sufficient to fulfill the ophthalmologic criterion. Finally, in his 1972 article, the internist claims to have discovered circumstantial evidence that, at least in his mind, "suggested a cardiac lesion" in Abraham Lincoln that would further confirm the diagnosis, a heart defect reflected in a physical finding a full two years before the president's assassination, a problem that would virtually "preclude completion of his second term in office even if he had not been assassinated." [23]

The evidence produced by Dr. Schwartz to confirm the president's cardiovascular disease is found in a photograph, reproduced in figure 5,

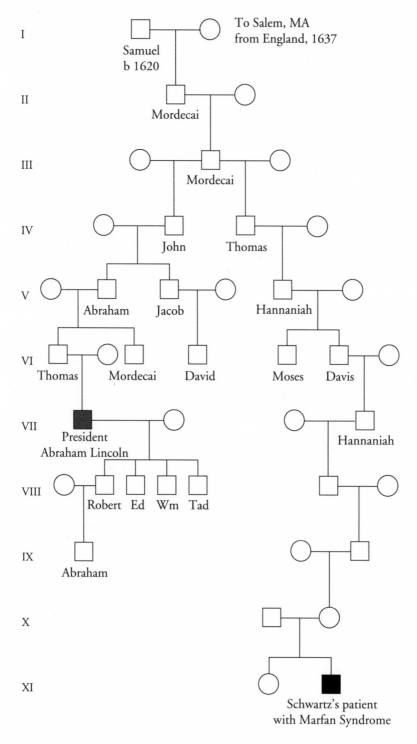

Figure 4. Abraham Lincoln's pedigree (from Schwartz[22])

taken by Alexander Gardner in Washington on November 15, 1863. In the picture, Lincoln is seated with his legs crossed. While reviewing this photograph with Noah Brooks, a newspaperman, the president comments:

> "I can understand why that foot should be so enormous. It's a big foot anyway, and it is near the focus of the instrument. But why is the outline of it so indistinct and blurred? I am confident I did not move it."
>
> Brooks suggested that the throbbing of the arteries may have caused an imperceptible motion.
>
> The President crossed his legs and watched his foot. "That's it! That's it!" he exclaimed. "Now that's very curious, isn't it?" [25]

Based on this "evidence," Dr. Schwartz concludes that, at least in his latter years, Lincoln suffered from a condition known as aortic insufficiency, caused by a defect in the valve that separates the left ventricle from the first, or ascending portion of the aorta. Aortic insufficiency, a common accompaniment to the dilatation of the aorta that occurs in Marfan syndrome, would be expected to lead to the presence of sharp, bounding pulses, cardiovascular impulses so strong that they could shake an entire foot when the legs were crossed. Thus, in Dr. Schwartz's opinion, Lincoln's aortic insufficiency, another manifestation of his Marfan syndrome that fulfilled the fourth criterion necessary for confirming the diagnosis, directly led to the blurring of the president's left shoe in Mr. Gardner's photograph. Therefore, Lincoln had evidence of every major criterion. Dr. Schwartz's conclusion was easy to reach: he believed that, without a doubt, Abraham Lincoln had Marfan syndrome.

––––––––

The publication of Dr. Schwartz's articles did not exactly meet with jubilation, dancing in the streets, and universal acclaim. In fact, in 1981, our old friend, Dr. John Lattimer, the chairman emeritus of urology at Columbia University and the man who bought Napoleon's penis at auction (see the preceding chapter on Napoleon), in an article succinctly and

Figure 5. A photograph of Lincoln, taken Nov. 15, 1863, showing the president with his legs crossed. Note that his left foot (the one suspended in the air) appears blurry. Schwartz argues that this blurriness is caused by bounding pulses in Lincoln's leg, a consequence of aortic insufficiency.
From Stefan Lorant's *Lincoln, A Picture Story of His Life* (W. W. Norton). Photo by A. Gardner, November, 1863.

unambiguously entitled "Lincoln Did Not Have the Marfan Syndrome,"[24] refuted each and every one of Dr. Schwartz's claims. Dr. Lattimer concluded that, although Lincoln did in fact have an unusual body
habitus with long, spider-like legs, he did not have the typical skeletal
manifestations of Marfan syndrome. First, his personal examination of
the plaster casts of the president's hands that had been made by sculptor
Leonard Volk in 1860 revealed that Lincoln's distal upper extremities
were thick and muscular, unlike the thin spider-like distal extremities
clearly illustrated in Dr. Marfan's drawing of Gabrielle's hands and reproduced in figure 3. Next, Dr. Lattimer pointed out that Lincoln was a
strong man, "a champion rough-and-tumble wrestler," who was able to
"hold his own" with Jack Armstrong, the wrestling champion of New
Salem, Illinois, the village in which Lincoln lived as a young man;[26] this
fact, Lattimer concluded, is a "powerful argument against his having the
weak connective tissue of the hands and arms of a patient with the Marfan syndrome." Finally, although, as previously mentioned, William
Herndon described the president as having a "sunken breast,"[10] a condition that seems to be consistent with the chest deformity expected in an
individual with the Marfan syndrome, Dr. Lattimer stated that no specific mention of pectus excavatum is made by any of the physicians who
viewed Lincoln's naked body during the autopsy that followed his assassination. For these reasons, Dr. Lattimer was forced to conclude that Abraham Lincoln simply did not have the skeletal manifestations commonly
associated with the Marfan syndrome.

Next, Dr. Lattimer, who, as mentioned in the previous chapter,
actually owns the eyeglasses that Lincoln was wearing at the time of his
assassination, refuted the claims of his Marfan-like eye problems. As already discussed, ectopia lentis, or dislocation of the lens of the eye, is
seen in up to 80 percent of individuals with the disorder. It is therefore
highly unlikely (although technically still possible) that, had he actually
had Marfan syndrome, Lincoln would have lived to the age of fifty-
six without suffering from this complication. Further, Dr. Lattimer
correctly pointed out that the president was farsighted, and that characteristically people with Marfan syndrome are extremely nearsighted.
Therefore, in Dr. Lattimer's view, this criterion is also left unfulfilled in
the case of Abraham Lincoln.

In his article, Dr. Lattimer launched his most vehement argument against Dr. Schwartz's claim that Alexander Gardner's photograph, reproduced in figure 5, provides any evidence whatsoever that Abraham Lincoln suffered from aortic insufficiency or, for that matter, from any other cardiovascular condition. The surgeon from New York claims that, rather than being caused by abnormally bounding pulsations of the arterial system, the blurring of the president's left foot was actually a natural consequence of the photographic process. With his legs crossed, the toes of President Lincoln's left foot "would have been at least three feet closer to the camera than the plane of Lincoln's face, on which the camera was focused," thus placing the entire foot essentially out of focus. This, plus the fact that exposure time was as long as twelve or thirteen seconds, combined to cause the boot to appear blurred. Therefore, rather than representing aortic insufficiency, the blurring of Lincoln's boot actually represents nothing more than a photographic artifact. Since no other evidence exists indicating that Lincoln suffered from cardiovascular compromise, Dr. Lattimer argued that this third criterion is also left unfulfilled.

Last to be considered is the matter of Lincoln's supposedly positive family history. Dr. Lattimer pointed out that a review of their physical descriptions by contemporaries and examination of photographs of both Lincoln's parents and his sons fail to confirm or to even suggest that any first-degree relatives had any of the features associated with the Marfan syndrome. Dr. Lattimer concluded that, rather than representing an abnormal gene that has been passed along, basically undiagnosed, through generation after generation of the Lincoln family, the presence of Marfan syndrome in Dr. Schwartz's original patient actually was the result of a spontaneous mutation, a naturally occurring change in the genetic material, that occurred at the time of conception of the young boy. The finding of the disorder in this young boy, at least in Dr. Lattimer's opinion, in no way adds credence to the argument that Abraham Lincoln might have had Marfan syndrome.

So when it comes to the question of whether Abraham Lincoln's unusual body morphology was caused by Marfan syndrome, the medical community is divided into two camps: the pro-Marfan camp, followers of Drs. Schwartz and Gordon, who claim that the sixteenth president fulfilled each and every one of the four criteria necessary for making the diagnosis; and the anti-Marfan camp, who, trusting Dr. Lattimer's evidence, believe that none of the four criteria were present in the case of Abraham Lincoln. How can we justify these two diametrically opposed positions? Did Lincoln have Marfan syndrome or didn't he? And if he didn't have it, what accounted for his unusual morphology?

In reality, I believe there is a common ground between the two extreme positions. In examining the evidence presented by Drs. Gordon, Schwartz, and Lattimer, I can't help but believe that Abraham Lincoln did have one of the criteria for making a diagnosis of Marfan syndrome: the skeletal manifestations. Lattimer's finding of the strong, well-muscled appearance of the casts of the president's hands, coupled with the historical accounts of his prowess at wrestling, log-splitting, and weight lifting, are not necessarily inconsistent with the diagnosis. Although Dr. Marfan's original sketches of Gabrielle's hands did show spider-thin, wasted-appearing distal extremities, since the disorder's characteristic features are quite variable, some individuals with Marfan syndrome are, in fact, reasonably well muscled. This point is underscored by the existence of athletes, including Flo Hyman and Chris Patton, a University of Maryland basketball player who died suddenly of a ruptured aortic aneurysm while in the midst of a game,[16] who were strong and well-coordinated enough to excel in sports at a national or even international level, in spite of being affected with the disorder. Therefore, based on descriptions of his physical appearance by contemporaries, and on examination of the available photographs and measurements, I am convinced that Abraham Lincoln did fulfill the skeletal criterion necessary for making the diagnosis of Marfan syndrome.

But, as far as I can judge, this is the only criterion that is satisfied. I agree with Dr. Lattimer's conclusion regarding the president's vision: had he had Marfan syndrome, it is highly unlikely that Abraham Lincoln would have survived to be fifty-seven years of age without having developed either dislocated lenses or significant myopia. It is probably even more unlikely that, had he had Marfan syndrome, Lincoln would have even survived to be fifty-seven years of age in the first place: as already mentioned, prior to the availability of treatment, the average age at death in patients with Marfan syndrome is the mid-thirties. The fact that he lived to be fifty-seven (and presumably would have lived to be a lot older had he not been shot in the head by John Wilkes Booth on the night of Good Friday, April 14, 1865) and suffered from no symptoms or signs of heart disease—except, perhaps, for the remote possibility that he had a pulse so bounding that it caused his foot to shake when his legs were crossed—is strong evidence against the possibility that Abraham Lincoln had the underlying cardiovascular weakness that is a virtually inevitable concomitant of the disorder. No, the lack of eye and heart features in a man of fifty-seven virtually assures, at least in my mind, that Lincoln was not affected with Marfan syndrome.

And a review of photographs and descriptions of members of his immediate family pretty much confirms this impression. Neither of Lincoln's parents appeared to have had any of the features of Marfan syndrome. Thomas Lincoln, the president's father and direct relative of the seven-year-old boy in whom Dr. Schwartz diagnosed Marfan syndrome, was, according to Carl Sandburg, a man of about 5 feet 9 and 180 pounds. Thomas Lincoln had "a round face,"[27] and bore none of the gaunt appearance nor the hollowness of the cheeks that caused little Grace Bedell to write her letter to his son. And the elder Lincoln lived to be seventy-three years of age, dying in 1851 following a long illness, again a highly unlikely longevity for a person affected with Marfan syndrome prior to the advent of the recent aortic replacement surgery.

Less is known about Abraham Lincoln's mother. No known photographs exist of Nancy Hanks Lincoln, who, although described by Sandburg as "tall, slender" and "dark complexioned,"[28] was actually shorter than her husband. The woman who bore two children in addition to Abraham (Sarah, who was healthy, and Thomas, who died a few days after birth) herself passed away at the age of thirty-four, an age not inconsistent with a diagnosis of Marfan syndrome. However, Nancy Lincoln's death was not caused by a catastrophic explosion of her aorta; rather, she died of an infectious disease known as "the milk sick," an illness that had apparently reached epidemic proportions in Pigeon Creek, Indiana, the town in which the family had settled.[30] Although the information is scanty, there is no clear-cut evidence pointing toward a diagnosis of Marfan syndrome in Lincoln's mother.

Having parents who are not affected does not necessarily rule out the presence of Marfan syndrome in the child; in 15 percent of cases, the disorder seems to appear suddenly, without any previous history, the result of a spontaneous mutation.[29] But if Abraham Lincoln had had Marfan syndrome caused by a spontaneous mutation, it would be expected, at least empirically, that he'd have passed the disorder along to approximately one-half of his children. Photographs of three of Abraham Lincoln's four sons are reproduced in figure 6. The children, including Willie, who died at the age of twelve of an infectious illness;[31] Eddie, who died at four years of age after a two-month illness;[32] Robert; and Tad, who spoke with a lisp because of a "misshapen" (probably cleft) palate,[33] with their full, round faces and well-proportioned bodies, appeared to more closely resemble their mother, Mary Ann Todd Lincoln, than their father. None of the children had any feature that in any way suggested the possibility that he carried the gene for the Marfan syndrome. Accordingly, it must be concluded that Abraham Lincoln had no first-degree relatives with Marfan syndrome: he therefore failed to meet the fourth criterion necessary for the diagnosis.

After review of the data at hand, it can be concluded that Abraham Lincoln did not suffer from the disorder. But if not Marfan syndrome, then what did he have? What exactly caused him to look the way he did?

The possibilities are limited to only a few disorders. In 1975 Dr. Jurgen Herrmann and his colleagues at the University of Wisconsin suggested that two members of the Lincoln family might have been affected with another autosomal dominantly inherited disorder, this one known as the Stickler syndrome,[33] an entity that combines specific craniofacial abnormalities, such as clefting of the palate, with a "Marfanoid habitus" and ophthalmologic abnormalities. The authors of this article argue that the presence of the gene that causes Stickler syndrome could have caused Tad Lincoln's cleft palate and contributed to the boy's father's skeletal findings. However, they quickly point out that, as

Figure 6. Abraham Lincoln's sons Willie, Robert, & Thomas (Tad). None illustrate any features suggestive of Marfan Syndrome.
All three photographs from Stefan Lorant's *Lincoln, A Picture Story of His Life* (W. W. Norton).

in Marfan syndrome, Stickler syndrome is associated with nearsightedness and Abraham Lincoln was farsighted. Also, although affected individuals have arms and legs that are disproportionately long when compared with their trunks (the so-called Marfanoid habitus), their overall height is usually normal or, in fact, shorter than normal. Although not unheard of, it would be unusual for an individual with Stickler syndrome to attain an extraordinarily tall height. For these reasons, it is unlikely that it was Stickler syndrome that caused Lincoln's morphologic abnormalities.

The panel of leading experts in the field of Marfan syndrome who assembled in Berlin in 1986 listed three disorders other than Stickler syndrome that were most often considered in the differential diagnosis of Marfan syndrome. In reviewing these entities, I believe that Abraham Lincoln was affected with another disease that affects connective tissue, a disease that has come to be known as mitral valve prolapse syndrome. Although in the past this disorder was often considered to be a *forme fruste* (that is, a milder form) of the Marfan syndrome, recent work performed by physicians at Johns Hopkins in Baltimore has revealed that mitral valve prolapse syndrome is a separate entity, with features that overlap with the disorder initially described by Dr. Marfan.[34]

Occurring in 3 or 4 percent of the population, mitral valve prolapse is the most common congenital malformation of the heart. Usually causing few if any symptoms, the term describes a "ballooning" or billowing out of the valve that separates the heart's left atrium from its left ventricle, or pumping chamber. Mitral valve prolapse causes an unusual clicking sound when the heart is examined with a stethoscope; sometimes it leads to irregularities in the heart rate; occasionally it leads to more serious cardiac pathology, such as congestive heart failure. But in the majority of cases, the individual affected with mitral valve prolapse is unaware that he or she has the condition.

Most of the time, mitral valve prolapse is an isolated finding in an otherwise healthy individual. In a small percentage of patients, however, the defect of this heart valve is associated with skeletal findings such as arachnodactyly, tall stature, disproportionately long limbs, as well as abnormalities of the chest and the spine—features that, at first glance, might lead one to suspect the diagnosis of Marfan syndrome. However, individuals with mitral valve prolapse syndrome lack the ocular findings that occur in Marfan syndrome and usually have normal aortas and negative family histories. As such, based on the evidence presented above, it appears as if a diagnosis of mitral valve prolapse syndrome best fits the picture that has been painted of Abraham Lincoln both during his life and subsequent to his death.

Having settled upon a diagnosis, the next question that must be asked is: What difference does any of this make? Who really cares if the sixteenth president of the United States was affected with the Marfan syndrome, the Stickler syndrome, mitral valve prolapse syndrome, or no syndrome at all? What really must be determined is whether the presence of the features of a particular genetic disorder actually played any role in the formation of the character of the man who came out of the Illinois wilderness in early 1860 as a virtually unknown lawyer and, on a platform that supported his inherent belief that slavery was morally and ethically wrong, was elected president of the United States.

One morning about five years ago, I was called to the nursery at our hospital to see a baby who had been born the previous night. On the phone, the resident who had been on call the night before told me that as soon as she'd laid eyes on the infant in the delivery room, she'd known that something was wrong with her: although her skin was pink and she was breathing comfortably and had a steady, normal heart rate, the baby "looked just like a daddy long-leg spider." "I've never seen a baby with Marfan syndrome before," she continued, "but if I had to guess, I'd say she's got it."

I left my office and immediately went up to the nursery. While examining the child a few minutes later, I rapidly came to the same conclusion that the resident had reached just hours before. The infant had the classic skeletal manifestations of Marfan syndrome: at 59 centimeters (or 23 1/4 inches, for those who need this "translated" into English) from the top of her head to the bottom of her heel, she was longer than any other baby I'd ever seen; she had dolichostenomelia, with extremely long arms and legs; arachnodactyly, with, as the resident had mentioned, spider-like fingers and toes; and even at that stage, there was an obvious caved-in appearance of the baby's chest. Although she was only a few hours old and we still had no information about either her heart or her eyes, I was willing to bet, based on what I was seeing, that the kid had Marfan syndrome.

After finishing my examination of the baby, I went to talk to the resident; I needed to find out about this child's parents. When I asked about the baby's mother, the resident told me that, although the woman was legally blind for reasons that hadn't been completely spelled out in the Obstetric Department's prenatal chart, Ms. Anderson, who was a little more than 5 feet tall, appeared to have none of the skeletal

manifestations of Marfan syndrome. Curious about the woman's eye
problem and what relationship it may have had to those seen in the disorder we were considering in the infant, I immediately went to speak
with Ms. Anderson.

I found her alone, lying apparently asleep in a bed on the post-
partum ward, and after a quick glance, I found myself again agreeing
with the pediatric resident's assessment: although her eyes looked abnormally small, the result, undoubtedly, of her blindness, Ms. Anderson had an otherwise normal appearance. "If this baby does have
Marfan syndrome," I found myself thinking, "she either inherited it
from her father or got a fresh mutation." While I was considering the
situation and studying her from across the room, the woman in the bed
began to stir. "Ms. Anderson?" I asked after seeing her raise her head
and look around.

"Who's there?" she asked, turning her head from side to side, trying to pick up some signal about the strange person who had invaded
her room. After introducing myself, shaking her hand, and congratulat-
ing her on the birth of her first child, I asked how she was feeling.

"I'm all right," she responded, rapidly, trying to focus on me. "Is
there something wrong with the baby?"

"She's absolutely fine right now," I replied. "She's pink and comfortable and her heart and lungs and all the rest of her organs seem to
be working just fine. But she looks a little unusual. She's very long and
thin. . . ."

"Is there something wrong with that?" the woman interrupted,
more anxious now.

"It looks to us like the baby might have something called Marfan
syndrome. Have you ever heard of Marfan syndrome?"

The new mother thought for a moment, and finally replied, "No.
Should I have?"

"It's a problem that sometimes runs in families. It's usually passed
along from parent to child. People who have it are very tall and thin
and sometimes have problems with their eyes and their hearts. Since
we're concerned about Marfan syndrome in the baby, I was just won-
dering whether you or her father might have it."

"No one's ever told me I have it," the woman responded. "I was
born with cataracts, that's why I can't see very well now, but as far

as I know, there's nothing else wrong with me. And my husband's never said anything about any syndrome or anything. He is much taller than me—"

"How tall?" I interrupted.

"I'm not sure," she answered. "Since my eyesight's so bad, I've never really had a good look at him. It's not something we've ever discussed. But he is very tall."

"Does he have any other problems with his health?" I asked.

"Well, he's got bad vision; it's not as bad as mine, though. He at least can get around by himself. I've been blind since birth. He only started to lose his vision when he was a teenager. I'm not exactly sure what happened to him."

With the additional evidence of tall stature and eye disease, I was now just about sure that Baby Girl Anderson's father had Marfan syndrome. But I was confused about why someone as close to the man as his wife had never heard the term, why she seemed to be unaware of her husband's disorder. Is it possible that the diagnosis had never been made in him? "Did anyone suggest that you get genetic counseling during the pregnancy?" I asked.

"I did get genetic counseling," the new mother replied. "When I was about two months pregnant, the midwife who was taking care of me told me to go and speak to someone about whether my baby might be born with the same eye problem I had. She sent me to see this genetic counselor in Manhattan. They did some tests and told me they couldn't find anything wrong except that I'd been born with cataracts. They said they didn't think my baby would have any problems with her eyes, but they couldn't be 100 percent sure because they didn't know what was wrong with my husband's eyes. They told me whatever he's got might be genetic."

"Oh, he didn't go with you to see the geneticist?" I asked.

"No," she replied, smiling. "He refused to go. He doesn't like doctors or medical people very much."

Just then, in the time it took me to formulate my next question, while I was trying to comprehend how, during the second half of the twentieth century, a man with Marfan syndrome living in New York City could have made it into adulthood without having had such an obvious diagnosis made, Carl Anderson slipped into the room. At least

113

6½ feet tall, painfully thin, with enormously long arms and legs and spidery fingers, he looked like a photograph out of a textbook of clinical genetics. After greeting his wife, he kissed her on the cheek and, trying his best to ignore me, took a seat in a chair by the bedside.

I fell silent upon seeing the man, and Ms. Anderson began to fill him in about what I was doing in the room: "This is one of the doctors who's taking care of the baby. They're worried that she might have some problem; something called Murphy's syndrome."

"Marfan syndrome," Carl corrected, still ignoring me. "And they're right; she does have it. I have it, too."

This statement apparently shocked the man's wife, but it put me back on track. "Where do you go for your medical care?" I asked.

"I used to go to New York Hospital," he replied, "but I stopped going there about five years ago. They weren't doing anything for me. Every time I went down there for an appointment, all they ever did was stare at me like I was some kind of a freak and tell me I was going to die when I was thirty-five. Who needs that? I know how I look and I don't need someone to keep telling me how much longer I have to live."

"Why didn't you tell me you had this thing?" the man's wife asked.

"Sure, and what would you have done? I tell you I've got Marfan syndrome and I'm going to be dead within ten years, and the first thing you'd do is take off. And more than anything else in life, I wanted to have a kid. If you found out that this disease was inherited, and there was a fifty-fifty chance that any kid I had could get it, you'd have never gotten pregnant in the first place. And if you did happen to get pregnant, by some accident or something, you'd have had an abortion. By not saying anything, at least now we have this baby."

During the next hour, Ms. Anderson tried to explain to her husband that she loved him regardless of whether or not he had Marfan syndrome, and I told him about all the breakthroughs that had occurred in the management of the cardiovascular complications of Marfan syndrome, advances that could, with good medical care, offer new hope for Carl's longevity, virtually guaranteeing that he would live past his thirties. That very afternoon, we had echocardiographic examinations performed on both father and daughter, who had been named

Valerie by her parents. Thankfully, although both had widening of their aortas, a finding that confirmed the diagnosis of Marfan syndrome, neither's aortic diameter was in the danger range. Valerie left the hospital after an uncomplicated three days in the nursery. With frequent follow-up, she and her father have done exceedingly well; to this point, neither has required surgical intervention. And last year, Ms. Anderson had a second child, another girl, this one named Katherine. Like her sister and father, Katherine is also affected with Marfan syndrome.

During the period since Valerie's birth, I've come to know Carl Anderson pretty well. An intelligent, sensitive man, he reads a great deal, in spite of his poor vision, and is one of my only patients who keeps up on developments in the research being conducted about the disease that affects him and his two daughters. During one of his visits, we've even discussed the question of Abraham Lincoln's diagnosis. Unlike me, Carl believes that Lincoln was affected with what he calls "my disease."

But of all the discussions we've had, the most poignant, the ones I've remembered most vividly, have involved what having Marfan syndrome has meant to Carl Anderson. "From as far back as I can remember," he told me at one of his regular six-month check-ups a couple of years ago, "even before they told me I had this thing, I knew I was different. When I was real little, five or six, the kids around our neighborhood used to call me names all the time: spider boy, four-eyes, freak face, scarecrow, ugly. It always tore me apart inside. I didn't know what to do, so I'd just start crying and run home to my mother. Neither of my parents had Marfan syndrome, so they had no idea how to handle me. My mother'd just tell me to stay home and find something to do around the house, rather than go back out into the street where all the other kids played.

"But it got harder for me to just stay home once I started going to school. That's when things really got tough. I used to get into fights nearly every day. A kid would call me 'freak,' or 'ugly,' and I'd be on him in a second. Only problem was, I was so weak, I'd always get the crap beat out of me. Nobody would stand up for me; I never had any friends; anytime I showed any interest in a girl, she'd just make fun of

me. By the time I was in fourth grade, I'd had it; I never wanted to go
to school anymore. I'd wake up every morning and complain to my
mother that I was sick, hoping she'd let me stay home. Lots of times, I'd
whine so much, she'd finally give in to me. I'd stay home in bed, crying
to myself. I was always depressed. And the school certainly never gave
a damn about whether I showed up or not: they thought of me as a
troublemaker, so they were happy to have me out of there. I'm not
dumb, but I was always a rotten student; I never made it to school
enough days in a row to learn anything."

In fact, the cumulative effects of having Marfan syndrome affected nearly every aspect of Carl Anderson's life. It was his Marfan syndrome that had caused him to develop cataracts at age sixteen, a
complication that ultimately led to the loss of most of his vision and,
thus, severely limited his career opportunities and his ability to work
(he currently works as a clerk at a candy stand in a New York City
branch post office, a job provided by a city agency that serves the hand-
icapped). His Marfan syndrome, because of the predicted early demise
that accompanies the illness, had caused him to adopt a fatalistic attitude toward life, to take unnecessary, potentially dangerous risks when
a more cautious course might have seemed more appropriate. And the
Marfan syndrome had caused him to appear different, to look, in his
words, like a freak, in the eyes of those around him. The skeletal manifestations had caused him to become the brunt of endless teasing from
his peers; the Marfan-induced body habitus had led to his lifelong
episodes of depression, as well as the fits of crying during early childhood and the nearly daily fights of later childhood, fights that were in-
evitably lost because of the weakness of his musculature, another
contribution of the syndrome. And his unusual morphology and the
toll taken by all of these other contributing factors had led Carl Anderson to develop such a poor self-image, to have such low self-esteem that
he was reluctant, even afraid, to admit to his wife—a woman whom
he'd undoubtedly chosen in the first place because her vision was so
poor that she would not notice that he was so different—that he was
afflicted with this disorder, for fear that she would immediately aban-
don him, refuse to bear his children, choose to abort a fetus rather than
risk having it born similarly affected. Although smart and sensitive,

Carl Anderson was the man he was largely because he carried the gene for Marfan syndrome.

And Abraham Lincoln became the man he was at least partly because he was afflicted with a Marfan-like syndrome. Although the twin specters of a life spent in total darkness due to blindness and of an unexpected, explosive premature demise did not present themselves in early life to him, Lincoln suffered some of the verbal and psychological abuse experienced more than a hundred years later by Carl Anderson. Although records of most of the insults hurled at the future president have been lost, some examples persist: when Lincoln was six or seven, a neighbor referred to him as "a tall spider of a boy."[35] When he was eleven, some homesteaders in the part of Indiana in which the Lincolns then lived described Abraham as "lazy, awful lazy."[36] And, perhaps most telling, a young woman who knew Lincoln as an adolescent recalled that "all the young girls of my age made fun of Abe" because of his unusual appearance. She didn't think Lincoln minded the teasing, however, because he was "such a good fellow."[37] But regardless of what that woman or her friends believed, the toll taken by the name-calling cannot be so easily dismissed.

In this context, is it surprising that, like Carl Anderson, Abraham Lincoln was less than enthusiastic about his educational experiences? Times were difficult for the Lincolns of Indiana in the early 1820s, and Abraham was unable to attend school regularly because he was forced to stay home, assisting his father in tending the fields of their homestead farm. But the lack of opportunity to attend classes did not exactly meet with Abraham's disapproval because, on the rare occasions when he did make an appearance at the local "blab" school, "so called because pupils studied aloud so that the teacher, rod in hand, could grade their progress," the tall, gangly Abraham would show up wearing "a raccoon cap and buckskin clothes, his pants so short they exposed six inches of his calves,"[36] a vision that must have consistently brought down the house. Is it any wonder that later, as an adult, he would look back with scorn upon the brief periods of instruction he received in Indiana, recalling that "there was absolutely nothing to excite ambition for

education," words that Carl Anderson might have used to describe
his own education in the New York public school system of the 1960s
and 1970s?

The teasing Carl Anderson experienced during his school years led
to nearly daily fights with his peers. Of course, this was also true of
Abraham Lincoln. Much mythology has developed about Lincoln's
brawling during the years he lived in New Salem, Illinois. Legend has it
that, upon moving into town, the twenty-one-year-old Abraham fell in
with a bad crowd (apparently the nineteenth-century frontier equivalent
of a motorcycle gang) and got into "his share of fights." [37] The most
celebrated of these events pitted the future president against Jack
Armstrong, the village wrestling champion. According to Oates, the
two fighters, bared to the waist, "grabbed, grunted, wrenched, and
struggled." [37] Unlike Carl Anderson's many fights, the fight between
Lincoln and Armstrong ended in a draw, with the two fighters shaking hands.

Why did Abraham Lincoln get into all those fights? Was it simply
the way of the frontier at the time? It would seem not; rather, these
battles seemed to seek out the future president. And why? Probably because, at 6 feet 4 inches, with that unusual body shape and those
ill-fitting clothes, Lincoln must have been what would today be considered a "geek" and, as such, would have proved a natural target for
bullies.

Carl Anderson's relationships with women also seemed to parallel
Abraham Lincoln's. According to a friend, Lincoln knew he was "gawky
looking" and so "didn't take much truck with girls." [38] As already noted,
when Abraham was an adolescent, the girls made fun of him because
of his odd appearance. As a result, largely because of his insecurities,
and his fear of failure or rejection, during those early years in Indiana
and Illinois Abraham made it a point to avoid all eligible women, feeling comfortable only in the company of those, like Ann Rutledge, the
nineteen-year-old daughter of the keeper of the inn in which Lincoln
boarded, who were engaged or already married to other men. According to Stephen B. Oates, these women, probably sensing the man's vul-
nerability, tended to mother him. [39]

Lincoln's shyness around women continued well into adulthood,
until 1839, when at the age of thirty he met the twenty-one-year-old

Mary Ann Todd, the woman who ultimately would, on November 4, 1842, become his wife. According to the future Mrs. Lincoln's sister, Elizabeth Edwards, a virtual hypnotic spell would overcome Lincoln whenever he encountered Miss Todd: "He would listen and gaze on her as if drawn by some superior power. He never scarcely said a word." [40] But even this seemingly magical courtship was touched by Lincoln's insecurity and poor self-esteem. Within weeks of their engagement in December 1840, their agreement to marry was broken because Mary's sister, Elizabeth, and her husband, Ninian Edwards, disapproved of the marriage, on the grounds that Lincoln was "from nowhere, that his future was nebulous, and that by marrying him, Mary would be marrying beneath herself." [41]

Another man might have chosen to stand up for himself, to challenge his future sister- and brother-in-law, to argue with them, or at least to attempt to convince his fiancée that her relatives were wrong. But Abraham Lincoln's reluctance to believe in his own desirability would not have allowed any such thing to happen. Instead, he slunk off and sunk into a profound depression, or as it was known at the time, a fit of "hypochondria." As Stephen B. Oates recorded:

> For a week in mid-January, Lincoln lay in his boarding room in acute despair. . . . He couldn't sleep, and his insomnia and weariness only aggravated his depression. After a week of "making the most discreditable exhibition of myself in the way of hypochondriaism," . . . he looked emaciated. . . . "I am now the most miserable man alive," he sighed. [42]

Although the couple was brought back together again in 1842 by the actions of Mr. and Mrs. Simeon Francis, friends of both Mr. Lincoln and Miss Todd, [43] and ultimately married, much of the storminess that battered this courtship, many of the trials and tribulations that caused both members of the couple such heartache, resulted directly from the insecurity that Abraham Lincoln felt, insecurity that, at least in part, must have been drilled into him because of the teasing he'd undergone in childhood.

The episode of depression into which the future president sank following the rupture of his engagement was far from an isolated event. From early childhood, Lincoln experienced these fits of "hypochondria," or "the hypo," episodes of melancholy that lasted from a few days to months and left him virtually incapable of working. My patient, Carl Anderson, also spent a good deal of his time depressed. In his case, the depressions were a direct result of the teasing he received because of his appearance; was the same true in the case of Abraham Lincoln?

Of course there were other significant factors that played important roles in the development of Abraham Lincoln's low self-image. Embarrassed by his background, by the simpleness of his parents and their progenitors, and by the poverty in which he was raised, he severed ties with his father at an early age, failing to visit the man as he lay on his deathbed in early January 1851, even refusing to attend the funeral when he finally passed away on January 17 of that year.[44] Ashamed of his lack of formal education and social training, he acted shy and withdrawn around the more cosmopolitan residents of Springfield, Illinois, and later, Washington, D.C.[45] But the effect that his appearance had on the image Lincoln developed of himself cannot be ignored. In fact, it may have played a role in the development of his hatred of slavery.

———————————

Abraham Lincoln was taught early in life that human bondage was wrong, a lesson passed on to him, not unlike the way he learned the Ten Commandments or the Golden Rule, by both his father and the preacher at the Pigeon Creek Baptist Church in Indiana.[46] But it wasn't until later, in early adulthood, that he first commented on the moral and ethical realities of slavery. Soon after the breakup of his engagement to Mary Todd in 1841, Lincoln went to visit his old friend Joshua Speed in Kentucky. On the return trip to Springfield, Illinois, the two friends encountered a group of twelve slaves, chained together, who, having been ripped away from their family and friends in Kentucky, were being transported to the Deep South, to be sold "into perpetual slavery where the lash of the master is proverbially more ruthless and unrelenting than any other where."[47] The image of these twelve slaves stayed with the future president for many years, proving to be "a continual torment to me. . . . Slavery . . . had the power to make me miserable."[47]

But the roots of Lincoln's hatred of the institution of slavery can also be found in some notes he wrote to himself, fragments that were meant to be used at a future time in speeches:

> If A. can prove, however conclusively, that he may, of right, enslave B.—why may not B. snatch the argument, and prove equally, that he may enslave A.?
>
> You say A. is white and B. is black. It is *color* then; the lighter having the right to enslave the darker? Take care. By this rule, you are to be a slave to the first man you meet, with a fairer skin than your own.
>
> You do not mean *color* exactly?—You mean the whites are *intellectually* the superiors of the blacks, and therefore have the right to enslave them? Take care again. By this rule, you are to be slave to the first man you meet, with an intellect superior to your own.[48]

The message that emerges from these fragments is clear: the opposition to the concept of slavery that was held so strongly by the man who would become known as the Great Emancipator was based not on any political dogma, but rather on his moral and ethical belief that it was simply wrong to discriminate against a fellow human being because of the way he looked. And, when viewed from a geneticist's perspective, one of Lincoln's influences in adopting this stance becomes equally clear: at 6 feet 4 inches tall and bone thin, with legs that made him appear to be standing on stilts and arms that made him look like a scarecrow, with a face that caused one male to describe him as "ugly, but not repulsive,"[48] and another, little Grace Bedell, to write an unsolicited letter asking that he immediately grow a beard, he was a man who, during his early life, had faced more than his fair share of discrimination, of teasing and name-calling, simply because of the way he looked.

And so, a genetic flaw had caused Abraham Lincoln to develop his
unusual "Marfanoid" body habitus. That unusual body morphology,
and the effect that it had on his early life, was a factor leading to Lincoln's lifelong hatred of slavery. And, finally, that hatred of slavery, that
intolerance for the concept of human bondage, led in fairly rapid succession to his candidacy for the presidency as an Abolitionist, to
his election as president of the United States, to the secession of the
southern states, to the start of the American Civil War, and, ultimately,
to the firing of the bullet from the gun held by John Wilkes Booth that
ended his life. When viewed from this perspective, the comments made
by Grace Bedell in her letter were not just the innocent impressions of
an eleven-year-old girl; rather, they were a key that help unlock one of
the mysteries of Abraham Lincoln.

References

1. H. Holzer, ed., *Dear Abe: Letters to President Lincoln* (Reading, Mass.:
   Addison-Wesley Publishing Co., in press).
2. Stephen B. Oates, *Abraham Lincoln: The Man Behind the Myths* (New
   York: Harper and Row, 1984), 35.
3. J. M. Tanner, Growing up, in G. Piel, D. Flanagan, F. Bello, et al., eds.,
   Life and Death and Medicine (San Francisco: W. H. Freeman and Co.,
   1973), 17–25.
4. Carl Sandburg, *Abraham Lincoln: The Prairie Years and The War Years,*
   one-volume ed. (New York: Harcourt, Brace and Co., 1954), 14.
5. Stephen B. Oates, *With Malice Toward None: The Life of Abraham
   Lincoln* (New York: Harper and Row, 1977), 12–13.
6. Oates, *Lincoln: Man Behind Myths,* 34.
7. A. Rothschild, *Lincoln, Master of Men* (New York: Houghton
   Mifflin Co., 1906), 26.
8. C. Shurz and J. H. Bartlett, *Abraham Lincoln* (New York: Houghton
   Mifflin and Co., 1907), 25.
9. Oates, *Lincoln: Man Behind Myths,* 35.
10. W. H. Herndon and J. W. Weik, *Herndon's Lincoln,* vol. 2 (Springfield,
    Ill.: Herndon's Lincoln Publishing Co., 1921), 408.
11. A. M. Gordon, Abraham Lincoln: A medical appraisal, *Journal of the
    Kentucky Medical Association* 60 (1962): 249.

12. V. A. McKusick, *Hereditable Disorders of Connective Tissue*, 4th ed.
(St. Louis: C. V. Mosby Co., 1972), 61.

13. A. B. Marfan, Un cas de deformation congenitale des quatre membres
plus prononcee aux extremites charicterisee par l'allongement des os avers
un certain degre d'amincissement, *Bull Mem Soc Med Hop Paris* 13
(1896): 220.

14. R. E. Pyeritz, The Marfan Syndrome, *American Family Physician* 34
(1986) 83–94.

15. V. Salle, Uber einem Fall von angeborener abnormen Grosse der extrem-
itaten mit einen an Akronemegalia erinnerden Symptomenkomplex,
Jahrbuch Kinderheilk 75 (1912): 540.

16. J. R. Jauchem, Advances in treatment of the Marfan syndrome, *Research
Resources Reporter* 10 (August 1986): 8.

17. McKusick, *Hereditable Disorders*, 146.

18. V. L. Gott, R. E. Pyeritz, G. J. Magovern, et al., Surgical treatment of
aneurysms of the ascending aorta in the Marfan syndrome, *New England
Journal of Medicine* 314 (1986): 1070.

19. Weve H., Über arachnodaktylie (Dystrophia mesodermalis congenita,
typus Marfanus), *Archiv Augenheilkrauk* 104 (1931): 1.

20. K. Kainulainen, L. Pulkkinen, A. Savolainen, et al., Localization on
chromosome 15 of the gene defect causing Marfan syndrome, *New
England Journal of Medicine* 323 (1990): 935.

21. B. Lee, M. Godfrey, E. Vitale, et al., Linkage of Marfan syndrome and a
phenotypically related disorder to two different fibrillin genes. *Nature*
(1991): 330–334, 353.

22. H. Schwartz, Abraham Lincoln and the Marfan syndrome, *Journal of the
American Medical Association,* 187 (1964): 473.

23. H. Schwartz, Abraham Lincoln and aortic insufficiency: The declining
health of the president, *California Medicine* 116 (1972): 82.

24. J. K. Lattimer, Lincoln did not have the Marfan syndrome, *New York
State Journal of Medicine* November 1981: 1805.

25. Oates, *With Malice Toward None,* 16.

26. Sandburg, *Lincoln: Prairie Years,* 3.

27. Ibid., 6.

28. Ibid., 11.

29. R. J. Gorlin, M. M. Cohen, Jr., and S. Levin, *Syndromes of the Head and
Neck,* 3rd ed. (New York: Oxford University Press, 1990), 267–73.

30. Oates, *With Malice Toward None,* 289–90.

31. Ibid., 93.

32. S. Lorant, *Lincoln: His Life in Photographs* (New York: Duell, Sloan and Pearce, 1941), 53.

33. J. Herrmann, T. D. France, J. W. Spranger, et al., The Stickler syndrome: Hereditary arthroopthalmopathy, *Birth Defects Original Article Series* 11 (1975): 100.

34. M. J. Glesby and R. E. Pyeritz, Mitral valve prolapse syndrome and Marfan syndrome: A Phenotypic continuum, *American Journal of Medical Genetics* 32 (1989): 251.

35. Oates, *With Malice Toward None,* 6.

36. Ibid., 10.

37. Ibid., 18.

38. Ibid., 17.

39. Ibid., 19.

40. Ibid., 53.

41. R. P. Randall, *Mary Lincoln: Biography of a Marriage* (Boston: Little Brown and Co., 1953), 47–48.

42. Oates, *With Malice Toward None,* 57.

43. Randall, *Mary Lincoln,* 64.

44. Oates, *With Malice Toward None,* 95.

45. Randall, *Mary Lincoln,* 12.

46. Oates, *With Malice Toward None,* 8.

47. Ibid., 59–60.

48. Ibid., 126.

The Molecular Genetics of the Russian Revolution

On October 6, 1912,[*]

PART I

Tsarevich Alexis Nicolaievich, the only son of Tsar Nicholas II, Emperor of Russia, and his wife, Alexandra Feodorovna, was riding in a carriage between his mother and her closest friend, Anna Vyrubova. It was a beautiful early-autumn day in the village of Spala, the ancient hunting grounds of the kings of Poland where the Romanovs, the imperial family of Russia, were vacationing, and Alexandra, concerned that the eight-year-old tsarevich had been spending too much time cooped up in his room, decided to take her son, the heir to her husband's empire, out for some fresh air and sunshine. A few weeks earlier the boy had injured his left thigh in a boating accident and had been ordered by his physician to remain off his feet until the wound had completely healed.

Unfortunately, the road was fairly bumpy, and as they sat in the imperial carriage, the three passengers were continually tossed from side to side.[1] Just a few minutes after they'd set out, little Alexis winced

---

[*] All dates noted with an asterisk correspond to the Julian calendar, which was in use in Russia until 1918. The Julian calendar was twelve to thirteen days behind the more widely used Gregorian calendar, which was finally adopted in Russia after the revolution.

125

and began to howl at the top of his lungs. When asked what was wrong, the tsarevich explained, through his moans and groans, that he'd experienced a sharp, knife-like pain in the region of his previously injured left thigh. Panicking, Alexandra ordered the driver to immediately turn the carriage around and head for home as fast as he could. During the ride back to the villa (which, of course, was just as bumpy as the ride out) the tsarevich continued to scream and cry. "Every movement of the carriage, every rough place in the road, caused the child the most exquisite torture," Anna Vyrubova later recalled. "By the time we reached home, the boy was almost unconscious with pain." [1]

Alexandra's panicked reaction to her son's sudden pain was certainly understandable, considering what she knew about the young boy's medical condition. Although seemingly normal and healthy at the time of his birth on August 12, 1904,* Alexis, the fifth and last child born to the tsar and tsaritsa, at six weeks had suddenly begun to bleed from his umbilical region. In the words of his father, writing in his diary: "Alix [Empress Alexandra's real name] and I have been very much worried. A hemorrhage began this morning without the slightest cause from the navel of our small Alexis. It lasted with but a few interruptions until evening." [2]

Over the weeks that followed this initial, unexplained hemorrhage, the tsarevich experienced similar episodes. Without any obvious cause, the infant would simply begin to spout blood as if he were a fountain. In addition, during this same period, the tsar and tsaritsa noticed the sudden development of mysterious purplish lumps under Alexis Nicolaievich's skin, lumps that had the frightening tendency to rapidly enlarge. In the next few months, the cause of these distressing symptoms became clear: Alexis had been born with classic hemophilia, a hereditary disorder in which the blood fails to clot. From the time of his initial diagnosis in early infancy until that October eight years later when he and his family had been vacationing in Spala, the tsarevich's life had consisted of long periods of excellent health and normal development, punctuated by unpredictable episodes of acute, persistent, life-threatening hemorrhage. So, when Alexis unexpectedly began to scream during the early part of that leisurely carriage ride in the coun-

126

try and complained of a sharp pain in his thigh, his mother knew all too well how serious the problem might be.

Upon their return to their villa, the tsarevich was carried to his room and immediately examined by Dr. Eugene Botkin, the imperial family's official physician. Dr. Botkin confirmed what the empress already knew: Alexis Nicolaievich had suffered a hemorrhage in the area of his thigh and hip. He'd started to bleed, probably as the result of an acute injury to the fragile, friable blood clot that had begun to form weeks earlier at the site of his boating injury. He'd begun to hemorrhage, and worse still, the doctor reported that the leakage of blood from the injured vessel was continuing unchecked, pouring fresh, irritating fluid into the soft tissue of the tsarevich's thigh and into his abdominal cavity even as the doctor and his mother stood helplessly by watching the young boy moan and writhe in his bed. Understanding what probably would lie ahead, having learned the difficult lesson from past experiences just like this one, Dr. Botkin without delay sent an urgent call for help.[1]

His colleagues did not delay in answering Dr. Botkin's call. From their offices in the hospitals of St. Petersburg, specialist after specialist canceled his patients, freed up his schedule, and began boarding trains to Spala. There was Dr. Vladimir Derevenko, the tsarevich's regular doctor, and Dr. Federov, a physician who had also frequently treated Alexis Nicolaievich; there was Dr. Ostrogorsky, a specialist in the relatively new field of pediatric medicine, and Dr. Rauchfuss, a general surgeon. One by one, these learned men, some of the most respected medical authorities in all of Russia and Europe, reached the bedside of the suddenly gravely ill tsarevich; each man noted the striking pallor of the boy's skin and of the conjunctivae of his eyes; each commented on the rapidity of the boy's ever-weakening pulse; each gingerly palpated the tender and enlarging hematoma, the collection of blood that was growing in Alexis's upper thigh. Then, after completing their examinations, each member of this distinguished group gathered around the boy's bedside and spoke softly to the others, arguing about the course of action that should be taken. And during those hours spent "davening" (a term, derived from the Hebrew word for praying, used to describe the long periods of time often spent by a group of physicians in seemingly pointless discussions of the pros and cons of a given treatment plan) about what should be done to save the life of the heir to the throne of all of Russia, the doctors each began to realize how utterly futile their efforts were likely to prove. For despite their accumulated knowledge and years of experience, they were forced to stand by helplessly as the tsarevich—crying in agony as his blood continued to slowly leak out of the injured vessel in his thigh, pool in his hip joint, and flow over into his abdomen—was literally bleeding to death in front of them.[1]

The agony continued day and night, without letup, through the next four days. As the young boy, moaning in pain, unable to sleep or to attain even a single moment of comfort, grew steadily weaker, the physicians became more and more desperate and frustrated. On numerous occasions it appeared as if the end had finally arrived, as if the boy was at last about to die, but each time Alexis Nicolaievich somehow managed to rally, continuing to cling to life. Outside the villa, a single official announcement of the serious illness from which the tsarevich was suffering caused all of Russia to begin to pray for their future tsar's survival. But neither the people's prayers nor the doctors' ministrations seemed to do any good.[1]

Although these four days were grueling for everyone who played a part in the drama, the ordeal was clearly worst for Alexandra Feodorovna, who steadfastly remained at her young son's bedside, listening to the doctors' pessimistic words and witnessing the steady deterioration of her only son's strength and the weakening of his will to survive.[1]

Given the desperateness of the situation, it's fairly safe to say that near the end of that four-day period, Alexandra, like virtually any other mother facing a similar circumstance, would have done anything, given up any of her possessions or power or wealth, if in return she could have obtained even the smallest amount of relief for her son from his unbearable pain. And so, understanding that the doctors had failed, and realizing that the end was unquestionably at hand, it's not surprising that Alexandra took the only path that she might have viewed as being open to her at that point: she begged her friend, Anna Vyrubova, to call on her acquaintance, the *starets* (holy man) Grigory Rasputin, and beg that he pray for the tsarevich's life.[1]

Although Rasputin, a disheveled, unwashed, mystical peasant from the town of Pokrovskoe in western Siberia, was only thirty-three in 1912, he had already managed to achieve something of a national reputation. A man who had spent his youth apparently dedicated to the commitment of sin, Father Grigory, as he later came to be known to members of the imperial family, was said to possess miraculous, unexplainable curative powers. After receiving the desperate cable from the empress's friend, Rasputin apparently lost no time in cabling back a response: "God has seen your tears and heard your prayers," Father Grigory answered. "Do not grieve. The Little One will not die. Do not allow the doctors to bother him too much."[1]

In a bedroom surrounded by pessimistic physicians and the difficult reality of the small body of her dying son, that reassuring message from this strange holy man immediately lifted the tsaritsa's spirits; and unexplainably, within hours of the initial contact with Father Grigory, the rate of Alexis Nicolaievich's hemorrhage appeared to slow and finally to cease altogether. In the days that followed what had to be considered by the members of the imperial family nothing short of a miracle, the tsarevich began to rally, regaining his strength and stamina, slowly replenishing the color in his cheeks and the twinkle in his eyes. Somehow, through coincidence or truly through divine intervention, Grigory Rasputin had apparently saved the life of the tsarevich. Not surprisingly, Empress Alexandra became an instant and permanent believer in Father Grigory: for the rest of her life, she would accept with all her heart the incredible powers of this strange unwashed peasant from Siberia.

Clearly, the origins of the Russian revolution of 1918, like those of the American Revolution nearly 150 years earlier, were complex, traceable to a large number of disparate causes. It is indisputable that social upheaval, worldwide economic change, and international political intrigue all played major roles in the start of the struggle that ultimately ended the Romanov family's nearly three centuries of rule. But the circumstances that surrounded Alexis Nicolaievich's surprising recovery and, more important, what happened between Nicholas, Alexandra, and the bizarre Grigory Rasputin in the aftermath of his recovery contributed to the family's ultimate downfall. For when the cable from

Father Grigory was received by the imperial family on that night in October 1912, an important seed was sown: it would eventually sprout into the Russian Revolution.

———————

Like inhaling and exhaling without giving the process a single, conscious thought, the clotting of blood is one of those small miracles of biology that most people take for granted, but without which human life would not be able to exist. Illustrated in figure 1, the process by which clotting occurs appears to be the biochemical equivalent of a Rube Goldberg cartoon, a mechanism in which a long series of complicated and intricate steps must occur in an exact sequence in just the right environment in order for the process to succeed at all.

For the purpose of understanding the disorder that affected Tsarevich Alexis Nicolaievich and had such a profound effect on the history of modern Russia, it's not really necessary to comprehend each of these complex biochemical steps. To summarize the process as simply as possible, the injury of a blood vessel causes collagen, a protein normally buried deep within the wall of the vessel, to come into contact with the circulating blood. This exposure of collagen to certain elements in the plasma, the liquid portion of the blood, automatically triggers a series of interconnected chemical reactions. These complicated reactions ultimately result in the generation of a substance called *fibrin,* a tough, insoluble protein that forms the actual hardware of the plug that, like the little Dutch boy's thumb on the water leaking through the hole in the dike, actually stops up the hole in the blood vessel's wall and prevents further bleeding. As can be seen in figure 1, at least nineteen separate chemical compounds are necessary for the entire coagulation cascade to function. Twelve of these nineteen compounds have come to be known as clotting "factors"; numbered I through XIII (through some fluke in the system of nomenclature, or simply because the person who initially developed the system had some difficulty counting, there is no "factor VI"), these factors are encoded by different genes spread around the human genome, and most are produced by the cells of the liver.

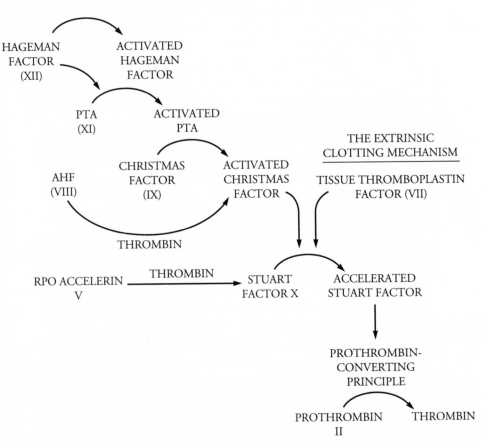

THE INTRINSIC
CLOTTING MECHANISM

HAGEMAN
FACTOR
(XII)

ACTIVATED
HAGEMAN
FACTOR

PTA
(XI)

ACTIVATED
PTA

THE EXTRINSIC
CLOTTING MECHANISM

AHF
(VIII)

CHRISTMAS
FACTOR
(IX)

ACTIVATED
CHRISTMAS
FACTOR

TISSUE THROMBOPLASTIN
FACTOR (VII)

THROMBIN

RPO ACCELERIN
V

THROMBIN

STUART
FACTOR X

ACCELERATED
STUART FACTOR

PROTHROMBIN-
CONVERTING
PRINCIPLE

PROTHROMBIN
II

THROMBIN

Figure 1. The Intrinsic and Extrinsic Clotting Pathways (after Ratnoff, reference 4)

At one time or another in human history, deficiencies of virtually all the substances involved in the clotting process have been described in humans. These deficiencies may be either acquired—due, for instance, to a disease such as hepatitis that destroys the cells in the liver responsible for producing that factor—or inherited, passed along from parent to child. An inborn error of the clotting pathway may cause a bleeding disorder so severe that, because of the complete inability to

131

arrest a hemorrhage once it's begun, it nearly always results in the premature death of the affected individual; or the deficiency may cause clinical features so mild that, in most cases, the condition will remain undiagnosed throughout the lifetime of the affected individual. Finally, lack of a specific clotting factor may result in an entity that is easily treatable through replacement therapy (artificially supplying the missing protein through transfusion of whole blood, blood plasma, or infusion of just the specific factor), or it may be impossible to treat, at least with the methods currently available.

Of the hereditary bleeding disorders, classic hemophilia, which affects one out of every 10,000 males in the United States, is the most common.[3] One of the first human genetic disorders ever described, classic hemophilia appears in its earliest example in the Tract Yebamoth of the Babylonian Talmud. According to the text of that tract, during the second century A.D., Rabbi Judah (possibly the world's first human geneticist) exempted from the necessity of ritual circumcision a boy whose two older brothers had inexplicably bled to death after undergoing the procedure.[4]

Although this biblical case obviously recognized the familial nature of the disorder, it wasn't until 1803 that Dr. John Conrad Otto, a young physician from Philadelphia, accurately described for the first time the peculiar inheritance pattern that occurs in classic hemophilia. In that year, Dr. Otto reported the case of a family in which multiple members suffered from a "hemorrhagic predisposition" characterized by spontaneous bleeding into the joints (a condition known as hemarthrosis), muscles, and internal organs. Dr. Otto noted that "the males only are subject to this strange affliction, and all of them are not liable to it." He further reported that although female members of the family were exempt from the tendency to bleed spontaneously, "they are still capable of transmitting it to their male children."[5]

At the time that he wrote the article, neither Dr. Otto nor any other contemporary physician or scientist could offer an explanation for the unusual pattern of distribution of the bleeding disorder in this family. After all, the three principles that form the basis of our understanding of heredity would not be formulated for another sixty-two years, when the work of the Austrian monk Gregor Mendel first appeared in an obscure scientific journal;[6] and it would be nearly one hundred years until three scientists, Drs. de Vries in Holland, Corens in Germany, and Tschermak in Austria, working independently, would re-discover the Austrian monk's article and understand for the first time his work's profound significance.[7] However, in spite of any difficulty they may have had in explaining the mechanism of inheritance, several other physicians soon confirmed Dr. Otto's observations. By 1820, following an independent report by Dr. Christian Friedrich Nasse, pro-fessor of medicine in Bonn, Germany,[8] this peculiar pattern of distri-bution, in which males are affected and females, who may carry the disorder and pass it along to some of their sons, are apparently spared, had become well established in the medical literature. Because this method of inheritance is so important in understanding what hap-pened in Russia in the second decade of the twentieth century, it's nec-essary to review the mechanism involved in what's now come to be known as X-linked recessive inheritance. To do that, we'll need to review basic Mendelian genetics.

As has already been mentioned in this book, the nuclei of all nor-mal human cells contain a total of forty-six chromosomes, the actual blueprints of the human body. Composed of deoxyribonucleic acid, or DNA, and arranged in discrete units called genes, these chromosomes, when viewed through a microscope, can be seen actually to consist of twenty-three distinct pairs. At the time of conception, one member of each of these chromosome pairs is contributed by the father via the sperm that has penetrated the egg's outer membrane, while the other member, originating from the mother, is transmitted to the new indi-vidual by virtue of the fact that it's already present in the egg that has matured and become fertilized. Thus, the entire process of conception consists of nothing more than the coming together of a new mix of chromosomal material, with half paternally derived and half maternally derived.

Of the twenty-three pairs of chromosomes, twenty-two are identi-cal, indistinguishable under normal conditions in individuals of differ-ent races, different ethnic backgrounds, even different sexes. In fact, it is only the pair that has come to be known as the sex chromosomes that distinguishes male from female; it is the X and the Y chromosomes, as the two sex chromosomes have come to be known, that in fact dictate whether a fertilized egg will ultimately develop into a man or a woman. Normal females possess two copies of the X chromosomes; males have one X and one Y.

This simple difference between the chromosomes of males and females accounts for the unusual pattern of distribution of symptoms first noted by Dr. Otto in 1803, and now known as X-linked recessive inheritance, that occurs in classic hemophilia. As has already been mentioned, the DNA that composes the chromosomes is arranged in a series of units known as genes; thousands of individual genes are arranged on each chromosome, something like beads on a necklace. Through a series of complex processes known as transcription and translation, each gene gives rise to a protein, which serves some essential function within the body. Proteins can be tough, structural substances, such as the fibrillin that appears to be deficient or defective in Marfan syndrome (see the chapter on Abraham Lincoln); they can be enzymes, compounds that drive chemical reactions, as is the case with protoporphyrinogen oxidase, the substance that is deficient in porphyria variegata (see the chapter on George III), and 17-ketosteroid reductase, the enzyme that catalyzes the final step in the production of testosterone (see the chapter on Napoleon); or they can be regulatory signals that form and control virtually every function that keeps the human body alive.

The genes themselves are modeled out of the actual building blocks of the DNA, chemical compounds known as bases. It has been estimated that there are three billion pairs of these bases (one member of each pair residing on each member of the chromosome pairs) within the human genome, three billion pairs that exist in the nucleus of each and every cell of the body. Although the vastness of this number is itself staggering, consider this fact: a change in a single one of these billions of bases, an alteration such as the accidental deletion or insertion of a base, or the mistaken substitution of one base for another, can result in the production of a defective protein, a protein that either cannot assemble itself properly or is incapable of performing the task for which it was intended. Such a change in a single base or in a small group of bases, technically called a mutation, is the cause of all genetically transmitted diseases.

In many cases, a mutation within a gene will cause no discernible clinical disorder: after all, chromosomes and genes are present in pairs, and production of one-half of the normal amount of a protein may be all that's needed for the maintenance of good health. There are clearly situations, however, such as in both Marfan syndrome and porphyria variegata, in which the presence of a single dose of an abnormal gene is enough to produce symptomatology; such entities are said to be "dominantly inherited." When a disease results only when both the maternally derived and paternally derived copies of the gene are defective, the entity is termed "recessively inherited."

When a mutation occurs in a gene located on one of the twenty-two pairs of chromosomes that are indistinguishable in males and females, the disorder that results from the genetic alteration will occur equally, and in most cases with equal severity, in both males and females; this is clearly the situation in both Marfan syndrome and porphyria variegata. But when a gene on the X chromosome is altered, an unusual sex distribution of affected individuals will result. Since females possess two copies of the X chromosome, they are less likely to be affected by a mutation involving a single X-linked gene (since they possess a second copy of that gene that is presumably normal). However, since males possess only one X chromosome (and one Y), the presence of an abnormal gene on the X chromosome will *always* give rise to the disease entity in question. Thus, females who carry an X-linked recessive disorder, such as classic hemophilia, would be expected to be externally normal in every discernible way; their daughters, since they have a one-in-two chance of inheriting their mother's X chromosome that bears the abnormal gene, may also be carriers, but will, like their mothers, not be affected. It is the sons of these female carriers, boys who have inherited the X chromosome with the abnormal gene from their clinically normal mothers, who will actually manifest the disease entity. Since such boys inherit one X chromosome from their mother and the Y chromosome carried by their father, they possess no normal gene to compensate for the presence of the abnormal gene. These individuals wind up expressing these X-linked recessively inherited diseases, and thus fulfill the pattern initially described by Dr. Otto in 1803.

In recent years it's become clear that the clinical condition called classic hemophilia actually represents two separate but very similar X-linked recessively inherited disorders. The vast majority of men with the bleeding disease have what's come to be called "hemophilia A"; a much smaller percentage of affected individuals have what's now known as "hemophilia B." Because it is the more common, most of the remainder of this discussion will focus on hemophilia A.

Since the time of Dr. Otto's description of its inheritance pattern, we've learned a tremendous amount about what causes hemophilia A. In 1937 two British biochemists, Drs. A. J. Patek and F. H. L. Taylor, isolated and studied the component of whole blood that is missing from the blood of boys with the disease, naming the protein "anti-hemophilic globulin," or AHG.[9] When the entire Rube Goldberg–esque mechanism of the clotting cascade was finally elucidated, it was realized that AHG, now renamed factor VIII, was the protein that reacted with Christmas factor (the protein currently known as factor IX) and then activated Stuart factor (now called factor X) near the end of the entire clotting process (see figure 1). Analysis of factor VIII has revealed a large and complex protein, a compound that must be produced by what was believed to be a huge segment of DNA.

In fact, in recent years this prediction about the size of the gene that codes for factor VIII proved to be right on the money. Molecular genetics is very much like the study of ancient civilizations: like their colleagues in archaeology, geneticists, using complicated techniques to carve the DNA into small segments and laboriously sequence each base, dig through the genome at sites at which a gene is expected to exist, hoping to uncover the "buried treasure." Using this approach, a major breakthrough in our understanding of the genetics of hemophilia A occurred in 1984 when two groups of scientists, digging through the DNA under the auspices of separate biotechnology companies, independently isolated and sequenced the gene responsible for producing the factor VIII protein for the first time.[10, 11] Located near the very tip of the long arm of the X chromosome, this gene, composed of 186,000 bases, turns out to be one of the largest genes in humans.[12]

Since the discovery and elucidation of the gene, research has centered on attempting to identify the changes in the genetic code that give rise to a deficiency of factor VIII and therefore cause hemophilia A. Numerous genetic changes, including point mutations (substitutions of one base for another) and deletions (in which one or more bases are missing), have been found in different affected males. But regardless of the changes in the DNA, the result of each mutation has been the same: a deficiency of factor VIII, and thus the bleeding disorder.

It's clear, then, that hemophilia A, a disorder in which a large gene on the X chromosome is altered, is a classic, X-linked recessively inherited disorder and as such is passed along from carrier mother to affected son. Thus, it can be assumed that, at the time of his conception, the Tsarevich Alexis Nicolaievich received an X chromosome from his mother that possessed the defective gene. But where did this abnormal X chromosome come from? Was the appearance of the gene a new event, the result of a spontaneous mutation, a change in the genetic material that occurred at the time of Alexis's conception? Or was the abnormal gene already present in Empress Alexandra's family, carried on the X chromosome that was passed along to Alexandra from her mother, a situation that would suggest that the disorder might have manifested itself in other relatives?

The answers to these questions are clear: Tsarevich Alexis Nicolaievich was far from the first member of the empress's family to be affected with the deadly bleeding disease. By the time of his birth in 1904, the ruling family of Great Britain had experienced a full fifty years of what Alexandra's grandmother, Queen Victoria, once referred to as "this awful disease." [13]

———————————

Queen Victoria hated childbirth. The woman who ruled Great Britain from the time of the death of her uncle, King William IV (one of the sons of George III who apparently was not affected with porphyria variegata) on June 20, 1837, until her own death sixty-three years later, clearly dreaded the pain, mess, and most of all, the inconvenience caused by the process of bringing children into the world. So much did she resent the task that, according to her biographer, Cecil Woodham-Smith, the queen was "capable of feeling something approaching rage against" her beloved husband, Prince Albert, simply because as a man, he was physiologically exempt from such responsibilities.[14]

But even though she hated the process, Queen Victoria understood, at least intellectually, that having a large number of children was one of her most important duties. Bearing a horde of royal offspring would fulfill two essential tasks: first, it would ensure that, at the time of her own death, a qualified successor would be available and in place; and second, and nearly as important, a large number of princes and princesses would allow the queen, through carefully arranged marriages, to establish important bloodbased alliances with members of the other powerful ruling families spread throughout the remainder of the civilized world. And although she may have detested the job, the queen, demonstrating almost superhuman dedication and determination, fulfilled her duty in exemplary fashion: by the time she finally brought down the curtain on her reproductive career, in 1857, Victoria had given birth to four sons and five daughters, a legacy so sizable that, following their own marriages, Victoria became known as "Granny" to most of Europe's ruling families.[15] But although she put up with having all those children, on the occasion of none of their deliveries did Queen Victoria come close to enjoying the experience.

Or perhaps she enjoyed it just once. In 1853, when she was pregnant with her eighth child, a new era was dawning in medicine. Just six years previously, James Young Simpson, a physician in Edinburgh, Scotland, had used the drug chloroform as an anesthetic agent during surgery for the first time.[13] Understanding that this newly developed medication could dull her pain, and realizing that such a wonder drug might conceivably offer her some measure of respite and relief from what she viewed as the misery of labor and delivery, Victoria sought out the best anesthesiologist then practicing in London and requested his assistance. That physician was Dr. John Snow and, after agreeing with the queen's proposal, he administered to her chloroform by inhalation on April 7, 1853, as the queen went into labor.[13]

According to the entry made later that month in her diary, the anesthetic agent proved to be everything the queen had hoped it would be: "the effect was soothing, quieting and delightful beyond measure" [14] Under the influence of the inhaled chloroform, Queen Victoria, apparently in the highest of spirits and suffering none of the pain or agony that she'd experienced seven times before, swiftly and easily gave birth to an apparently healthy child, a boy quickly named Prince Leopold.[14]

But unfortunately the queen's delight with the chloroform-assisted delivery soured rapidly, ultimately turning to dismay. In the days following his birth, Leopold, described by his mother in a letter as the "jolly fat little fellow,"[14], developed a series of purplish bumps and bruises just under his skin, hematomas whose appearance occurred mysteriously, without signs of any significant antecedent trauma. Over the course of the hours that followed their appearance, the bumps and bruises grew alarmingly in size. A diagnosis of hemophilia was soon made; needless to say, the presence of this lethal condition in their infant son came as a horrible shock to both Queen Victoria and Prince Albert.[14]

Prince Leopold's diagnosis created two immediate public-relations problems for the royal family. First, because of the unsightly hematomas, it was decided that the child was simply too unattractive to show off to the queen's subjects. Citing the excuse that the newborn infant was too delicate and frail, the prince's baptism was postponed for nearly three months.[13] But more significant, the diagnosis of hemophilia created a sensation in the British press. Although other inherited diseases, the most celebrated being the Royal Malady, were certainly no strangers to members of the family that ruled Great Britain, a bleeding disorder had never previously appeared in a member of any branch of the Stuart or Hanoverian dynasties. Furthermore, because chloroform was then so new and its effects on children born while their mothers had been under its influence were so unknown and unstudied, a cause-and-effect relationship between the wonder drug and the then-dreaded bleeding disease was quickly assumed. Some contemporary Christian fundamentalists went so far as to suggest that the presence of hemophilia in the newborn prince was the direct result of divine intervention: the queen, these people argued, had betrayed the scriptural admonition that "In sorrow thou shalt bring forth children"; as such, Leopold's disease was interpreted as a punishment from God.[13]

Of course, members of the medical establishment knew better. Exactly fifty years had passed since Dr. Otto's description of the inheritance pattern of classic hemophilia, and since that time, as has been already stated, its familial nature had been repeatedly demonstrated and verified. Even the queen had some understanding of the genetic peculiarities of the disorder; upon receiving confirmation of Prince Leopold's diagnosis, she asked how something like this could happen. After all, she argued, "this disease is not in our family." [15]

Like so many other individuals affected with classic hemophilia, like his great-nephew Alexis Nicolaievich half a century later, Prince Leopold enjoyed relatively long periods of good health, but they were punctuated by episodes of spontaneous, painful hemorrhage into his joints and muscles, episodes that led to prolonged incapacity and, because of the arthritic changes that occurred in affected joints, some degree of permanent disability. According to his mother, by the time the prince was twenty-six years old, he had already been "*four or five times at death's door*" [italics the queen's]. Victoria added that Prince Leopold had never spent more than "hardly a few months without being laid up." [13]

As is the case in some other families in which a son is affected with classic hemophilia, Leopold and his mother developed what would have to be considered an unusual and at times pathological relationship. Perhaps because of her extreme concern regarding the seriousness of her son's medical condition, her fear that he could die at any time of an overwhelming, unceasing, unstoppable hemorrhage after what would amount to only minor trauma, and also her probable feelings of guilt at having passed along the disorder to the boy, Queen Victoria became unusually attached to and markedly overprotective of her hemophilic son. [15] This overprotectiveness manifested itself in the queen's attempting to prevent Leopold from doing virtually anything that might cause him harm. Into adulthood, Prince Leopold was forbidden to travel alone; unlike his brothers, he was given no position of authority or any significant governmental responsibilities. Through most of his life, his mother essentially kept her youngest son locked in the palace, literally a prisoner of his disease.

Not surprisingly, and as often happens in such situations, this coddling engendered nothing but progressive and deepening resentment in the son for his mother. Once, while in his twenties, Prince Leopold, who was then being sequestered on the upper floor of Buckingham Palace, actually ran away from home; he spent two weeks in Paris before finally being returned to his luxurious prison. And although, unlike his brothers and sisters, his parents sought no match for him with a daughter from a powerful or wealthy ruling family, the prince independently managed to find himself a wife. In 1882, at the age of twenty-nine, against the wishes of his mother, the prince married Helen of Waldeck, a German princess. The marriage between Leopold and Helen ultimately bore two children. The first, a daughter named Alice, was born in 1883; as the daughter of a man affected with classic hemophilia, it's certain that the sperm that formed Alice had to carry her father's X chromosome, the chromosome that obligatorily bore the gene that causes hemophilia. As such, Alice was an obligate carrier of the hemophilia gene; although clinically normal in every way, she was nevertheless capable of passing the disease along to her sons. In 1907 Alice delivered a son who turned out to be affected with the disease: this child, named Prince Rupert, the grandson of Victoria's son Leopold, lived to be twenty years old before he ultimately died of a cerebral hemorrhage following an automobile accident.[13]

The second child born to Leopold and Helen was a boy. As such, having by necessity inherited his father's Y chromosome and not his X, this child was guaranteed his freedom from the familial disease. But unfortunately, Prince Leopold never had the opportunity to see his healthy son. While on a vacation in Cannes on March 28, 1884, some months before Helen was due to deliver this second child, Prince Leopold accidentally fell and hit his head. Although at the time the injury was believed to be only minor, a hemorrhage had immediately begun within the substance of Leopold's brain. Within hours, the thirty-one-year-old prince was dead.[13]

Had Prince Leopold's hemophilia occurred as the result of a spontaneous mutation in the sequence of bases that composed the gene for the important clotting factor within the previously "normal" X chromosome he received at the time of conception from his mother, the death of Prince Rupert would have ended forever the drama that hemophilia A had introduced into Victorian England. But in fact, the death of Rupert was only one in a series of tragedies caused by this aberrant gene that occurred in the royal family. Hemophilia spread through the royal gene pool like wildfire, ultimately affecting, as shown in the pedigree in figure 2, three of Victoria's grandsons and at least six of her great-grandsons, children who all were descendants of three of Victoria and Albert's nine children.

From analyzing the pedigree, it appears clear that, although Prince Leopold was the only child of the queen and the prince consort who himself was affected with classic hemophilia, two of the couple's daughters, Princess Alice of Hesse, who, born in 1843, was her mother's third child, and Princess Beatrice, the last of Victoria's offspring, proved to be carriers and transmitters of the abnormal gene. Except for Prince Leopold and his grandson, Prince Rupert, all of the males within the pedigree who were affected with classic hemophilia stem from either Alice or Beatrice.

Following her marriage to Henry, Prince of Battenburg (who, after having permanently settled in Great Britain and becoming an English citizen, translated his last name into English as "Mountbatten"), Beatrice gave birth to four children: the first two, a son and a daughter, spent their lives in excellent health; the third child, however, a boy who, like his hemophilic uncle, was also named Leopold, was found early in life to be affected with the bleeding disorder. In actuality, it was the birth of Leopold Mountbatten that confirmed that, at the time of her birth, Beatrice had received from her mother the X chromosome that bore the mutated gene.[13]

But Leopold was not the only child of Beatrice and Henry Mountbatten affected with the bleeding disease. After the birth of Leopold, the princess became pregnant again. This time she delivered another boy, named Maurice, who, early in life, was also found to be affected with the disorder. Although both of Princess Beatrice's hemophilic sons survived into adulthood, managing to serve their country during World War I, both were plagued throughout their lives by episodes of spontaneous bleeding. And, as was inevitable in sufferers of hemophilia prior to the 1960s, both of Princess Beatrice's sons died young: Leopold passed away in 1922 at the age of thirty-three, following an emergency surgical procedure; and Maurice died a war hero in

142

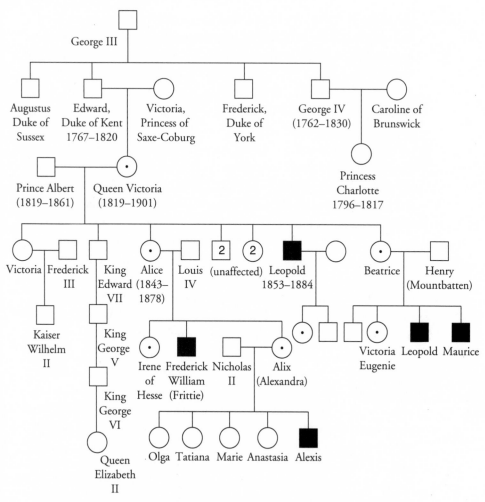

Figure 2. Queen Victoria's pedigree (after McKusick, reference 13).

October 1914 at the age of twenty-three, having been killed in action near Ypres during the early months of World War I. Neither Leopold nor Maurice left any surviving children.[13]

And as it turned out, Leopold and Maurice were not the only children of Princess Beatrice who bore the abnormal gene. Although she was healthy in every way, Victoria Eugenie, the only daughter of the marriage between Beatrice and Henry Mountbatten, also proved to be a carrier of the abnormal gene. Following her marriage to Alfonso XIII, the King of Spain, in 1906, Victoria Eugenie bore seven children. At least two of the offspring of this union, the couple's sons Alfonso, born in 1907, and Gonzalo, born in 1934, were also affected with hemophilia.[13]

Like her younger sister Beatrice, Alice, Queen Victoria's other daughter who proved to be an obligate carrier of the gene for hemophilia, learned firsthand about the tragedy of the disease by caring for her own affected son. In 1870, after her marriage to Louis IV, the Grand Duke of Hesse, Alice delivered Frederick William, the fifth of her seven children. Nicknamed Frittie by his parents, the boy was described from infancy as being "delicate," and his tendency to bleed spontaneously became obvious very soon after birth. Unlike the other members of Victoria's family who were affected with hemophilia, Frittie did not survive early childhood. One morning in 1873 while playing with his older brother, Ernst, the boy, who was only three years old at the time, accidentally fell out of a window in his mother's bedroom, landing heavily on a stone terrace twenty feet below. Although he broke no bones and it initially appeared as if he'd received only minor trauma, he soon fell into a deep coma. The fall from the window had resulted in a cerebral hemorrhage. Within a few hours, Frittie was dead.[16]

The only logical way to explain the fact that one of Queen Victoria's sons and two of her daughters were carriers of the gene that causes hemophilia is to postulate that she was a bearer of the mutant gene. Since the queen's father, Edward, Duke of Kent (a son of King George III who also was clearly affected with the Royal Malady, porphyria variegata), had no problems with bleeding and clotting, and there's no evidence that any of the relatives of her mother, Victoria of Saxe-Coburg, were afflicted with the bleeding disease, it's most likely that the mutation occurred in the X chromosome carried in either the egg or, as is genetically more likely, the sperm that initially formed the queen.

Although there is no way to prove conclusively that the mutation occurred in Edward's sperm cell, there is some circumstantial evidence involving the story of Queen Victoria's conception that suggests that this is in fact the case. An only child, the queen was conceived in a desperate attempt to provide an heir to the throne of England that would perpetuate the Hanoverian dynasty. Such an offspring became necessary after the principal heir to the throne, Princess Charlotte, the only child of King George IV (and granddaughter of King George III), and yet another member of the Hanover family who was affected with the Royal Malady, died unexpectedly during childbirth in 1817, most likely as the direct result of complications arising from an attack of porphyria variegata. Following his niece's unexpected death, Edward, who was then fifty and had never married, quickly sought a wife and prayed that she'd be fertile. Edward and his wife succeeded in their important task: the Duke of Kent was fifty-two when his daughter, Victoria, was born.[13] He died less than a year later.

The genetic literature is replete with instances in which new mutations leading to the presence of disease have occurred in offspring born to older fathers.[17, 18] Apparently, for reasons that are not clearly understood, such alterations in the genetic material are more likely to occur in the germ cells of men who are thirty-five years of age or older at the time of their child's conception. Therefore, because of this unexplained genetic peculiarity, it appears probable that the mutation that ultimately introduced classic hemophilia into the royal families of England, Germany, Spain, and finally Russia occurred in the X chromosome carried in the sperm cell of the desperate Duke of Kent.

Alix of Hesse, the younger sister of Frittie, who died at age three as a result of a cerebral hemorrhage, was herself an infant at the time of her brother's death, too young really to carry any lasting image of the boy in her mind or to understand the tragedy of his passing. But unfortunately Alix, like her mother Alice, her Aunt Beatrice, and her grandmother Victoria, would come to learn firsthand of the realities of classic hemophilia: during her marriage, she, too, would give birth to a son afflicted with the disease. That son was Tsarevich Alexis Nicolaievich, who was born after his mother, having adopted the Russian name Alexandra Feodorovna, had married Tsar Nicholas II.

Like our expanding knowledge of the molecular basis of hemophilia A, in the years since the birth of Alexis, a tremendous amount has been learned about the care and management of children with this disorder. Since Dr. Thomas Addis first demonstrated in 1910 that spontaneous hemorrhaging in boys with classic hemophilia could be abruptly terminated by simply transfusing the whole blood of unaffected individuals into the affected person's vein, major breakthroughs in the treatment of this deadly disease have been accomplished on a fairly regular basis. As previously mentioned, in 1937, two British biochemists, A. J. Patek and F. H. L. Taylor, isolated antihemophilic globulin, or AHG, the component of that transfused whole blood that caused the hemorrhaging to stop.[9] In 1965, Drs. J. G. Pool and A. E. Shannon developed a simple, inexpensive method of isolating and concentrating antihemophilic globulin from whole blood, a technique that permitted the substance, called "cryoprecipitate" because of the way in which it was isolated, to become readily available to patients.[19] This major advance, which through its rapid infusion into the bloodstream could control spontaneous bleeds, revolutionized the lives of boys and men with hemophilia by allowing them to start an intravenous line and mix and administer the cryoprecipitate themselves at home at the earliest sign of a hemorrhage. The marketing of this medication has significantly diminished the numbers of episodes of life-threatening hemorrhage, as well as decreasing the number of serious side effects, such as painful and chronic arthritis, that used to interrupt and endanger the lives of most such individuals.

Although control of the disease has been markedly improved, there remains no permanent cure for hemophilia A. And in addition to the threat of a huge, uncontrollable, life-ending hemorrhage that in spite of the presence of self-administered cryoprecipitate still lurks around every sharp corner, mothers of affected boys today have yet another, more modern problem with which to cope, another worry to keep them awake through the long hours of the night: since cryoprecipitate is prepared from pooled donor blood, material that we now know was infected with the human immunodeficiency virus (HIV) prior to 1984, along with the protection from hemorrhages carried by this medication, the virus that causes acquired immune deficiency syndrome was also passed on to these unsuspecting boys and men. By 1978 some men with hemophilia were already infected with HIV;[20] the number of hemophilic men testing positive for HIV ballooned to 10,000 by 1985, and in the 1990s, it is estimated that more than 70 percent of all men with the bleeding disease are infected with the deadly virus.

So today, thirty years after the introduction of Pool and Shannon's miraculous cryoprecipitate offered what was believed to be a cure for classic hemophilia, it's not difficult to imagine what must have been going through the mind of Empress Alexandra Feodorovna as she sat at the bedside of the tsarevich in the Romanov family's vacation villa in Spala during those dark days of October 1912, watching her son slowly, painfully, and uncontrollably bleeding to death.

It's still not clear exactly what Grigory Rasputin did on that night in October 1912 at his home in Siberia after receiving the cable from Anna Vyrubova begging for his assistance. We know that Father Grigory cabled back that he had prayed and that God had answered those prayers; but was it prayer alone that caused the torn blood vessel in Tsarevich Alexis's left thigh to cease its leakage of blood, and to ultimately heal, or was it simply coincidence? And on those subsequent occasions when, as an invited guest of the tsar and tsaritsa, he was called upon to stop the tsarevich's hemorrhages or to prevent them from occurring in the first place, did Father Grigory continue to use prayer in his healing? Or was it hypnosis that the *starets* utilized in treating Alexis Nicolaievich? In his book *Nicholas and Alexandra,* Robert Massie suggests two possible alternate explanations, both of which probably served to contribute at least in part to Father Grigory's still-inexplicable therapeutic success.

The first suggestion cited by Massie is that the optimistic words, the messages of encouragement from Father Grigory, had a significant, soothing effect on the frazzled psyches of both the tsarevich and his frightened mother.[21] Physiologically, there is some evidence that emotional stress can exacerbate bleeding in individuals with classic hemophilia; the converse of this, that the relief of that stress might improve clotting, is also a possibility.

147

The presence of stress, whether derived from the pain of a broken bone, from exposure to intense heat or cold, or through severe emotional upheaval, leads within seconds to an outpouring of adrenocorticotropic hormone, or ACTH, a substance manufactured by the cells of the pituitary gland, the so-called master gland of the human body. Through its function as a messenger, ACTH acts upon the cells of the adrenal cortex, a gland sitting atop the kidney that produces the hormones testosterone, cortisol, and aldosterone (for a full explanation of the production and functioning of these hormones, see the chapter on John F. Kennedy that follows).

Aldosterone and cortisol are amazing chemicals. They control and regulate a wide range of vital bodily functions, including heart rate and blood pressure. When stress causes an outpouring of ACTH, the adrenal glands respond by manufacturing more hormone; this increase in production of cortisol and aldosterone causes, in turn, an elevation in blood pressure and an increase in the amount of blood pumped by the heart. In the presence of a spontaneous hemorrhage, these two physiologic changes would be expected to increase the amount of bleeding.

So now imagine this scene: it's the sickroom of the Tsarevich of Russia. The empress, Alexandra Feodorovna, is trying her best to keep up her spirits, to remain hopeful and optimistic so that her son, believing that everything will be all right, will retain his will to live. But as the hours pass, the task becomes more and more difficult; the empress sees her son growing weaker; she can almost measure, as the hours pass, his life ebbing away. Surrounded by Russia's most eminent physicians, the empress can find no one who will offer even a single word of encouragement or hope. And, as her false front of optimism is slowly replaced by hopelessness and exhaustion, Alexandra finally comes to accept that the end is truly in sight, that the tsarevich is really going to die.

And through all this, Alexis Nicolaievich, lapsing in and out of consciousness, recognizes the gradual change in his mother's demeanor. With the empress's developing sense of hopelessness, her increasing emotional stress and turmoil are transmitted to her suffering son. Alexis begins to sense that the situation is hopeless; as a result, his pituitary gland produces massive amounts of ACTH; his adrenal glands increase the amount of aldosterone, cortisol, and testosterone circulating in the boy's bloodstream; and as a result, Alexis's blood pressure rises, his cardiac output is increased, and the amount of blood passing through the ruptured blood vessel and into his hip joint and his abdomen increases.

But then, when all seems lost, a cable arrives from this mysterious Father Grigory. "Do not grieve," the *starets* writes. "God has heard your prayers. The little one will not die." Suddenly, there is hope where there had been none; for the first time in days, the empress's spirits have reason to lift. Although the men of medicine continue to hold out no hope, the man of God has said that all will be well. Immediately, Alexandra's demeanor changes; she begins to smile; optimism returns. Coming into the drawing room smiling for the first time in a week, she tells those members of the court assembled there, "The doctors notice no improvement yet, but I am not a bit anxious myself now." [22]

And, like the pessimism of just hours before, the lifting of the empress's anxiety is also recognized by the dying boy; he sees his mother smiling and comes to realize that, despite what he himself has come to believe, all is not lost. According to this scenario, if over the next few hours samples of Alexis's blood could have been taken and the levels of ACTH, cortisol, and aldosterone analyzed, a marked reduction in each of these hormones would have been seen. And with the reduction in those levels, the tsarevich's blood pressure and cardiac output would have also dropped significantly. Within hours, the torn blood vessel stopped leaking; the hemorrhage, and with it, the crisis, gradually came to an end.

And so, by doing nothing more than sending an optimistic telegram, Father Grigory effected a cure of the tsarevich's seemingly terminal condition.

The second suggestion offered by Robert Massie to explain Rasputin's success in controlling the tsarevich's episodes of bleeding is that Father Grigory somehow successfully employed hypnosis. According to this theory, which is traditionally the most popular explanation for Rasputin's success in the episodes of bleeding following the one that occurred in Spala during October 1912, the *starets,* through the use of a posthypnotic suggestion, was somehow able to cause constriction of Alexis Nicolaievich's small arterioles, the tiny blood vessels in the limbs that, since their control normally resides in the autonomic nervous system, are not usually externally controllable;[23] constriction of the arterioles would allow less blood to reach the site of a hemorrhage and thus dramatically slow the bleeding.

This theory was supported by work performed in the precryoprecipitate era by Drs. O. Lucas, A. Finkelman, and L. M. Tocantins, three dentists from Philadelphia. In 1963, inspired by the story of Rasputin and Alexis, Dr. Lucas and his colleagues decided to try to use hypnosis in a group of 150 boys and young men with hemophilia who, for various reasons, required dental extractions. Although in the age prior to cryoprecipitate dental surgery in men with hemophilia was usually dangerous and complicated, Dr. Lucas's technique proved to be so successful that not one patient had to receive even a single unit of blood.[24]

Regardless of how and even if he was able to produce control of Alexis's spontaneous hemorrhaging, Rasputin was viewed by Alexandra Feodorovna as being the one and only savior of the tsarevich. As a result, the empress turned to Father Grigory not only for assistance with her son's medical condition, but also for advice in other aspects of her life. And it was these decisions in nonmedical areas that caused all the trouble.

During World War I, Tsar Nicholas, the commander-in-chief of the Russian army, chose to personally command his troops in their battles with the army of Kaiser Wilhelm of Germany. When he left for the front, the tsar turned over many of the responsibilities for the day-to-day operation of the government to his wife, the tsaritsa. Unsure of what needed to be done or exactly how to do it, Alexandra quite naturally turned with ever-increasing frequency to her "guru," Rasputin, for advice and guidance.

Although the decision to seek counsel was a good one, the person the empress chose to be her advisor left something to be desired. The advice Father Grigory offered Alexandra was uniformly horrible. According to the whim of the *starets,* government ministers whose jobs were essential to the well-being of the Russian people were hired or fired for little more reason than that they had recently pleased or angered Rasputin; decisions about the timing and the location of the Russian army's attacks were sometimes made based on Rasputin's dreams.[25] Soon many people in the country's capital assumed that Rasputin and Alexandra (who, after all, was German by birth) were spies, who, rather than trying to maintain any semblance of normalcy within the Russian Empire while the tsar was away, were in fact attempting its overthrow from within.

When Rasputin was assassinated by Prince Felix Yussoupov and his colleagues on the night of December 29, 1916,* the news was greeted with nearly uniform joy by the populace of Moscow. However, the hatred and resentment that Rasputin had caused were not quelled by his death. A year and a half later, more than a year after the tsar had been forced to abdicate his throne, the entire former imperial family, who for months had been held prisoner in a compound in the city of Ekaterinburg in the Ural Mountains, were themselves savagely murdered by their Bolshevik captors. Many people played a role in those gruesome deaths; indirectly, Grigory Rasputin was one of them.

It might seem like oversimplification to imply that a single gene defect, a disorder that resulted from an error in a single one of the three billion base pairs that compose the human genome, might be responsible for the political upheaval, turmoil, and destruction of life and property brought about by the Russian Revolution. However, it is undeniably true that this simple mutation that occurred in one of the X chromosomes that gave rise to Queen Victoria and that was transmitted through Victoria's daughter Alice, her granddaughter Alix, and that finally came to rest within the genome of Alexis Nicolaievich, the last tsarevich of the Romanov dynasty, played an important role in the political drama that occurred in Russia during the latter portion of the second decade of the twentieth century. Without hemophilia, there would have been no Rasputin. And without Rasputin, there would undoubtedly have been less unrest among the people, unrest that ultimately erupted into war.

PART II

At approximately nine o'clock on the evening of Tuesday, February 17, 1920, exactly nineteen months after the deposed Tsar Nicholas II and the remainder of the former imperial family of Russia had, according to the team of officers from the White Army charged with investigating the incident, "been shot, stabbed, and bludgeoned to death by their Bolshevik captors"[26] in the basement of the house in Ekaterinburg that had been their prison, a distraught young woman, apparently attempting to commit suicide, threw herself off the Bendler Bridge in Berlin, landing in the cold water of the Landwehr Canal. At that early hour of the evening, there were many other people in the area, and many of these eyewitnesses immediately came to her aid. After assuring themselves that she was alive and relatively well, her rescuers wrapped the woman in a dry blanket and brought her to a nearby police post, where, after she was given something warm to drink, intensive interrogation was begun.[27]

Intentionally or not, the soaking wet and apparently terrified young woman, who spoke German with a foreign accent, was unable to answer virtually any of the questions. She could recall neither her name, her age, nor her address; she couldn't explain why she had jumped from the Bendler Bridge, nor even whether she had actually jumped, been pushed, or had simply lost her balance. Further, the woman carried absolutely no identification: no purse, no papers, not even any laundry marks on the labels of her soaking garments she continued to wear. Frustrated, and with no other options, the police decided to bring the woman to Elisabeth Hospital, where she was admitted to a charity ward and put to bed.[27]

After a night's sleep, the unknown woman seemed stronger and more in control of her faculties. But despite her apparent recovery from the fright of the night before, she continued to have trouble coming up with answers to even the simplest questions: although the doctors charged with her care interrogated her in multiple languages, the woman remained absolutely silent.

This pattern of intense questioning by the authorities and stone silence by the patient was repeated every morning during the six weeks that the woman remained at Elisabeth Hospital. Finally, frustrated with their lack of progress, the physicians decided to transfer the woman from the acute care hospital to the Dalldorf Asylum, a facility for the mentally unbalanced. Admitted to Dalldorf as "Fraulein Unbekannt" (Miss Unknown), the silent woman was placed in a bed in House 4 Ward B, a unit that housed fourteen other women.[27]

While she was a patient at Dalldorf, the remarkable story of Fraulein Unbekannt slowly began to emerge. Reluctantly, over the course of months, with tiny bits leaking out at a time, and while talking with a wide variety of both reliable and unreliable witnesses, the woman's tale grew in scope and significance. And when the story was finally completed, it was truly a blockbuster, a tale that has since been translated into books and film.

Although she would admit it only reluctantly, Fraulein Unbekannt let it be known to some of those around her that she was, in actuality, Grand Duchess Anastasia, the fourth child and youngest daughter of Nicholas and Alexandra. Of course, this was somewhat difficult to believe: after all, in light of the White Army investigation team's report, the entire imperial family had been violently slaughtered nearly two years before. In attempting to account for her continued existence, Fraulein Unbekannt explained that although most of the information contained in that report had in fact been true, there were actually some important flaws. For instance, she contended that although it was true that, beginning in the late night of July 16, 1918, and stretching on into the early-morning hours of July 17, her parents, her brother, and her three older sisters had been mercilessly assassinated by their captors, Anastasia herself had been rescued by a young man named Alexander Tschaikovsky. A Bolshevik soldier who had been part of the force guarding the imperial family during their captivity in Ekaterinburg, Tschaikovsky had apparently fallen in love with the then-seventeen-year-old grand duchess, and somehow the couple had begun an illicit affair (according to another account, Anastasia claims to have been raped by the soldier). When the order to assassinate the Romanov family had finally been given, a command that had ostensibly come down from none other than Vladimir Ilich Lenin himself,[26] Alexander

Tschaikovsky, panicked by the thought of losing his beloved Anastasia, kidnapped the girl and deserted his post.

Accompanied by his mother, Maria, his sister, Veronica, and his brother, Serge, the fugitive Alexander Tschaikovsky hid Anastasia in a farm cart and fled toward the west. Successfully crossing the border into Rumania, the unusual extended family settled in the capital city of Bucharest, where, on or around December 5, 1918, just five months after the terrible slaughter at Ekaterinburg had occurred, the young woman gave birth to a healthy son, whom the couple named either Alexis, after the grand duchess's deceased brother, or Alexander, after his father.[28] Soon after the child's birth, the couple married in a Catholic church in Bucharest (although no records of this union are known to exist) and lived together, apparently happily, for a year, until, according to her story, tragedy once again struck Anastasia's life: in late 1919, for reasons that Fraulein Unbekannt never revealed, Alexander Tschaikovsky was shot and killed in the streets of Bucharest.

Suddenly widowed at age eighteen, with a young child, no family to rely on except her in-laws, who apparently intensely disliked her, and frightened that she'd be caught and murdered by the Bolsheviks, Anastasia went searching for help. Leaving her one-year-old son with his paternal grandmother in Bucharest, the young grand duchess claimed that she traveled to Berlin by herself, in an attempt to seek the aid of her mother's surviving relatives. Whether she actually had the opportunity to speak with those relatives or not, Anastasia (or more accurately, Fraulein Unbekannt) had been in Berlin for less than a week before she jumped, or possibly was pushed, off the Bendler Bridge.

From the time that the basic shell of Fraulein Unbekannt's remarkable story first came to light during her early years in Germany to the time that the woman, who had legally become known as Anna Anderson in 1928, died in New York in 1984, the question of whether she actually was Grand Duchess Anastasia was never convincingly answered. Many factors supported Fraulein Unbekannt's claim: the woman physically resembled the grand duchess (see figures 3 and 4); she had scars that corresponded to sites of injuries the grand duchess had putatively sustained during her childhood, and very strikingly, she

Figure 3. (a) Grand Duchess Anastasia in 1916. (b) Fraulein Unbekannt at the Dalldorf Asylum in 1921.

Figure a from the Ian Lilburn Collection, London; Figure b from the Houghton Library, Harvard University.

had a somewhat unusual foot deformity, called hallux valgus, in which the great toe deviates laterally, toward the outside portion of the foot, that Anastasia was also noted to have had. Further, Fraulein Unbekannt knew obscure facts about the everyday lives of members of the Romanov family, facts that those outside the royal court could not have possibly known. All of these factors went a long way to strengthen the belief of many observers that Fraulein Unbekannt actually was Grand Duchess Anastasia.

Unfortunately, there were other factors that prevented the widespread acceptance of Fraulein Unbekannt's claim by those interested in the fate of the Romanov family. There seemed to be major holes in the woman's long-term memory, lapses that prevented her from remembering some simple facts about daily life in Tsarskoe Selo, the site of the official residence of the imperial family. Perhaps more important, these lapses in her memory apparently prevented the woman from being able to recognize the faces of friends and acquaintances from the old days

Figure 4. (a) Grand Duchess Anastasia in 1915 (b) Fraulein Unbekannt in Berlin in 1925.
Figure a from Mrs. John J. Weber Collection. Figure b from the Ian Lilburn Collection, London.

who, having settled in Europe after having managed to escape the Bolshevik uprising, had come to inspect this mystery woman.

Her inability to remember information and to recognize faces might be explainable on the basis of the fact that, as a result of her months of captivity, the murder of her family, her subsequent flight from Ekaterinburg, and the experiences derived from her short, sad marriage, the grand duchess had suffered a series of major traumas so severe and significant that they had adversely affected her memory. Yet another factor made the unknown woman's story much more difficult to believe. Some of those old friends and acquaintances who came to Berlin to visit this Anastasia also failed to recognize *her*, and most damning of all, declared that the woman was in fact an out-and-out imposter, one of the many phony grand duchesses who had surfaced both in and out of institutions housing the insane since July 1918. The three most significant members of this group who doubted Unbekannt's story were the Dowager Empress Maria Feodorovna, widow of Tsar Alexander III, mother of Tsar Nicholas II, and grandmother of Grand Duchess Anastasia; Grand Duchess Olga Alexandrovna, Nicholas's sister and aunt of Anastasia; and Baroness Sophia Karlovna Buxhoeveden, maid of honor to Empress Alexandra Feodorovna. Without the acceptance of these three women, Fraulein Unbekannt had no chance of convincing the world of her claim.

There are several possible reasons why these members of the imperial court might not have been overjoyed to declare that the woman who would eventually become known as Anna Anderson was actually Grand Duchess Anastasia. The first and most obvious explanation is that perhaps Fraulein Unbekannt really wasn't the grand duchess. She may have been an imposter; or perhaps she was psychotic and delusional. There's some evidence to support this latter conclusion: after all, she did first come to the public's attention following what was probably a suicide attempt, an act that would immediately call the woman's sanity into question.

But either of these possibilities leaves many facts unexplained. If she wasn't Anastasia, how did Fraulein Unbekannt know all those obscure facts about the Russian imperial family? If she wasn't the grand duchess, how is it that she bore all those scars and was affected with that striking and unusual foot deformity? Could all this be coincidental? Or is it possible that Fraulein Unbekannt was actually the victim of a silent conspiracy? Perhaps the surviving Romanovs electively chose to ignore the claims of this woman who really was Grand Duchess Anastasia, perhaps because they disapproved of, or were embarrassed by the fact that, according to her story, she had had an illicit affair, had borne a child out of wedlock, and had ultimately married a man who was both a peasant and, even worse, had been a Bolshevik soldier. Undoubtedly, the Romanovs realized that as the only surviving grandson of Tsar Nicholas II, Alexander Tschaikovsky, the child of Grand Duchess Anastasia, would possess legal claim to the throne of Russia when the monarchy was restored, an event that the family believed was inevitable and would occur virtually any day. Because of the lowly origins of his father, and because of the questionable circumstances surrounding his birth, it's very likely that the accession of Alexander Tschaikovsky was

157

an event that the Romanovs felt had to be avoided at all costs, even if it meant that Grand Duchess Anastasia would be forced to live the remainder of her life in poverty and obscurity.

The puzzle of Anna Anderson has never been convincingly solved. Although the report of the White Army's investigation team is probably correct, a nagging doubt persists even today, because, until recently, no definitive physical evidence of the assassination, no weapons nor remains of the tsar and his family, had ever been recovered.

This situation has recently changed. In 1991, nine bodies were discovered in a mass grave in Ekaterinburg. Although the bodies were believed to have included five members of the imperial family, confirmation of this fact took an additional two years. In 1993, using techniques that had only recently been developed, a team of British geneticists led by Dr. Peter Gill compared samples of DNA isolated from the Ekaterinburg remains with samples taken from living relatives of the imperial family, and concluded with greater than 98% assurance that the skeletons in question were in fact those of Tsar Nicholas, Tsarina Alexandra, and four of the couple's five children.[29]

Although this discovery laid to rest a mystery that existed for more than 75 years, it also raises two tantalizing questions. First, what became of the fifth of the imperial couple's children? And second, is it possible that Fraulein Unbekannt actually was Anastasia?

The answers to these questions will undoubtedly rest in the study of genetics. Clinically, there are two trails that may be followed in attempting to prove that Fraulein Unbekannt belonged to the imperial family. The first involved the gene for hemophilia A; and the second, somewhat surprisingly, involves the gene for porphyria variegata, the Royal Malady.

As a daughter of Empress Alexandra Feodorovna, an obligate carrier of the gene for hemophilia A, Anastasia, in addition to receiving a "normal" X chromosome from her father, had a one-in-two chance of having gotten her mother's "normal" X chromosome and a one-in-two chance of receiving the X chromosome that bore the abnormal gene for hemophilia. If by chance she received this latter X chromosome, it's possible that she herself could have had sons who, like her brother, Tsarevich Alexis Nicolaievich, were affected with classic hemophilia.

Although from the moment that she splashed down in the icy waters of the Landwehr Canal until the time of her death, Fraulein Unbekannt bore no children, she did admit to having delivered one son, the aforementioned Alexis or Alexander Tschaikovsky, during the time that she and the elder Alexander Tschaikovsky were living in Bucharest. After leaving the child with her mother-in-law prior to beginning her trip to Berlin in 1920, Fraulein Unbekannt never saw that child again.

No information is available concerning whether the boy was affected with hemophilia; if he had been affected with the bleeding disease, this would have been virtually indisputable proof that Fraulein Unbekannt was, in fact, Grand Duchess Anastasia. However, even if her only son was free of the disorder, the woman's claim still could not simply be dismissed: as the son of a possible carrier of a gene for classic hemophilia, the boy himself would have had only a 50 percent chance of being affected.

But clinically, there is still a second possible method of solving the puzzle of Anna Anderson, a method that uses some clues already known but somehow overlooked by historians. These clues involve the disease porphyria variegata, the hereditary Royal Malady that affected King George III (and, it seems, just about every other King or Queen of England prior to the start of the twentieth century), which is extensively discussed in the first chapter of this book.

To recap, porphyria variegata is an autosomal dominantly inherited condition caused by an enzymatic defect in the biochemical pathway through which heme, an essential component of hemoglobin, is produced. Although the majority of people who carry the gene that causes porphyria variegata spend their life in excellent health, not even knowing that they bear the abnormality, the disorder can, under certain stressful situations, manifest itself with episodes of illness characterized by severe, colicky abdominal pain often accompanied by vomiting, constipation, and diarrhea; lightning-like arthritic pains in the limbs, head, neck, and chest; neurologic symptoms such as muscle weakness, loss of sensation and seizures, skin sensitivity; and psychiatric disturbances, including anxiety, restlessness, insomnia, delusions, hallucinations, paranoia, and depression. In addition, during these acute episodes, affected individuals will often be noted to excrete red or brown urine.

Now although Empress Alexandra Feodorovna clearly had genetic ties to the Hanoverian dynasty, the British royal family in which the gene for porphyria variegata was known to be present, she was linked to the family only through her grandmother, Queen Victoria, who appears not to have been affected with the entity. As such, she probably did not pass the gene along to any of her children. It's well known that Tsar Nicholas II was also related to the Hanoverians, linked by blood through his grandmother, great-grandmother, and other ancestors. Is it possible that the Romanov family also had members who were affected with the Royal Malady?

Amazingly, the answer to this question seems to be yes. In 1894 Nicholas's own father, Tsar Alexander III, became ill with a mysterious disease. At forty-nine years of age, Alexander, a tall, Herculean figure[30] who had always enjoyed excellent health, suddenly developed intractable headaches, insomnia, and weakness of his legs. Ignoring his doctor's advice that he spend a few weeks resting, Tsar Alexander loaded his family, including his eldest son, Tsarevich Nicholas, onto the imperial train and headed for the Romanovs' hunting lodge in Spala, the same lodge at which, nearly twenty years later, Alexander's grandson, Alexis Nicolaievich, would experience the severe episode of spontaneous hemorrhage that led to the apparently life-saving intervention of Grigory Rasputin.[31]

But once in Spala, Alexander III did not feel well enough to hunt. His illness worsened, and after his own doctors had failed to make a diagnosis, the eminent Professor Ernst von Leyden, a specialist from Vienna, was called in to offer his opinion. After evaluating the tsar, Dr. von Leyden made a diagnosis of nephritis, which he believed had resulted from a minor injury, actually nothing more than a bruise on his side, that the tsar had sustained in a train accident six years earlier.[32] Although the professor from Vienna could offer neither treatment nor cure for the tsar's condition, he believed that rest and relaxation were essential for recovery. At Dr. von Leyden's insistence, Alexander and his family traveled by train to Livadia, the imperial summer palace in the Crimea, where the tsar was ordered to spend time convalescing.[31]

Now although Dr. von Leyden's clinical acumen was virtually unparalleled in all of Europe, we, viewing the tsar's illness exactly one hundred years later, have one major advantage unavailable to the eminent doctor: we have the articles that summarize the work done by Drs. Macalpine, Hunter, and Rimington, the three British psychiatrists who studied the Royal Malady and concluded that King George III was actually affected with porphyria variegata.[33] In light of their work, Dr. von Leyden's diagnosis must be reconsidered.

Nephritis, an inflammation of the kidney, is characterized by the presence of hematuria, or red blood cells in the urine. In the late nineteenth century, there was little or no capability to examine the urinary sediment for the presence of red blood cells or other impurities. In other words, it's likely that, prior to making his diagnosis, Dr. von Leyden did not actually see red blood cells in a specimen of urine obtained from the tsar. Rather, it's probable that the doctor made his diagnosis based solely on the presence of burgundy-colored urine, a feature we have already mentioned as being present during times of the episodic illness characteristic of porphyria variegata. The other features Alexander suffered prior to Dr. von Leyden's diagnosis—the insomnia, weakness in his legs, and pain in his head—were also consistent with the diagnosis of porphyria. Therefore, like so many other close and distant relatives of the Hanoverian kings of England, Tsar Alexander III most probably was affected with the Royal Malady.

The remainder of the course of Alexander's illness further supports this contention. Following his arrival in the Crimea, the tsar rested and his condition improved somewhat, but this slight recovery proved to be shortlived. According to Robert Massie, "after a few days, he again began to have trouble sleeping, his legs gave way and he took to his bed."[31] From that point on, the tsar's condition traveled rapidly downhill; his legs became swollen and his heart was described as "weak"; on October 17,* the daily official medical bulletin reported that "a little blood appeared in his urine." And finally, on October 20, 1894,* just two weeks after he'd found it necessary to return to his bed, Tsar Alexander III suddenly died.[34]

If Tsar Alexander III did indeed suffer from porphyria variegata, this may be nothing more than a footnote in Russian history, yet another piece of evidence illustrating how little Russian blood actually

161

flowed through the veins of the later Romanov tsars. (The historian Maurice Paleologue once calculated that, genetically, Tsar Nicholas II was only 1/128 Russian, a result of the "habit" of the Russian tsars to marry German and Danish princesses.[35]) Outwardly, none of Alexander's children, including Tsar Nicholas II, manifested any signs of the disease; but as has already been emphasized, the majority of individuals who carry the gene for porphyria variegata never show any symptoms. Is it possible that Tsar Nicholas (who, if his father was affected, had a one-in-two chance of obtaining the abnormal gene) inherited the gene from his father and passed it along to his daughter Grand Duchess Anastasia (who, if her father carried the gene, also had a one-in-two chance of inheriting it)? Did Fraulein Unbekannt manifest any symptoms that might indicate that she was affected with porphyria variegata?

Of all the symptoms and signs that occur in porphyria variegata, it would seem that the psychiatric features would be the easiest to confirm in the case of Fraulein Unbekannt. After all, after she was fished out of the waters of the Landwehr Canal following what was believed to be a suicide attempt, she was admitted to the Dalldorf Asylum, an institution for the insane. And while she resided at Dalldorf, it was believed by the professionals charged with caring for her that she was, in fact, deranged. During her prolonged stay at the Dalldorf Asylum, a diagnosis of *Einfache Seelenstoerung* ("simple psychic disturbance") was made; at various times during that hospitalization, the woman was noted to be "dangerously depressed," to have psychopathic symptoms and chronic insomnia, and when she could sleep, she was nearly always awakened by terrifying nightmares. And of course, when, after more than two years of hospitalization, she finally reluctantly admitted to being Grand Duchess Anastasia, she was believed by most people to be delusional.[35] All of these symptoms are well-known features of porphyria variegata.

But in trying to make this point, we're faced with something of an historical catch-22. If we believe the story that Fraulein Unbekannt ultimately told, that in fact she was Grand Duchess Anastasia and that, through extraordinary circumstances, she had managed to survive the enormous tragedy of her family's slaughter, then a great many of the features that led to her diagnosis of a psychiatric disorder must be accepted as normal. If she was Grand Duchess Anastasia, then Fraulein Unbekannt was neither delusional nor psychotic; and her other symptoms, including the severe depression, the chronic insomnia, and the frightening night terrors, would have been expected, extrinsically induced problems caused by her struggle, rather than intrinsically triggered complaints, as would be the case in an individual affected with porphyria.

So the presence of the psychiatric component of porphyria variegata is not so well established in the case of Fraulein Unbekannt. But how about the other symptoms and signs of porphyria? Did Anna Anderson manifest any of these?

In the early years following her release from the Dalldorf Asylum, the young woman did suffer from some unusual, poorly defined problems that resemble those that occur in the Royal Malady. For instance, in May 1922, after she'd been "rescued" from the asylum by the von Kleists, a prominent Berlin family who, after hearing of the woman's plight, had been sympathetic, Fraulein Unbekannt became quite ill. During an examination in the late spring of 1922, Dr. T. A. Schiler, the von Kleist family's regular physician, found the woman to have acute anemia, to be "very pale," and to have a weak pulse. During visits during the next month, Dr. Schiler noted that she had intense pain over her skull when even mild pressure was applied, that she occasionally spit up blood, and that she often refused to eat.[36]

Although Fraulein Unbekannt's unexplained illness continued without causing much concern through the early part of the summer, this all changed on June 30, when, without warning, the woman fell suddenly to the floor, choking. Her mental status took a sudden turn for the worst: she was found to be dazed, confused, and very restless. During her sleep, she was noted to mutter in Russian.[36]

Fraulein Unbekannt was confined to bed during much of that summer. Treatment with digitalis, a medication that improves the efficiency of the heart, and morphine proved to have little effect on her condition. But then, in the middle of August, the woman suddenly and unexpectedly rallied; according to Dr. Schiler's notes: "Patient is up, extraordinarily cheerful."[37]

This illness, with its sudden onset, prolonged course, mysterious, unexplained symptoms and signs, and rapid, unexpected resolution, is reminiscent of some of the milder episodes of the Royal Malady suffered by King George III and so many of his illustrious relatives. But there are some serious flaws with this diagnosis: although it's true that some of the features of Fraulein Unbekannt's illness, such as the intense head pain, the psychiatric components, the sudden collapse, and respiratory symptomatology, are all consistent with the diagnosis of porphyria variegata, other cardinal components are missing, features such as the severe abdominal pain, many of the neurologic symptoms, and perhaps most important of all, the discoloration of the urine. Still, it's possible that this illness represented an episode of porphyria variegata, a link with Anastasia's grandfather, Alexander III, that would virtually confirm that Fraulein Unbekannt actually was the last surviving daughter of Nicholas and Alexandra.

Although the whole issue may seem frivolous, there actually is at least one important reason why it's important to prove the validity of the story told by Fraulein Unbekannt: money. The Romanov family, perhaps anticipating that their reign might end dramatically and suddenly, stored a portion of their enormous wealth in bank accounts and vaults outside of Russia. If, during her lifetime, she could have convinced the world that she was Anastasia, Anna Anderson would have become legal heir to that fortune. Unfortunately, with the death of this mysterious woman in the early 1980s, the opportunity to use our knowledge of molecular genetics to confirm or discard her claim has been lost.

Or has it?

There still is one possibility, one longshot that might allow confirmation of this woman's identity. The British team who recently confirmed that the bones lying in the mass grave in Ekaterinburg belonged to Tsar Nicholas, Tsarina Alexandra, and three of the couple's children has managed to obtain a lock of hair taken from the head of Anna Anderson before her death in 1984.[29] These scientists are currently attempting to extract minute quantities of DNA from this hair sample. If they succeed, it is possible that they will be able to compare Anna Anderson's mitochondrial DNA (a tiny component of the genetic material that is always inherited from the mother) with that of other known relatives of the imperial family. It is only through the use of this technique that the riddle of Anna Anderson may finally be solved.

References

1. Robert Massie, *Nicholas and Alexandra* (New York: Laurel Books, 1967), 183–86.
2. Ibid., 113.
3. G. A. Vehar, R. M. Lawn, E. G. D. Tuddenham, et al., Factor VIII and Factor V: Biochemistry and pathophysiology, in Scriver, A. Beudet, W. Sly, et al., eds., *Metabolic Basis of Inherited Diseases,* 6th ed. (New York: McGraw Hill Book Co., 1988), 2155–70.
4. O. D. Ratnoff, Hereditary disorders of hemostasis, in J. B. Stanbury, J. B. Wyngaarden, and D. S. Fredrickson, eds., *Metabolic Basis of Inherited Diseases,* 4th ed. (New York: McGraw Hill Book Co., 1978), 1755–91.
5. J. C. Otto, An account of an [sic] hemorrhagic disposition existing in certain families, *Medical Reports* 6 (1803): 1.
6. G. Mendel, Experiments in plant hybridization, reprinted in J. A. Peters, ed., *Classical Papers in Genetics* (Englewood Cliffs, N.J.: Prentice Hall, 1959).
7. J. S. Thompson and M. W. Thompson, *Genetics in Medicine,* 4th ed. (Philadelphia: W. B. Saunders Co., 1986), 1–2.
8. C. F. Nasse, Von einer erblichen Neigung zu todtlichen Blutungen, *Archivur medizinische Erfahrung im Gebiete der praktischen Medizin staatsarzneikunde, hrsg von Horn, Nasse, und Henke.* Berlin, Mai-June 5 (1820): 385.
9. A. J. Patek and F. H. C. Taylor, Hemophilia II: Some properties of a substance obtained from normal human plasma effective in accelerating the coagulation of hemophilic blood, *Journal of Clinical Investigation* 16 (1937): 113.
10. W. I. Wood, D. J. Capon, C. C. Simonson, et al., Expression of active human factor VIII from recombinant DNA clones, *Nature* 312 (1984): 330–37.

11. J. J. Toole, J. L. Knopf, J. M. Wozney, et al., Molecular cloning of a cDNA encoding human antihaemophilic factor VIII gene, *Nature* 312 (1984): 342–47.

12. J. Gitschier, The molecular basis of hemophilia A, *Annals of the New York Academy of Sciences* (1991), 614, 89–96.

13. Victor A. McKusick, The royal hemophilia, *Scientific American* 213 (August 1965): 88–95.

14. Cecil Woodham-Smith, *Queen Victoria: From Her Birth to the Death of the Prince Consort* (New York: Alfred A. Knopf, 1972), 328.

15. Massie, *Nicholas and Alexandra*, 148.

16. Ibid., 150.

17. L. E. Karp, Older fathers and genetic mutations, *American Journal of Medical Genetics* 7 (1980): 405–406.

18. C. Stoll, M. P. Roth, and P. Bigel, A re-examination of paternal age effect on the occurrence of new mutants for achondroplasia, *Progress in Clinical and Biological Research* 104 (1982): 419–26.

19. J. G. Pool and A. E. Shannon, The production of high potency concentrates of anti-hemophilic globulin in a closed bag system, *New England Journal of Medicine,* 273 (1965): 1443.

20. H. R. Robert, Factor VIII replacement therapy: Issues and future prospects, *Annals of the New York Academy of Sciences* (1991), 614, 106–113.

21. Massie, *Nicholas and Alexandra,* 202–203.

22. Ibid., 186.

23. J. B. S. Haldane, *Heredity and Politics* (New York: Norton, 1938).

24. O. Lucas, A. Finkelman, and L. M. Tocantins, Management of tooth extractions in hemophiliacs by the combined use of hypnotic suggestion, protective splints and packing of sockets, *Journal of Oral Surgery, Anesthesia and Hospital Dental Services* 20 (1963): 32–34.

25. Massie, *Nicholas and Alexandra,* 354.

26. P. Kurth, *Anastasia: The Riddle of Anna Anderson* (Boston: Little Brown and Co., 1983), xiv.

27. Ibid., 3–6.

28. Ibid., 34.

29. John Darnton, "Scientists Confirm Identification of Bones as Czar's." *The New York Times,* Saturday, July 10, 1993, 3.

30. Massie, *Nicholas and Alexandra,* 12.

31. Ibid., 41.

32. D. Radzinsky, *The Last Tsar: The Life and Death of Nicholas II* (New York: Doubleday and Co., 1992), 36.

33. W. B. Lincoln, *The Romanovs: Autocrats of All the Russians* (New York: Anchor Books, 1981) 454.

34. Massie, *Nicholas and Alexandra,* 243.

35. Kurth, *Anastasia: The Riddle,* 7–10.

36. Ibid., 32.

37. Ibid., 41.

JFK
and Compound F:
The Making of the
President, 1960

I PART I
n September 1947, while
visiting his ancestral homeland in southern Ireland, John F. Kennedy,
then a little-known freshman congressman from the eleventh district in eastern Massachusetts, fell ill with a disorder that ultimately
would have a major impact not only on his life and career, but also on
the future of American history. Weak and nauseated, suffering from
bouts of vomiting and prostration, Jack Kennedy, then just thirty years
old, found himself unable to rise from his bed in Linsmore Castle,
the twelfth-century structure that had been serving as the base of operations for the search for "lost" relatives that had brought the congressman to Ireland. Convinced that he was merely suffering from
gastroenteritis and that his condition would undoubtedly improve with
a couple of days of bed rest, a bland diet, and the continued visits with
his companion, Pamela Churchill, Kennedy decided to extend his stay
for a while longer and remained in his bed at Linsmore.

But unexpectedly over the next few days, Jack Kennedy's condition failed to improve. The young congressman actually became sicker,
his weakness and prostration worsening, his general health deteriorat-
ing, so that within seventy-two hours he had actually become critically
ill. He was evacuated to London by airplane and admitted in serious
condition to the London Clinic, where he came under the care of

168

Sir Daniel Davis, the personal physician of Lord Beaverbrook, a close friend of the congressman's father, the wealthy and powerful Joseph P. Kennedy.[1] Even on very brief examination, Dr. Davis could tell that Jack Kennedy was in trouble; the combination of marked hypotension (low blood pressure) and dehydration told the physician that Kennedy was in shock and suggested that his circulatory system was close to collapse.

A limited evaluation of Kennedy's blood was performed; in addition to confirming Dr. Davis's clinical impression, the tests revealed that the patient's serum electrolyte levels were all out of whack: the serum sodium was extremely low, and the potassium and blood urea nitrogen were dangerously elevated. But if they'd been able to measure it, the most striking abnormality in John F. Kennedy's blood would have been the serum level of cortisol—or as it was known then, Compound F—a hormone that stabilizes the functioning of the human body during times of extreme stress. It would have been expected that, in response to the congressman's as-yet-unexplained but already clearly life-threatening illness, Kennedy's adrenal glands would have manufactured buckets of cortisol. But instead, upon his admission to the London Clinic, little cortisol would have been detectable in the congressman's serum. On the basis of the clinical picture and the test results, Dr. Davis concluded that Jack Kennedy was afflicted with Addison's disease, a disorder caused by the complete destruction of the adrenal cortex, and that the congressman was at that moment suffering from a condition known as acute Addisonian crisis, a true medical emergency. "That young American friend of yours," Dr. Davis told Kennedy's companion, Pamela Churchill, "he hasn't got a year to live."[2]

Dr. Davis's pessimistic comments to Pamela Churchill were based on sound medical experience. Although the onset of Jack Kennedy's illness in September 1947 occurred more than ninety years after Dr. Thomas Addison, a British physician, first described the clinical manifestations caused by insufficient functioning of the adrenal glands,[3] at that time no adequate long-term treatment of the disorder had yet been developed. All eleven patients described by Dr. Addison in the original monograph he published in 1855 died as a result of their disease. In fact, up until the time that the young John Kennedy had been admitted to the London Clinic, every patient with adrenal insufficiency had died within a few years of his or her diagnosis.[4]

To comprehend exactly what happened to Jack Kennedy during his stay in Ireland and England, one must understand some of the basic physiologic functioning of the endocrine organs. The two adrenal glands, weighing an aggregate of only about eight grams in the adult human, sit, one each, atop the kidneys. Essential to the functioning of multiple systems, the tiny adrenals produce a series of hormones that are vital for the regulation of the body.

Each adrenal gland is actually composed of two separate organs. The inner portion, known as the medulla, is the site of production of the hormone epinephrine. Also known as adrenaline, epinephrine is essential for the "fight-or-flight" response that occurs in people under acute stress. Surges of epinephrine, released during such episodes of stress, have been known to infuse ordinary people, for at least short periods of time, with what amounts to superhuman strength. Under the influence of these surges of epinephrine, individuals have been documented to become so strong that they can singlehandedly lift an automobile that has pinned their child beneath it, or to be able to swim extraordinary distances against strong currents in short periods of time when the individual or a loved one is in danger of drowning.

But it is the outer portion of the adrenal gland, known as the cortex, that is destroyed in Addison's disease. The adrenal cortex produces three separate hormones: testosterone, the male sex hormone (though under usual conditions in the normal male, the testes manufacture the bulk of the hormone); aldosterone, originally called Compound Q, a hormone whose presence provides a signal to the kidneys that they need to retain sodium, necessary for maintenance of blood pressure within a steady range; and cortisol. Originally known as Compound F, cortisol plays many essential roles in the proper functioning of the human body and, as already mentioned, like epinephrine, is important in humans' physiologic response to massive stress.[5]

Addison's disease results when all or most of the cells that compose both of the adrenal cortices are destroyed, thus rendering the organs unable to produce these three hormones. In the 1940s, when Jack Kennedy fell ill, destruction of the glands resulted most commonly from either infection with tuberculosis or some other bacteria, or from a phenomenon known as autoimmune adrenalitis, a condition in which, for reasons still not completely understood, the immune system considers the cells of the adrenal cortex "foreign" or invading intruders and, in an attempt to protect the host, produces antibodies that destroy the adrenocortical cells.[6] Because Jack Kennedy never had a documented case of tuberculosis nor suffered from infections with meningococcus or any of the other bacteria or fungi known to cause Addison's disease, it is most likely that his disorder resulted from autoimmune adrenalitis.

Usually a disorder of gradual, insidious onset, typically found to smolder for months or years, the most striking physical feature noted in nearly every patient with Addison's disease is the deposition of dark pigment in the skin, as if the patient has developed a deep, rich tan. In fact, this increased pigmentation does result from the deposition of melanin, the substance that produces the dark bronze appearance of a suntan. However, rather than having the healthy glow that usually comes from spending time lounging on the beach, the patient with Addison's disease typically looks and feels awful: weak and lethargic, such individuals often manifest symptoms of endogenous depression and malaise. Gastrointestinal symptoms, such as nausea and vomiting, are not uncommon, and these patients usually have little or no appetite. As a result, patients almost always lose weight.[7, 8]

But occasionally, rather than the typical insidious onset, the patient with Addison's disease will be stricken as Jack Kennedy was, in spectacular fashion, with a profound, life-threatening, and often life-ending illness. The illness he suffered during his trip to Ireland, termed Addisonian crisis, represents an acute exacerbation of the chronic, underlying manifestations of the disorder. At times of acute stress, as might occur during an intercurrent illness, an emergency operation, or even during severe emotional upheaval, episodes during which the adrenal glands would be expected to rapidly produce an enormous surge of cortisol, the glands completely shut down, resulting in shock, and ultimately in death.[9] Undoubtedly, Jack Kennedy had been close to death at the time of his admission to the London Clinic. If it hadn't been for the rapid, precise care he received at the hands of Sir Daniel Davis and his colleagues, he almost certainly would not have survived.

But was Jack Kennedy's episode of Addisonian crisis during his trip to Ireland in 1947 really the beginning of his illness? The evidence suggests not. A review of the early life of the man who would become the thirty-fifth president of the United States reveals that, by the time of his trip to Ireland in 1947, he had probably been suffering from the symptoms of Addison's disease for nearly two decades.

From early in his life, Jack Kennedy's body was the target of numerous illnesses: both those, like whooping cough, measles, chicken pox, and scarlet fever, that typically affect children, and others, more mysterious and unexplained in origin, that are not so common in young people. Beginning in his early teenage years, Kennedy was hospitalized on numerous occasions for unusual symptoms and signs that seemed to defy diagnosis. Although complete medical records from this period have not been released to the public, there is evidence that some of the symptoms of Addison's disease may have been present in the future president from the time he was age thirteen.

During Kennedy's thirteenth year, while a student at the Canterbury School in New Milford, Connecticut, Jack wrote to his mother complaining about his inability to gain weight. All during this period, Jack was thin, frail, and somewhat gangly. In that letter, he informed his mother that despite every effort he'd made to fatten himself up, gorging on ice cream and other high-caloric foods, he had actually lost a pound. Trying to explain this unusual phenomenon, he wrote, "the only thing wrong with me is that I am pretty tired." To his father, he related an episode during Mass in which he "began to get sick dizzy [sic] and weak. I just about fainted and everything began to get black."[10] Although very generalized and nonspecific, this inability to gain weight, accompanied by frequent lethargy, and the near-fainting episode are all symptoms and signs consistent with early adrenal insufficiency. Although documentation is unavailable, it is quite possible that these mundane clinical features, related innocently to his parents in his weekly letters home, represent the first evidence of adrenal insufficiency in the adolescent Jack Kennedy.

And later, at the age of sixteen, after he'd left Canterbury and enrolled at Choate, another prep school in Connecticut, Jack Kennedy again became ill, this time with a mysterious disorder that caused him to develop hives all over his body, to have nausea and anorexia, and to have significantly abnormal findings on blood tests (the actual abnormalities are not known; they are part of the unreleased medical records). Because of the illness, Jack was admitted to New Haven Hospital, where despite spending nearly the entire month of February 1934 as an inpatient, no diagnosis could be established. At the end of that month, with his skin finally clear of its itchy rash but with his body emaciated from his inability to tolerate food, his continued blood abnormalities, and his general condition still weak and debilitated, he was finally discharged from the hospital. Forced because of all the work he'd missed during his hospitalization to take a leave of absence from school, Jack spent the rest of that winter at his parents' now-infamous estate in Palm Beach, Florida, having his blood monitored on a regular basis and, so that he would not fall far behind his classmates, receiving daily tutoring.

Although these winter months spent in the warm and soothing sun of southern Florida offered a period of convalescence for the inexplicably ill adolescent, his medical condition apparently failed to show any significant improvement: during the early part of the summer of 1934, a full six months after his initial admission to New Haven Hospital, Jack was again admitted to a hospital, this time to the world-famous Mayo Clinic in Rochester, Minnesota. And again, despite a month spent as a patient in that renowned facility, undergoing what must have amounted to a mammoth number of state-of-the-art tests, Jack Kennedy's underlying condition continued to remain undiagnosed. But while no definitive treatment could be offered and no explanation given, the young man's clinical condition gradually began to improve. By September 1934 he was back at Choate, having somehow managed, despite all the work he'd missed, to get himself promoted from the fifth to the sixth form.[11]

Could this mysterious, persistently difficult-to-diagnose illness also have represented the early manifestations of Addison's disease? Most of the symptoms and signs from which Kennedy suffered during the first half of 1934, including his unexplained lethargy, weakness, anorexia, and his continued emaciated appearance, all point in that direction. But what of the rash that apparently heralded the onset of the illness, the symptom for which Jack was initially admitted to the hospital in Connecticut? Hives are not a cardinal feature of Addison's disease; however, it's possible that this complaint represented the dermatologic manifestations of some viral illness, an infection such as chicken pox or rubella (so-called German measles) that provided a sufficient amount of physical stress to trigger Jack Kennedy's clinically smoldering adrenal insufficiency. As already mentioned, such stressful events are known to produce clinical flare-ups in individuals affected with Addison's disease. And what of the aberration found on testing of Kennedy's blood? Unfortunately, because the records are currently unavailable, it is impossible to offer any coherent clinical explanation for these findings. However, it certainly is possible that the abnormality actually represented a disturbance in Jack's blood electrolyte level, a change that may have reflected an incipient deficiency of aldosterone.

Even though he was well enough to return to school in September 1934, Jack was far from cured of the mysterious illness that had led to his two hospitalizations in February and July of that year. After his return to Choate, his condition continued to wax and wane over the next few years. Relapses of the illness, a disorder that George St. John, the headmaster at Choate, referred to as "that rotten bug,"[12] occurred repeatedly during the remainder of Kennedy's high school career. And following his graduation from Choate in June 1935, at the start of a planned year of study at the London School of Economics, Jack Kennedy's health again took a dramatic turn for the worse. Feeling too ill to continue, he was forced to drop out of his program and return home. This time, in addition to the lethargy and weakness, the weight loss and anorexia, a new feature was added. While in England, Jack was said to have developed "jaundice," a yellow discoloration of the skin.[13] Thus, during this illness, which quite likely represented yet another flare-up of his adrenal insufficiency, note was made for the first time of the darkening of Jack Kennedy's skin, the increase in pigmentation that is a hallmark of Addison's disease.

Following his return from England in November 1935, Jack Kennedy again attempted to continue his schooling, this time as a freshman at Princeton University. And once again, his health refused to cooperate; in December of that year, after becoming so lethargic and weak that he simply did not have the strength to continue at school, Kennedy was admitted to the prestigious Peter Bent Brigham Hospital in Boston, where he remained as an inpatient under the care of Dr. William P. Murphy, a Boston internist, for two months. And yet again, despite this stay at the hospital, during which time still more testing was performed, the cause of Kennedy's condition apparently continued to elude detection.[14]

Kennedy's hospitalization at the Brigham, and his subsequent convalescence in Arizona, cost him an entire school year. After withdrawing from Princeton, he gained admission to Harvard, where, in the fall of 1936, he began his freshman year. Described at that time as a "lank, bony six-foot-tall youth who looked even lighter than his 149 pounds,"[15] Jack was clearly embarrassed by and somewhat sensitive about his painfully thin physique. He continued to work hard at gaining weight, consuming massive amounts of ice cream, but his gawkiness and inability to add any bulk to his frame persisted all through his college years.

During his years at Harvard, Jack Kennedy managed to remain relatively healthy. In fact, his time in Cambridge was punctuated by only a single recurrence of the mysterious illness. During the spring of 1937, he was again hospitalized, this time in Harvard's Stillman Infirmary. The symptoms were apparently short-lived during this episode, and Kennedy lost no school time as a result of his incapacity.[16] But following his graduation from Harvard, Jack's health again deteriorated, forcing him, once again, to take a year off; during this period, Jack moved to California and audited classes at the Stanford School of Business Administration.

Following the outbreak of World War II, after his older brother, Joseph P. Kennedy, Jr., having enlisted in the Naval Aviation Cadet Program, had been sworn in as a seaman second class in the U.S. Naval

Reserve, Jack tried desperately to enlist in the armed forces. Because of his chronically poor health and the weakened condition of his body after years of suffering from this mysterious disease, Jack failed his physical examination for the Army Officers' Candidate School and was rejected outright by this branch. Initially, when he attempted to enlist in the navy, his application met with the same fate. But following the helpful intervention of his politically powerful father, Jack reapplied to this branch and finally was accepted to the Navy Officers' Training School. After his swearing-in on September 25, 1941, he received his commission as an ensign.[17] "Thus, a young man who could certainly not have qualified for the Sea Scouts on his physical condition, entered the U.S. Navy," Clay and Joan Blair noted in their biography of Kennedy.[18]

Despite his well-documented poor health and the question of whether he should have been admitted to the armed forces under any conditions, John F. Kennedy's well-publicized exploits in the South Pacific as the commander of *PT Boat 109* during the summer of 1943 made him an undeniable war hero, an attribute that would ultimately strongly boost his future career in politics. The combination of heroism, responsibility for the men under his command, and the leadership skills he exhibited during those stressful days in the South Pacific provided all the proof the American public would need to convince them that Kennedy had the "right stuff" to be president of the United States. But the toll the episode took on Kennedy's body, especially on his already-damaged adrenal glands, would prove to be incalculable.

The subject of a book written by Robert Donovan that was made into a popular film in the early 1960s, the story of *PT 109* is well known. After his patrol ship was literally split in two by the Japanese destroyer *Amigari* during the early morning hours of August 2, 1943, Kennedy expended tremendous, perhaps superhuman, strength and energy, demonstrating remarkable stamina and determination, in his efforts to save himself and the men under his command. Swimming by night, finding shelter during the day, hiding from both the Japanese and the sharks indigenous to those waters, and surviving on little more than their wits and the kindness of the natives, Kennedy and his crew were finally rescued on August 7.[19] During the five-day ordeal, Jack

Kennedy suffered numerous injuries. Superficially, he had festering wounds on his skin, the effect of stepping on exposed coral. But below the surface, he had sustained some unseen but extremely serious medical problems that would plague him for the remainder of his life.

First, there was his back injury. Soon after he and his men were rescued, X-rays of his back revealed that the commander of *PT 109* had suffered significant damage to one of the jelly-like disks that separate two of the vertebrae in the lumbar region of his spine.[20] This injury, though not life-threatening, could, because of its critical location in the lower portion of the spine, lead to chronic, unremitting pain and life-long disability; thus, the damaged disk required prompt and expert attention. Surgery was indicated, and in order to get the best result, the procedure needed to be performed quickly.

The operation was carried out at the Lahey Clinic in Boston, and by all accounts it did not go well.[21] Following his discharge from the clinic, Kennedy required months of rehabilitation at the Chelsea Naval Hospital. But despite all that was done for him during those months in the hospital, the final result of the treatment was certainly much worse than had been hoped for: Jack Kennedy was in constant pain; he required the use of a cumbersome back brace and crutches for walking even the shortest distance. And the eight-inch wound that had been created by the surgeons never did heal properly: it remained open and painful for years afterward. A friend noted that "you could look into it and see the metal plate that had been put into his spine."[22] The back ailment proved to be so severe and so disabling that, less than ten years later, it would ultimately lead to a significant personal crisis in the life of Jack Kennedy.

Next, there is evidence that Kennedy came back from the South Pacific with a case of malaria, probably due to an infection with the protozoan known as *Plasmodium falciparum*.[23] This infection, characterized by episodes of high fever occurring in forty-eight hour cycles (corresponding to the life cycle of the protozoan), is amenable to treatment with antimalarial drugs such as chloroquine.[24] As would be expected of someone with adrenal insufficiency, without the necessary reserves of cortisol to mount an adequate response to illnesses, Jack Kennedy became quite ill when his malaria would periodically flare up:

"I've never seen anyone so sick in my life," Pat Lannan, a friend who was with Kennedy in London in 1945, wrote. "He had a hell of a high fever."[25]

But some controversy exists surrounding this illness, because one of the drugs Kennedy was given for control of his infection, Atabrine (quinicrine), is known to cause a yellow discoloration of the skin.[26] In his biography of Kennedy, Herbert Parmet notes: "His greenish complexion, a result of Atabrine . . . , was common gossip among the Washington correspondents who knew him at the time."[27] Whether the abnormal pigmentation of Jack Kennedy's skin following World War II was a consequence of his treatment with Atabrine or still another manifestation of his as-yet-undiagnosed Addison's disease is not clear.

Although we can't be certain of the exact events, it's not really difficult, in the mid-1990s, to imagine what must have gone through Jack Kennedy's mind back in the late 1940s after he'd been diagnosed with Addison's disease by Dr. Davis in London. In September 1988, while working with a group of first-year students in a course called "Introduction to Clinical Medicine," I interviewed Patrick Sullivan, a thirty-year-old man whose AIDS had only recently been diagnosed. Pat, a set designer for Broadway shows, had been in excellent health until three months before, when he'd developed pneumonia and had been placed on a ventilator in the intensive care unit of one of our affiliated hospitals. He had spent over a month in the hospital and, upon discharge, was too weak to work. But despite the grim prognosis and the fact that nearly a dozen of his friends had already succumbed to the disease, Pat remained surprisingly upbeat and optimistic. "I know there's nothing they can do to cure me right now," he told the group of students when I got around to asking him about the future, "but there's a lot of research going on all over the world. It's only a matter of time before somebody figures out something that'll help. So I know if I can just hold on long enough, something will come along to help me. If I can just stay healthy, I'm almost positive somebody will come up with a cure in the next few years."

Because of his intensity, conviction, and his striking physical presence (he had bright red hair and was 6 feet, 4 inches tall), the students were mesmerized by him. Pat went on to tell them his plans for remaining healthy. "I've pared down my life to only those things that I think are important. I've tried to cut out all external stresses. I've completely changed my diet: I've gone macrobiotic. I've given up meat and fish, and eat nothing that has any preservatives or chemicals in it. I try to go to the gym and work out whenever I'm feeling strong enough, and I've started meditating again. Even though I don't have the stamina I used to, I feel better than I have in years."

When the interview ended, I gave Pat my office phone number and asked him, if he didn't mind, to call and check in with me periodically, so that I could keep the students updated on his progress. During the weeks following the interview, the students and I discussed Pat again and again: he had convinced all of us that if anyone could beat AIDS, he would be the one.

During that academic year, I heard from Pat only once: he called in January to tell me that he'd recently been hospitalized with what was thought to be pneumonia but turned out to be only a bad case of bronchitis. "When I first got sick, I was feeling so bad, I thought, 'Please God, just let me die.' But then, by the next day, I was up and around again." Over the phone, his voice sounded different from the way I'd remembered it; I could almost feel that he had lost that exuberant optimism that had flowed from him just four months before.

Pat's final call came nearly one year later, in January 1990. He telephoned from his room in the hospital in which I work. Sounding weak and obviously short of breath, he asked me to come and see him. Without hesitation, I took the elevator up to the seventh floor, the ward that in recent years had been reserved for patients in the terminal stages of AIDS. After asking for his location at the nurses' station, I went to find his bed. If not for his still-bright red hair, I never would have recognized him.

He was obviously critically ill; emaciated, with an oxygen mask covering his face, Pat was using every bit of his strength attempting to get air into his lungs. Because of his shortness of breath, our

179

conversation was necessarily very brief. "I always saved your number," he told me, his voice not much louder than a whisper. "I wanted to call you so you could tell those students I was cured." He laughed a little at that point and shook his head. "What was I thinking about?"

Pat Sullivan died two days later.

In 1947, although affected with a markedly different disease, Jack Kennedy faced the same grim prognosis that Pat Sullivan faced in 1988. Like Pat, knowledge that he had an incurable illness had to color the way Jack Kennedy lived every day of his life. It had to affect not only the mundane decisions he made, such as what he would eat and how and when he would exercise, but also how he would approach his work and his personal relationships. But two factors probably created a difference between the way Pat Sullivan responded to his diagnosis and the way Jack Kennedy responded to his. First, because of the years of suffering that had preceded his diagnosis, Jack Kennedy already had a fairly well-developed understanding of what life with adrenal insufficiency was like. As a result, it is reasonable to think that he must have had a pretty good impression of what the future would bring: worsening symptoms, progressive weakness, until, ultimately, a serious infection, injury, or other stressful experience would come along and suddenly end his life.

A second factor that set Jack Kennedy's illness apart from Pat Sullivan's (at least at its outset) is that adrenal insufficiency is known to cause neuropsychological dysfunction. Lack of cortisol has been shown to cause symptoms such as depression, psychosis, and even delirium.[8, 28] These symptoms are reflected in abnormal patterns of brain waves: nearly every patient with untreated Addison's disease manifests abnormalities on electroencephalograms. So following his diagnosis, it is understandable that Jack Kennedy might not have gone through the same initial optimistic phase of his illness that Pat Sullivan apparently had.

In fact, the record shows that, in the days following his diagnosis, Jack Kennedy readily acknowledged the fact that he was dying. He adopted a fatalistic attitude, informing his friend, journalist Joseph Alsop, that he was suffering from "a sort of slow-motion leukemia" and that he expected to die in his early forties.[29] During this period,

Kennedy apparently lost a great deal of his political ambition as well, simply "going through the motions" of being a congressman. When the leaders of the Democratic Party in Massachusetts asked him to consider running for governor in 1948, Jack declined, choosing instead to remain in congress.[30] In fact, considering the depressed state he appeared to be in during early 1948, it's even possible that, had it not been for the pressure from his father and other family members, Jack Kennedy might have quit politics altogether, resigned his seat in Congress, and gone back to Hyannis or Palm Beach, to live out what remained of his life in relative obscurity.

But unlike Pat Sullivan, fate, in the form of a significant medical breakthrough, shined down on Jack Kennedy and spared him from what was believed to be the inevitable outcome of his disease. Before Kennedy had a chance to suffer a second Addisonian crisis, before his life was prematurely ended by the effects of his profound adrenal insufficiency, a treatment was developed and marketed, a "wonder drug" that, taken orally every day of his life, would ultimately give Jack Kennedy back his health, returning his stamina and strength, offering relief from his chronic inability to gain weight and other gastrointestinal symptoms, and, ultimately, changing him from a shy, withdrawn, and emaciated man into an outgoing, gregarious, moon-faced future president of the United States.

That "wonder drug" was orally administered Compound F, now known as cortisone. At the time of his diagnosis back in 1947, Jack Kennedy was offered treatment with the only adrenocortical hormone then available for replacement therapy, 11-desoxycorticosterone acetate, or DOCA. First synthesized in 1937, DOCA is a mineralocorticoid, one of the hormones essential for the maintenance of the body's salt balance.[31] As such, DOCA serves as a replacement for aldosterone, or Compound Q. But DOCA, which is administered not by mouth but as gravel-sized pellets implanted under the skin, gradually breaking down and releasing the hormone into the bloodstream over a prolonged period of time, has no glucocorticoid effect; as such, it therefore cannot function as a replacement for vitally important cortisone.

But Jack Kennedy was undoubtedly happy to get any treatment for his disease. The congressman began to implant these DOCA pellets, in 150-milligram concentrations, just under the skin of his thigh. To protect against a possible international shortage of the medication, the Kennedy family established secret stashes of the pellets in safety-deposit boxes throughout the United States.[32] By maintaining his blood sodium concentration within a relatively steady range, the DOCA pellets probably were effective in preventing the recurrence of an Addisonian crisis and, as such, undoubtedly lengthened Kennedy's life. But, as expected, they offered no relief from the other symptoms of adrenal insufficiency: even under the influence of DOCA, Jack Kennedy remained weak, lethargic, extremely underweight, and hyperpigmented. Photographs of him taken during the late 1940s (figure 1) show a gaunt, frail, sickly looking man who seems significantly older than his age.

In 1946, just one year before Jack Kennedy found himself lying helplessly near death in the London Clinic, Dr. Lewis H. Sarett, a biochemist working for the Merck Pharmaceutical Company, produced a partially synthetic form of cortisone, or Compound F, as it was then known.[33] By 1950 Sarett's preparation, having been tested, found to be effective, and approved for use by the Food and Drug Administration, reached the American market. One of the first patients to use the drug was Jack Kennedy. And, as would be expected, the cortisone had dramatic effects on virtually all aspects of the congressman's life. Within weeks of the first treatment, Kennedy's clinical state would have been expected to show striking improvement: the record shows that he began gaining weight, and for the first time since early childhood, his frame began to fill out. His anorexia, nausea, and other nonspecific gastrointestinal symptoms undoubtedly disappeared. Virtually overnight, he

Figure 1. (top) In the late 1940s, Jack Kennedy illustrated the cumulative effects of nearly two decades of adrenal insufficiency on his body: This photo shows the twenty-nine-year-old congressman in 1946, prior to the episode of Addisonian crisis that nearly ended his life in Ireland in September 1947; (bottom) a photo taken on February 10, 1948, shows Kennedy, standing among a group of candidates for U.S. military academies, just three months after his release from the London Clinic.
Photos from the John F. Kennedy Library, Boston.

183

184

must have developed renewed stamina and strength. His mood would also have been expected to dramatically lift, his depression and feelings of aimlessness and fatalism replaced by a newfound exuberance and strong sense of ambition. Even his libido was undoubtedly improved. Many of these changes are reflected in the appearance of his face in photographs from that period (figure 2): in these later pictures, Jack Kennedy looks like a new man, younger, huskier, and healthier than the pre-1950 model; his face, rounded into the "moon-shaped" appearance typical of individuals taking cortisone, displays the classic Kennedy smile. This simple pill containing 25 milligrams of cortisone, taken once daily,[34] turned Jack Kennedy's life around.

In her book *On Death and Dying*, Elisabeth Kuebler-Ross outlines the psychological stages through which an individual affected with a lethal disease passes from diagnosis to death. But what of the patient who expects to die but is ultimately spared by some miracle? How does such an individual respond psychologically to both his recovery and to the way he lives the rest of his life?

Because of the nature of the medication he received, Jack Kennedy's response may not have been completely typical. While, as stated above, cortisone deficiency is known to cause depression and other psychological disturbances, the onset of treatment replacing the missing hormones frequently leads to a state of euphoria lasting months or even years. But whether his reaction was drug-induced or a natural consequence of the unexpected resolution of his disease, or both, after cortisone treatment began, Jack Kennedy underwent a major personality change.

Figure 2. (top) During his candidacy for the U.S. Senate in 1952, Jack Kennedy is surrounded by his siblings (from left) Jean, Pat, Bobby, and Eunice; (bottom) Kennedy, in 1952. Just two years after the introduction of cortisone, the congressman's appearance is strikingly changed; now moon-faced and smiling, he looks more like the Jack Kennedy who would become our thirty-fifth president.
Photos from the John F. Kennedy Library, Boston.

In the early 1950s, three significant alterations occurred in Kennedy's life. The first was his marriage. Although he had met Jacqueline Bouvier a few times prior to 1950, neither had made much of an impression on the other. But then, in the spring of 1951, as guests at a dinner party in the Washington home of Charles and Martha Bartlett, Jack and Ms. Bouvier met again, and apparently Kennedy's interest was sparked. The courtship did not get off to a memorable start: Jacqueline was at that time romantically involved with John G. W. Husted, Jr., a Manhattan stockbroker.[35] But then, following his election to the Senate in 1952, Kennedy turned his now sharply focused attention and suddenly limitless energy to winning Ms. Bouvier's hand. And, as would become the rule for the post-1950 Jack Kennedy, he eventually got his way: the couple was married at St. Mary's Roman Catholic Church in Newport, Rhode Island, on September 12, 1953.[36]

The second major change in Jack Kennedy's life following the introduction of orally administered cortisone was the reemergence of his dormant political ambition. After the struggles of the late 1940s, when he'd failed to act on his party's support for a run at the governorship of Massachusetts, after he'd appeared to become complaisant in remaining as the congressman representing the eleventh district for the rest of his life, Jack Kennedy started to approach his political career as if he was going places. And so, on the evening of Sunday, April 6, 1952, Kennedy announced his candidacy for the Senate seat then occupied by Republican Henry Cabot Lodge.[37]

Kennedy ran his race at a breakneck pace. Despite the fact that, as a result of the chronic lumbar spinal injury that continued to plague him six years after his failed surgery at Lahey Clinic, he required the use of crutches to support himself while ambulating much of the time, and that he was in constant, often excruciating pain, the congressman drove himself on as never before. Jack did everything he could, and used all of the resources availed him by his rich and powerful father, to beat the incumbent Lodge. He traveled the state, from Boston to Pittsfield, shaking hands, giving speeches, working to convince the electorate that, rather than a spoiled, rich son of Joseph P. Kennedy, he was a man of the people.

There were times during that campaign when it appeared as if Jack Kennedy simply wasn't going to make it. "At a Springfield fire station he succumbed to the impulse to demonstrate his agility by sliding down a fire pole from the third floor to the first. When he hit the bottom, he doubled up in pain. But still he tried to keep his agony private."[38] There were times when he'd stand on receiving lines greeting the public for hours, while in unbearable discomfort. Merely walking to and from the podium during a speaking engagement was enough to cause him intense agony.[38] But somehow driven, he kept on to the end; all the while, his medical problems were kept from the people of the state, who were never even allowed a glimpse of Kennedy using crutches.

Why would Jack Kennedy endure all this? What would cause a man who was so severely impaired to carry on? Could simple political ambition alone have produced the dedicated campaigner that Jack Kennedy became in 1952? Such a conclusion would seem unlikely. After all, this was the same man who had passed up the opportunity to run for a similarly prestigious office when offered to him just four years before. Rather, it appears more probable that this newfound political ambition was in some way related to the medication that had commuted the death sentence imposed upon him in the early fall of 1947. Now, under the influence of adequate levels of cortisone, Jack Kennedy seemed to believe that he could accomplish virtually any goal in the world, and he propelled himself mercilessly. And in the general election on November 6, 1952, he went on to beat Henry Cabot Lodge by 70,000 votes.[39]

The campaigns Kennedy waged both for his Senate seat and for the hand of Jacqueline Bouvier took a significant physical toll on the young politician's body, and that led to the third significant change in his life during the early 1950s: the chronic back condition that had afflicted him since the *PT 109* episode deteriorated dramatically. Although during 1952 Kennedy was in nearly constant pain, requiring the use of crutches for ambulation, by 1954, the degenerative spinal condition had significantly worsened. The constant pain had become so intense that the senator could no longer bear to walk the long marble halls between the Senate chamber and his office. For the first time since his

187

election, rather than return to his office, he chose to remain in the Senate chamber between quorum calls.[40] Something clearly had to be done.

In January 1954 Kennedy visited Dr. Philip D. Wilson, a noted orthopedic surgeon affiliated with New York's Hospital for Special Surgery.[40] It appears that, because of the risks of operating on a patient with Addison's disease, Dr. Wilson was reluctant to recommend that Kennedy undergo any type of surgery; it is likely that the surgeon advised his patient, before committing to any type of operation, to explore all nonsurgical methods of alleviating the pain and debilitation. But despite all the bed rest, hot baths, and physical therapy recommended by Dr. Wilson, Senator Kennedy apparently found little, if any, relief. In early July 1954, his condition had deteriorated to the point that he required admission to the Bethesda Naval Hospital for intensive treatment. It seemed that surgery, in the form of a spinal fusion, could be put off no longer. So, on October 10, 1954, Jack Kennedy was admitted to the Hospital for Special Surgery in preparation for a life-threatening operation that, if successful, would return to him a portion of his life taken away eleven years before in the South Pacific.[41]

Dr. Wilson's hesitation to recommend surgery to Jack Kennedy certainly made a great deal of medical sense. As already mentioned, one of the more important roles played by the hormones secreted by the adrenal glands is to maintain the body's homeostasis during times of stress. Normally, during an acute illness or following severe trauma, the adrenals produce a surge of cortisol and epinephrine. Because their adrenal cortices have been destroyed, individuals with Addison's disease cannot produce such a cortisol surge; as a result, during such times of stress, they typically develop an acute Addisonian crisis.

Although by 1954, Jack Kennedy was being maintained quite well on a daily dose of cortisone, surgery still represented a major problem. Since his adrenal glands were unable to respond to stress, Kennedy was still at great risk for developing Addisonian crisis. Upon learning of Kennedy's medical history, the following scenario undoubtedly played itself out in Dr. Wilson's mind: anesthesia is induced; an initial midline incision is made in the lower portion of the senator's back; the spinal fusion is begun; suddenly the anesthesiologist shouts that he can't get a blood pressure reading; despite all efforts to resuscitate him, Senator Kennedy dies on the operating table almost before the surgery has even begun.

But faced with the combination of a chronic condition that was refractory to any form of nonsurgical treatment and a patient who, perhaps because he believed himself invincible, refused to take no for an answer, Dr. Wilson and his team probably felt that they really had little choice. Reluctantly, they decided to proceed.

Because of the rarity with which elective surgery had been performed in patients with Addison's disease, and because of surgical complications in such patients in the past, the operation performed on Senator Kennedy was notable enough to be reported in an article written by Dr. Wilson and his colleagues and published in the journal *Archives of Surgery*.[41] Although not identified by name, Kennedy appears in that article as Case 3, described as "a patient with adrenal insufficiency due to Addison's disease requiring elective surgery." Thus, perhaps for the first and only time in the history of the United States, a president-to-be, because of the ground-breaking work that was performed on him and not because of his celebrity, was included in a scientific article that appears in the medical literature.

The *Archives of Surgery* article identifies Case 3 as a "man 37 years of age" who has had "Addison's disease for seven years" and who, "owing to a back injury, . . . had a great deal of pain that interfered with his daily routine." The article reports that an orthopedist suggested that the patient's condition might be improved by "lumbosacral fusion together with sacroiliac fusion," but that "because of the severe degree of trauma involved in these operations" coupled with the fact that the patient had severe adrenal insufficiency, "it was deemed dangerous to proceed." Surgery was performed, however, only "reluctantly" as the paper points out, because the patient would otherwise become completely incapacitated.

After his admission to the Hospital for Special Surgery on October 10, Kennedy was seen in consultation by Dr. Ephraim Shorr, an endocrinologist on the staff of New York Hospital. A workup was performed and Kennedy's complete medical condition assessed. Dr. Shorr suggested a regimen for the management of the senator's Addison's disease that included a switch from his orally administered cortisone tablets to hydrocortisone, an intravenous form of cortisol. The reason for this change was simple: during the perioperative period, while under anesthesia, Kennedy would be able to take nothing, neither nourishment nor medication, by mouth. Intravenous medication for maintenance of his adrenocorticosteroid level was therefore imperative.

During the week prior to the surgery, Kennedy's intravenous hydrocortisone dose was fine-tuned. On October 20, twenty-four hours before the surgery was scheduled to begin, a large dose, consisting of 100 milligrams of hydrocortisone, was given in preparation for the oncoming stress. That evening, twelve hours later, a second "stress dose" of 100 milligrams of hydrocortisone was administered intravenously.

On the morning of October 21, 1954, Kennedy's surgery began. As his vital signs were carefully monitored, anesthesia was induced; the skin of his back was opened, and using a surgical-steel device he developed called, appropriately, a Wilson plate, Dr. Wilson surgically fused the bodies of the lumbosacral spine; because the senator's vital signs remained stable during this phase, with his blood pressure persistently in the range of 100/64 millimeters of mercury, his pulse around 72 beats per minute, the surgeons decided to proceed with the second part of the operation, the fusion of the sacroiliac, or terminal portion of the spine. (Apparently, although Dr. Wilson and his colleagues had been reluctant to promise anything, Kennedy had urged them to perform both procedures, usually done in separate operations, at the same time.) During the procedure, a marathon event that went on for most of the daylight hours of October 21, the anesthesiologist administered to the senator a third stress dose of hydrocortisone, two full liters of blood ("to compensate for a similar amount of blood loss produced by the" procedures), and a liter of normal saline solution (to prevent circulatory collapse due to loss of sodium), all given intravenously. Following closure of the skin, Kennedy was transported to the recovery room and eventually back to the floor.

Although the article in *Archives of Surgery* states that "the postoperative course was satisfactory in that no Addisonian crisis developed at any time," the days just after the surgery were not easy ones for members of the Kennedy family. On the third postoperative day, due to the presence of a Foley catheter, a tube placed through the urethra and into the bladder that allowed strict monitoring of urinary output, Kennedy developed a urinary tract infection that appeared to be resistant to conventional antibiotic therapy. According to Parmet, "the situation seemed grave. Kennedy slipped into a coma and was placed on the critical list. His father . . . weeping . . . said that he thought Jack was dying."[42] Sensing that the end was near, the family rushed to the senator's bedside and the last rites of the Roman Catholic Church were given. But then, one of the antibiotics finally began to work, the infection started to clear, and, yet again, for the third time in his life, Kennedy was rescued from what seemed like certain death.

During the postoperative period, Kennedy's condition was closely monitored by Dr. Shorr, the endocrinologist from New York Hospital. At the time of his urinary tract infection, and during two other postoperative complications (the development of an infection in the wound, and an allergic reaction to a blood transfusion), Kennedy was empirically treated with extra doses of steroids to cover the potentially stressful situations. The senator's recovery was almost agonizingly slow: gradually, he was switched back to his usual dose of orally administered cortisone; slowly, while he lay on his belly in a grossly uncomfortable position, his wound healed and the spinal fixation became firmer and more stable. Finally, on December 21, 1954, he was well enough to leave the hospital. After more than ten weeks as an inpatient at the Hospital for Special Surgery, two months to the day after the team of surgeons led by Dr. Wilson had fused his spine, Jack Kennedy was discharged. Lying face down on a stretcher, he was flown by private plane to Florida, where, as he had done twenty-one years before following his discharge from New Haven Hospital while a student at Choate, he spent the winter recuperating in his parents' home in Palm Beach.

His winter was punctuated by two more hospitalizations: on February 10, he returned, as scheduled, to the operating room at the Hospital for Special Surgery to have the Wilson plate removed from his spine and to have a bony fusion of the region performed; and on April 26, he was admitted to New York Hospital for some further endocrinologic

191

testing administered by Dr. Shorr. Then on Tuesday, May 24, 1955, after months of recuperation, Jack Kennedy returned to the floor of the Senate.[43] But although he was back in Washington, the senator was far from healthy: the surgery had taken a tremendous toll on him.

During the next few months, surreptitiously, Kennedy was admitted for rehabilitation to both the New York Hospital (from May 26 to June 1) and to the New England Baptist Hospital (from July 3 to 10). He traveled from Washington to New York virtually every weekend for outpatient therapy under the supervision of Dr. Janet Travell, a New York Hospital–based physician who treated his recurrent muscle spasms, a biproduct of the spinal fusion and the prolonged period of inactivity that followed the surgery, with injections of Novacaine.[44] (Dr. Travell's treatment protocol would be controversial by current standards; today, instead of injecting the muscles with an anesthetic agent, such postoperative symptomatology would be treated with a course of vigorous physical therapy, directed toward exercising the affected muscles into proper functioning.) During all of this medically related activity, the driven Jack Kennedy's political activities were steadily increasing. There were speeches to give, hands to shake, fact-finding trips to take.

In October 1955, a full year after his admission to the Hospital for Special Surgery, Kennedy returned from a trip to Europe finally feeling better.[45] At last he had managed to put the surgery and the postoperative recuperative period behind him. Like his Addison's disease, against all odds, against the predictions of the physicians who had cared for him and advised against surgery, against the harsh realities of the reported outcome of such surgery in patients with Addison's disease that had appeared in the medical literature, Kennedy had licked his debilitating spinal injury. Although it had perhaps been more difficult than he'd ever imagined, the successful outcome of the spinal surgery may have had a secondary effect on John F. Kennedy: besides freeing him from pain and disability, conquering his back problem probably reinforced Jack Kennedy's feelings that he was invincible, that he could accomplish any goal.

And as would be expected of a politician who believed he'd been rendered invincible, the next four years saw the continuing, unprecedented rise of Jack Kennedy's political star. In rapid fashion, not only did he achieve national attention, but he and Jacqueline, according to reporter Fletcher Knebel, became Washington's "hottest tourist attraction."[46] At the 1956 Democratic National Convention in Chicago, Kennedy was awarded the honor of placing the name of Adlai Stevenson, the ultimate Democratic candidate for president that year, into nomination.[47] Kennedy delivered a rousing speech witnessed by tens of millions of television viewers, an event that immediately thrust him into the national spotlight. In 1957 he won the Pulitzer Prize in the category of biography for *Profiles in Courage*,[48] a book of case studies about senators who, acting with courage and patriotism, had chosen routes that were often unpopular and against conventional wisdom in order to achieve what amounted to the national good;[49] *Profiles in Courage* had remained on *The New York Times* nonfiction best-seller list for well over a year.[50] And in 1958, in a landslide victory over his Republican opponent, Vincent J. Celeste, Kennedy was reelected to the Senate.[51] By the late 1950s, it must have seemed virtually certain to Jack Kennedy that, after all he'd been through, after nearly dying in the shark-infested waters of the South Pacific and then later on the wards and in the operating theatres of both the London Clinic and the Hospital for Special Surgery, the next step in his career was inevitable: it was time to set his sights on the Oval Office.

> I dreamed about 1960 myself the other night, and I told Stuart Symington and Lyndon Johnson about it in the cloakroom yesterday. I told them how the Lord came into my bedroom, anointed my head, and said "John Kennedy, I appoint you President of the United States." Stu Symington said: "That's strange, Jack, because I, too, had a similar dream last night, in which the Lord anointed me and declared Stuart Symington President of the United States *and* outer space." And Lyndon Johnson said: "That's very interesting, gentlemen: because I, too, had a similar dream last night—and I don't remember anointing either of you."
> —John F. Kennedy, addressing the annual dinner of the Gridiron Club, Washington, D.C., 1958

And so it was. After announcing his intentions to seek the Democratic nomination on January 2, 1960, Kennedy, who probably only jokingly believed that God was actually talking to him, entered the primaries in West Virginia, New Hampshire, Indiana, Wisconsin, Nebraska, Maryland, Pennsylvania, and California, and he won them all. By the time the Democratic National Convention opened in Los Angeles on July 11, Jack Kennedy held a commanding lead over his only announced opponent, Senator Hubert H. Humphrey of Minnesota. Although Adlai Stevenson, the perennial Democratic presidential candidate of the 1950s, made an attempt to steal the nomination away from Kennedy, he fell far short.[52] Jack Kennedy won on the first ballot and went on to narrowly defeat Richard M. Nixon in the general presidential election of November 1960, thus becoming the thirty-fifth president of the United States.

While the conquest of his Addison's disease probably played a significant role in Jack Kennedy's political rise of the 1950s and early 1960s, sadly, his resulting feelings of invincibility may have played a role in his death at midday on November 22, 1963. For on that morning, apparently despite warnings from the Secret Service and the FBI, Kennedy vulnerably rode through the streets of Dallas in a convertible limousine that rendered him a proverbial sitting duck for his assassin. Apparently the president expected nothing untoward to happen to him that morning. "I thought they'd get one of us," Robert Kennedy told Ed Guthman immediately after learning of his brother's assassination. "But Jack, after all he'd been through, never worried about it."[53]

Although he was struck by at least two bullets, President Kennedy probably would have died after the first shot entered the soft tissue of his neck. After all, he had Addison's disease; his body wouldn't have been able to produce the cortisol necessary to respond to the stress that gunshot wound had caused. Of course, if that had been his only wound and he had been given an immediate infusion of intravenous hydrocortisone upon his arrival at the emergency room at Parkland General Hospital, he might have survived the initial injury. But since Kennedy's adrenal insufficiency had been largely kept a family secret, did the doctors who cared for him during those frantic minutes even know about it? Would they have even suspected that the president might lapse into immediate Addisonian crisis? Of course, this issue is moot: the wound caused by the second bullet that struck the president, the bullet that penetrated his skull, destroyed most of the right hemisphere of Jack Kennedy's cerebral cortex; no dose of steroids could have saved him from the effects of that mortal blow.

In the days before the start of the Democratic National Convention in Los Angeles in July 1960, Lyndon Johnson, never a declared candidate but a senator who had hoped to benefit from Adlai Stevenson's interference in the nominating process, began to circulate rumors that Kennedy, because of his history of poor health, was not fit to serve as president of the United States. Describing the Massachusetts senator as "a scrawny little fellow with rickets," Johnson had his lieutenant, John Connally, the governor of Texas—who, ironically, would be riding in the car with the president three years later on that fateful day in Dallas—begin a whisper campaign about Jack Kennedy's Addison's disease.[54] Kennedy, Johnson's supporters contended, could never effectively function in national office; his adrenal insufficiency rendered him disabled. The man simply would not be able to handle the stress that the office of president would place on his system; during the very first crisis he had to face, Kennedy would simply crumble, collapse, and quickly die.

Although it might seem impossible to believe in the 1990s, when a presidential candidate's entire social, medical, and financial history must, of necessity, become a matter of public record, Connally's disclosure of a potentially terminal illness affecting Jack Kennedy represented the first and only time in that or any other campaign in which he participated that Kennedy's medical condition was ever discussed. The secret was so thoroughly kept, the charade so well played out, that at the time of his death in Dallas, few Americans knew that their president was afflicted with adrenal insufficiency.

But Lyndon Johnson's accusation, passed on through Governor Connally, couldn't have been farther from the truth. Instead of preventing him from being able to serve as president, Jack Kennedy's Addison's disease seemed to have been a significant factor in driving him on during the ten years that led up to his election. It seems probable that, had it not been for his Addison's disease, or more correctly, for his triumph

over it, and his subsequent recovery from complicated back surgery in
the 1950s, Jack Kennedy might never have experienced the ambition
necessary to rise to the heights to which he ultimately rose. Undoubtedly, whether or not Kennedy's treatment with cortisone played a role
in enhancing his feelings, conquering his disease spurred him on, illustrating to him that he could achieve any goal, no matter how lofty or
difficult, to which he set his mind. In a sense, his conquest of the adversity caused by Addison's disease was John F. Kennedy's profile in
courage.

PART II

It was during his inaugural address, delivered on January 20,
1961, that President Kennedy spoke the line for which he's perhaps
most remembered: "Ask not what your country can do for you, ask
what you can do for your country."[55] Kennedy apparently "practiced
what he preached," and this sentiment of an obligation for assuring the
welfare of others was meant to pertain not only to matters of government, but to the field of medicine as well, because during his life and
even after it was over, Jack Kennedy and his family, either directly or indirectly, made two significant contributions to the field of pediatrics. In
the many tellings and retellings of the story of the Kennedy family published through the years, these two important contributions have, for
the most part, been overlooked.

The first contribution, made possible through charitable funding
supplied by the Joseph P. Kennedy, Jr. Foundation, involves the establishment of research and service facilities devoted to the study and care
of children with mental retardation, a condition that afflicts between
3 and 5 percent of the population. The main impetus for establishing
such centers was the fact that Rosemary Kennedy, the third child of
Joseph and Rose (and therefore the next in line after Jack), suffers from
multiple developmental disabilities.

Although her life has been guarded from the public, glimpsed
only through reports from her mother, other family members, and very
close family friends, some facts about Rosemary Kennedy are known.
In early childhood, her parents became concerned that their first
daughter was not acting quite like their two older sons: significantly
slower in her motor and cognitive development, Rosemary seemed to

learn things less easily than did either Joe Jr. or Jack.[56] The Kennedys, desperately searching for an explanation for their daughter's problems and, more important, for a treatment or a cure, brought Rosemary to a series of specialists; unfortunately, little help was forthcoming. Although, at the age of five, she entered a regular kindergarten class at the Dexter School in Brookline, Massachusetts, from the beginning Rosemary could not keep up with the other children. "Her lack of coordination was apparent," her mother writes in her autobiography, "and she could not keep up with the work."[56] From that point on, Rosemary was kept at some distance from the rest of the family, spending most of her time at boarding schools, such as the Sacred Heart Convent in Rhode Island, where she received special education.[57]

Her degree of disability appears to have been relatively mild in those days: she was able to participate in some games and activities with her siblings and their friends; she was able to carry on brief conversations and repeat simple messages, but even the smallest degree of complexity appeared to confuse her. Most visitors to the house, noticing Rosemary's reticence, were told simply that she was very shy: "only the closest family friends knew."[58] From these and other accounts, it appears as if Rosemary, at least during childhood and early adolescence, functioned in what today would be considered the borderline normal range. And as long as she functioned well and made attempts to keep up appearances, the Kennedys, like most families with a child who has a development disability, attempted with all their powers to deny that any problem existed and accepted her as a member of their family.

But as she reached her early twenties, Rosemary, and the entire situation, began to change for the worse. For the first time, the younger sister of Jack Kennedy began to show signs of developmental as well as social degeneration.[59] It is not known whether this represented the natural course of the underlying, undiagnosed condition that had led to her disability in the first place, or whether it resulted from the anger and frustration she must have felt at being different, at being set apart from her siblings for reasons over which she had no control. But during those years, which corresponded to the start of World War II, Rosemary lost the ability to carry out some of the tasks that she earlier had mastered. She gained a great deal of weight and became sexually

mature, and therefore was no longer able to "pass" as a normal but unduly shy child. She began to have tantrums, throwing and smashing
objects, and striking out against her parents, her siblings, and even,
during one particularly violent episode during the summer of 1941,
against her grandfather, John J. ("Honey Fitz") Fitzgerald.[60]

Bewildered and confused, worried about their daughter's well-
being, but also concerned about the consequences her sexuality and the
potentially "embarrassing" effects her developmental problems might
have on her siblings and their future careers both in and out of politics,
Rosemary's parents searched for guidance. They understood that something had to be done about their daughter; unfortunately, they had a
great deal of ambivalence about what that something should be.

The plight that the Kennedys faced during the early 1940s was
not unique. Even today, parents of children with developmental disabilities, no matter what the cause, struggle with these same issues, reluctantly making decisions that ultimately affect their child's future.
The range of emotions such parents experience is immense and often
quite conflicted. On the one hand, these children are loved because
they are their parents' flesh and blood; on the other hand, they are resented for the emotional and physical burdens they place on their parents and siblings. Such parents often feel guilty, blaming themselves for
causing their child's problems; but they also consume themselves with
concern about what will happen to the child after they're no longer able
to care for him or her, weighing possibilities such as institutionalization
or burdening a sibling or other family member with the affected child's
care, and even fantasizing about murdering their own offspring. Typically, these conflicted emotions terrify parents: "What kind of monster," they ask themselves, "would hate its own child?" And often,
because there are usually no friends or family members who have experienced this situation, these parents find themselves with no one to turn
to for advice or assistance.

Because of their enormous wealth, Rose and Joseph Kennedy, unlike most other couples in this same situation, had a great deal of support. After gathering all available information and consulting medical
and religious experts throughout the world, they finally made a firm decision about Rosemary's future. In the fall of 1941, the twenty-three-

year-old woman was admitted to St. Elizabeth's Hospital in the suburbs of Washington, D.C., for what Rose describes as "a certain form of neurosurgery."[61]

That neurosurgery was a prefrontal lobotomy.[62] The operation, performed as an attempt to control Rosemary's worsening behavior, has to be viewed, at least on the surface, as a success; it accomplished its stated goal. However, the procedure had a major, probably unexpected side effect on the young woman: in the words of Timothy Shriver, Rosemary's nephew, it "made her go from being mildly retarded to very retarded."[61]

It is almost inconceivable for us in the 1990s to understand how anyone could justify performing a prefrontal lobotomy or lobectomy on an individual like Rosemary Kennedy. It is now understood that the prefrontal areas, the portions of the frontal lobes of the cerebral cortex that lie directly in front of the portion of the brain that controls motor function, play essential roles in a number of vitally important functions. Not present in lower primates, the area has for years been considered a locus of higher intelligence. Their cells allow us to focus on specific tasks, preventing distraction from ambient stimuli; the region may be important in the retention of immediate memory, rendering the individual who lacks the prefrontal lobes unable to classify incoming information and "code" it for storage in the memory area of the brain. And finally, the lobes appear to be critical for the elaboration of thoughts, a center where ideas are "built upon" from simple concepts through an increase in depth and abstractness. It is now understood that after the prefrontal areas have been destroyed, either surgically or through disease or injury, the affected individual often acts precipitously, unable to consider the consequences of that action; in addition, such individuals lose their inhibitions, demonstrating little or no embarrassment in relation to excretory, sexual, or social activities, and they are prone to rapid and extreme swings of mood, quickly passing from overt friendliness to all-encompassing hatred, from passivity to violence in little or no time.[63]

But in 1941, the important roles played by this portion of the brain were not yet fully understood, and some optimism existed about the effect of surgical destruction of the cells of the prefrontal lobe on people who, because of their developmental disability, proved to be difficult to manage. Based on the information given them, the Kennedys apparently believed that, at least in the case of Rosemary, the potential benefits of the surgery were worth the risks documented in the medical literature.

The overall effect of the surgery on Rosemary was, to put it simply, that she ceased being Rosemary. Reduced, according to her mother, to forever acting at a "childlike level,"[61] no longer able to care for herself or to perform even the simplest of activities of daily living, Rosemary was sent away, with the blessings of Cardinal Cushing, the family's trusted religious advisor, to St. Colletta's Convent in Wisconsin, where she's lived, cloistered from the outside world, ever since.

As already stated, Joseph and Rose Kennedy experienced the same painful and disturbing mix of emotions concerning their oldest daughter's condition, the same anger and embarrassment, frustration and shame, that are shared by nearly every parent in their situation. But, unlike most parents of retarded children who find themselves facing a battery of medical, neurologic, and developmental experts who can offer no explanations, treatments, or cures, the Kennedys had two assets that could help both them and others who found themselves in this same situation: enormous wealth and power. In the years following Rosemary's prefrontal lobotomy, they managed to put both assets to good use.

In 1944 with the establishment of the Joseph P. Kennedy, Jr. Foundation, the Kennedy family began to support research, both at the basic science and the clinical level, in an attempt to find a biological basis and an effective treatment for mental retardation.[64] Kennedy Centers were established at medical facilities in major cities throughout the United States. During John F. Kennedy's years in the White House, a Presidential Panel on Mental Retardation was established.[64] Scientists who have been supported by funds donated by the Kennedy family have made major contributions to our understanding of brain growth and function in the developing human; and clinicians, also funded by the Kennedy Foundation, provide much-needed services to developmentally impaired children. Whether motivated by the desire to cure their daughter, or because of the great amount of guilt they must have carried with them as a result of what ultimately happened to Rosemary, the advances nurtured and supported by the Joseph P. Kennedy, Jr. Foundation have aided hundreds of thousands of infants, children, and adults afflicted with developmental disabilities throughout the world.

The second major medical advance brought about by a member of the Kennedy family was an indirect one. It resulted from the premature birth and, thirty-nine hours later, the tragic death of Patrick Bouvier Kennedy, the second son of Jack and Jacqueline, in August 1963.

Although he was the third child of the president and his wife, Patrick was actually the product of Jacqueline's fifth gestation. Her first pregnancy, in 1955, ended in a miscarriage.[65] The second one ended just as unhappily: on August 23, 1956, at Newport Hospital in Rhode Island, Jacqueline delivered a perfectly formed but premature, stillborn baby girl.[66]

The Kennedys' third and fourth pregnancies concluded on much happier notes: weighing 7 pounds, 2 ounces, Caroline was born by cesarean section at New York Hospital on November 27, 1957;[67] and John F. Kennedy, Jr., weighing 6 pounds, 3 ounces, also emerged via cesarean section at Georgetown University Hospital in Washington, D.C., on November 25, 1960.[68] But the fifth pregnancy was different from all of Jacqueline's previous ones; in fact, it was different from every other pregnancy that had taken place during the entire twentieth century. Occurring from the moment of conception to the time of delivery while the Kennedys were dwelling in the White House, it was a gestation that, in a sense, belonged to all of America. Patrick's intrauterine experience was given wide media coverage; stories about the pregnancy were carried on the front pages of newspapers, as well as on the nightly newscasts of all three television networks. His would truly be a birth that every American could celebrate.

But there would be no celebration following Patrick Bouvier Kennedy's delivery. Five-and-a-half weeks before her expected date of confinement, while accompanying Caroline and John, Jr., to a horseback riding lesson near Hyannis, Jacqueline felt a sudden sharp, stabbing pain in her abdomen. Fearing the onset of labor, she and her physician were taken by helicopter to the nearby Otis Air Force Base hospital. Upon hearing the news in the Oval Office at the White House, Jack Kennedy was rushed by helicopter to Andrews Air Force Base in Virginia, where he boarded one of the waiting fleet of presidential aircraft. After making a brief stop at LaGuardia Airport to pick up a well-known New York obstetrician whose services, in light of the impending emergency, had been urgently requested, the jet once again became airborne, finally coming to rest at Logan Airport in Boston. On the ground, the presidential party was transferred to another waiting helicopter, this one ready to ferry them on the last leg of the journey, to the hospital at Otis Air Force Base.[69]

By the time Jack Kennedy arrived, Jacqueline was being prepared for surgery. Another cesarean section was necessary (at that time, the conventional wisdom was "once a c-section, always a c-section"), and, with the obstetrician from New York assisting, the surgery was carried out flawlessly. Weighing 4 pounds, 10½ ounces, Patrick was well grown for an infant born five-and-a-half weeks prematurely. But his course became complicated almost from the time he took his first few breaths.[69]

Taking those breaths proved to be the problem. It soon became apparent that Patrick had respiratory distress syndrome (also known as hyaline membrane disease), a condition not uncommon in premature infants, in which, because of the absence of surfactant, a chemical naturally produced by specialized cells within the alveoli (air sacs), the lungs cannot adequately perform their normal function of providing oxygen to the blood while eliminating carbon dioxide. As a result of his condition, Patrick lay in his bassinet, gasping for air like a fish out of water, while his father, the most powerful man in the free world, looked on helplessly.

Because of the newborn's ever-worsening respiratory symptoms, the physicians at the air force hospital who were caring for Patrick Bouvier Kennedy decided that the infant needed to be transferred immediately to the Children's Hospital Medical Center in Boston. There, at one of the most prestigious pediatric facilities in the world, the child would be sure to receive state-of-the-art care, delivered by some of the nation's finest pediatric specialists. If anybody could get

Patrick through his respiratory distress syndrome, it was the members of the staff at Boston Children's.

But it was not to be. The problem was simply that, in 1963, there was no state-of-the-art care available for infants with respiratory distress syndrome: there were then no neonatologists, physicians specializing in the intensive-care management of critically ill newborns. Even at Boston Children's Hospital, there was no neonatal intensive care unit, nor any ventilators designed to aid babies who had been born before their lungs had matured enough to perform the normal functions of respiration; there were no intravenous solutions, no cardiac monitors, no oxygen saturation monitors. All that was available was supplemental oxygen, released from huge compressed-air tanks, passed through thin plastic tubes, and blown into the faces of these unfortunate tiny newborns. The physicians at Boston Children's did not even have the ability to control the quantity of oxygen that came out of those tanks: the valves were either open or closed. The baby would either get better on his own or he would die.

In the case of Patrick Bouvier Kennedy, of course, the result was the latter. During the day and a half that composed Patrick's life, President Kennedy remained at his infant son's side. Pediatricians who had developed some sort of expertise in the management of newborns, the people who would, within a few years, become known as the mothers and fathers of neonatology, were flown in from around the country to offer advice. But nothing helped; Jack Kennedy's secretary, Evelyn Lincoln, described the end of Patrick's life in this way: the president "was holding Patrick's hand and the nurse said, 'He's gone.' And tears came into his eyes. I had never seen tears in his eyes before." [69]

Although tragic, the death of Patrick Bouvier Kennedy also proved to have one major positive consequence. By focusing attention in both the public and the private sector on the grossly inadequate level of care that physicians were able to offer premature babies, Patrick's death literally forced the founding of neonatology as a medical specialty. Federal funds began to pour into research; neonatal intensive care units were established throughout the world; equipment designed specifically for the needs of these critically ill babies was invented and widely distributed. And today, babies weighing less than one-third of what Patrick

203

weighed at birth, with lungs far less mature and less able to cope with the needs of the extrauterine world, not only routinely survive, but are able to go on and lead normal lives.

Because this outcome has proved so vital to so many infants and children since 1963, it is safe to say that, as a result of his tragically short life, Patrick Bouvier Kennedy has become one of the most important figures in the field of pediatrics during the twentieth century.

References

1. Herbert S. Parmet, *Jack: The Struggles of John F. Kennedy* (New York: The Dial Press, 1980), 190.
2. Joan Blair and Clark Blair, Jr., *The Search for John F. Kennedy* (New York: Berkeley Publishing, 1976), 560–61.
3. T. Addison, *On the Constitutional and Local Effects of Disease of the Suprarenal Capsules* (London: Highley Publishing Co., 1955).
4. J. E. Bethune, The diagnosis and treatment of adrenal insufficiency, in L. J. deGroot, ed., *Endocrinology,* 2nd ed. (Philadelphia: W. B. Saunders Co., 1989), 1647.
5. J. Tepperman, *Metabolic and Endocrine Physiology,* 3rd ed. (Chicago: Year Book Medical Publishers, 1973), 133–51.
6. Bethune, Diagnosis and treatment, 1651.
7. Ibid., 1648–49.
8. P. C. Whybrow and T. Hurwitz, Endocrine disorders and hormone therapy, in E. Sachar, ed., *Hormones, Behavior, and Psychopathology* (New York: Raven Press, 1976), 127–28.
9. Bethune, Diagnosis and treatment, 1656–57.
10. Parmet, *Jack: The Struggles,* 28.
11. Ibid., 39–40.
12. G. St. John to J. F. K. (letter), November 8, 1935 (in J. F. K. file, Choate School, Rosemary Hall).
13. Parmet, *Jack: The Struggles,* 42.
14. Ibid., 42–43.
15. Ibid., 43.
16. Ibid., 47.
17. Ibid., 86–87.
18. Blair and Blair, *Search for Kennedy,* 114.
19. Parmet, *Jack: The Struggles,* 103–107.

20. Ibid., 115.

21. Ibid., 121.

22. J. W. McCarthy, *The Remarkable Kennedys* (New York: Dial Press, 1960), 150.

23. Parmet, *Jack: The Struggles,* 116.

24. E. Jawetz, J. L. Melnick, and E. A. Adelberg, *Review of Medical Micro-biology,* 12th ed. (Los Altos, Calif.: Lange Medical Publishers, 1974), 503–506.

25. Blair and Blair, *Search for Kennedy,* 337, 387.

26. Physician's Desk Reference, 47th Ed. (1993), Montvale, NJ: Medical Economics Co. p213b.

27. Parmet, *Jack: The Struggles,* 116.

28. M. Bleuler and W. A. Stoll, Psychological manifestations of hyper- and hypo-activity of the adrenal cortex, in H. W. Deane, ed., *Handbuch der Experimentellen Pharmakologie* (Berlin: Springer, 1962), 638.

29. A. M. Schlesinger, Jr., *A Thousand Days* (Boston: Houghton Mifflin Publishing Co., 1965), 96.

30. Parmet, *Jack: The Struggles,* 198.

31. Bethune, Diagnosis and treatment, 1647–48.

32. Blair and Blair, *Search for Kennedy,* 567.

33. L. H. Sarett, Partial synthesis of pregnene-4-triol-17 (Beta), 20,21-dione-3,11 and pregnene-4-diol-17 (Beta), 21-trione-3,11,20 mono acetate, *Journal of Biological Chemistry* 162 (1946): 601.

34. J. A. Nicholas, C. L. Burstein, C. J. Umberger, et al., Management of adrenal insufficiency during surgery, *AMA Archives of Surgery* 739 (1955).

35. Parmet, *Jack: The Struggles,* 222.

36. Ibid., 261.

37. Ibid., 234.

38. Ibid., 239.

39. Ibid., 254.

40. Ibid., 308.

41. Nicholas, Burstein, Umberger, et al., Management of adrenal insufficiency, 739.

42. Parmet, *Jack: The Struggles,* 309.

43. Ibid., 316.

44. Ibid., 317.

45. Ibid., 319.

46. F. Knebel, *Minneapolis Morning Tribune,* May 9, 1957.

205

47. Parmet, *Jack: The Struggles,* 372.

48. Ibid., 394.

49. J. F. Kennedy, *Profiles in Courage* (New York: Harper and Row, 1956).

50. Parmet, *Jack: The Struggles,* 437.

51. Ibid., 458.

52. P. Collier and D. Horowitz, *The Kennedys: An American Drama* (New York: Summit Books, 1984), 236–44.

53. Ibid., 312.

54. Ibid., 241.

55. J. F. Kennedy, inaugural address, January 20, 1961.

56. Rose F. Kennedy, *Times to Remember* (Garden City, N.Y.: Doubleday and Co., 1974), 151–52.

57. Ibid., 156.

58. Collier and Horowitz, *The Kennedys,* 67.

59. Ibid., 114.

60. Ibid., 115.

61. Kennedy, *Times to Remember,* 286.

62. Collier and Horowitz, *The Kennedys,* 116.

63. A. C. Guyton, *Textbook of Medical Physiology,* 5th ed. (Philadelphia: W. B. Saunders Co., 1976), 748–49.

64. Kennedy, *Times to Remember,* 302–304.

65. R. G. Martin, *A Hero for Our Times: An Intimate Story of the Kennedy Years* (New York: MacMillan Publishing Co., 1983), 122.

66. Collier and Horowitz, *The Kennedys,* 209.

67. Parmet, *Jack: The Struggles,* 416.

68. Martin, *Hero for Our Times,* 247.

69. Ibid., 526–27.